THE SOUTHERN NEW HEBRIDES

THE SOUTHERN NEW HEBRIDES

AN ETHNOLOGICAL RECORD

BY

C. B. HUMPHREYS

CAMBRIDGE
AT THE UNIVERSITY PRESS
MCMXXVI

CAMBRIDGE
UNIVERSITY PRESS

University Printing House, Cambridge CB2 8BS, United Kingdom

Cambridge University Press is part of the University of Cambridge.

It furthers the University's mission by disseminating knowledge in the pursuit of education, learning and research at the highest international levels of excellence.

www.cambridge.org
Information on this title: www.cambridge.org/9781107455566

© Cambridge University Press 1926

First published 1926
First paperback edition 2014

A catalogue record for this publication is available from the British Library

ISBN 978-1-107-45556-6 Paperback

CONTENTS

INTRODUCTION

THE following account of some of the ethnological conditions of the Southern New Hebrides is offered with a certain degree of hesitation, especially since Speiser's able and elaborate treatment of the entire group, including these islands, has just been issued after a protracted delay due presumably to the war. There are three reasons, however, which support the venture. In the first place, no other effort has yet been made to set down the general cultures of this area in English: secondly, the German work referred to does not deal exhaustively with the southern islands, with the exception of Tanna: and thirdly, no account has hitherto been published of the ethnology of Eromanga, which, though poor culturally, is not unimportant. This survey of the five southern islands— Tanna, Anaiteum, Futuna, Aniwa and Eromanga—is therefore offered in the hope that it will prove to be an ethnological record in convenient form for reference, guiltless, it is perhaps needless to say, of any literary or popular claim, but not without a certain value for the student of the Pacific area.

A glance at the map of the Pacific will show that, while these five islands are included nominally in the New Hebrides, they are more so by chance than for any other reason. There appears to be no more justification for calling them a part of the New Hebridean group than for excluding the Banks' Islands, for example, from the same. Eromanga certainly has more affinity with the Efatese culture to the north than with that of Tanna and the other southern islands, but since geographically it is grouped with the latter, it will be included with them in the following pages.

Apart from the writings of explorers, such as Captain Cook and Erskine, and of missionaries, such as Gunn, Robertson and Gray, very little has ever been published about this region of the Pacific. Cook describes some of the things he saw when he visited these islands on his second voyage; some of his company have published their accounts; and Erskine, in his journal of a cruise among the islands of the Pacific, gives occasional references. The reports of Gunn, Robertson and Gray are necessarily more concerned with the missionary side of the question, though the last has recorded some extremely valuable information, as will be seen in the section dealing with Tanna. The work of Speiser has already been referred to, and although he gave some time to the southern islands, he was more concerned to study those lying north of the 18th parallel of S. latitude.

It must be confessed that it is a question if it is not too late even now for any perfect ethnological work to be done in these islands. Certainly four to five months spent in Tanna yielded extremely small returns, if judged by the results obtained in other remote parts of the world. The limited time at the disposal of the investigator is one reason for these rather meagre results; the sophistication of the natives, due to the length of time which has elapsed since they first came under the influence of the white man, is another and much more potent reason. In all ethnological work in the field the period devoted to getting one's bearings and to finding out which men are intelligent and willing to be questioned, and which men are not, consumes so much of the first part of the visit, that one has to leave, perhaps, just as these initial labours are beginning to bear fruit. As to the other reason, it is particularly true in the island of Tanna that the old order is just on the point of giving place to the new. The recollection of the ancient customs is still vivid in the minds of a few of the older men, but the difficulty of obtaining accurate information is extremely great, and the investigator has to be continually on his guard and check his results with unusual care.

This brings us to a consideration of the method adopted in the following pages. The division of the material obtained into subject groups is that suggested by Malinowski, and his plan of treatment of ethnological reports is followed throughout. The field work was largely carried on through the medium of long interviews with older men who were found, after repeated experiment, to be reliable in their recollection of ancient customs. After a sympathetic understanding was established with the native, matters generally went fairly smoothly. Usually several of the elder men stood or squatted around the old man being questioned. These were very ready to object to the statements of the latter, if they disagreed with him, and it is on this consensus of opinion that the field worker relies for the accuracy of his report. In certain cases, after mutual confidence had been established, interviews were conducted with one or two old chiefs alone, but this was only done after careful observation of the man and his mental processes, and was, with one exception, unusual. It must be admitted that there is constant danger of inaccuracy in this method of recording native customs, but no better method offers in a place where the field worker has not the time to acquire the language. Most interviews were carried on through an interpreter, and the writer considers himself fortunate that he had the willing and patient help of three men who had lived long enough in the islands (twenty-five, eighteen and ten years respectively) to ensure adequate knowledge of the native languages.

It is this question of the use of interpreters that is the crux of the whole matter in ethnological field work. To obtain the maximum result, the investigator must have an accurate knowledge of the language of the people among whom he is working, but this, for the average ethnologist, is impossible. Unless he has special linguistic attainments, a comprehensive understanding of a native dialect is obtained only after months, perhaps years, of patient effort, and is, for the ordinary field worker, out of the question. The only alternative is the use of the right man as interpreter. A man who has lived among the people, as missionary, as trader, as planter, or what you will, may have no knowledge of the native language beyond a few necessary words, or he may have a wide range of acquaintance with colloquialisms born of long and intimate association with the native in his special field. The writer counts himself fortunate that, in his case at least, the latter condition prevailed, and he finds it difficult to express his gratitude to the missionary and planter on Tanna, and the owner of the sheep station on Eromanga, for unlimited patience and unflagging interest in interviews that must have been, for the interpreter at least, periods of protracted and dreary monotony.

Cases occur, of course, where some of the older men had experience in the old days on the Queensland plantations, where they acquired a fair knowledge of English, of which use could be made, but, on the whole, the honesty and accuracy of the interpreter are, as noted above, the crux of the matter, and on these attributes, in the cases referred to, the writer is willing to stake his reputation.

It was only in Tanna and Eromanga that these methods of work were adopted. Futuna and Aniwa were not personally visited by the writer, while the few hours passed ashore on the island of Anaiteum served merely to give a general idea of the geography of the place and a cursory glimpse of the in- habitants. The detailed study of Tanna and Eromanga has more value, however, if short accounts of the cultures of the other three islands of the group, gathered from records of other observers, are added in convenient form for comparison.

The three largest islands, Eromanga, Tanna and Anaiteum, extend in the order named from north-west to south-east be- tween 18° 30′ and 20° 15′ S. and, roughly, from 168° 55′ E.— the approximate longitude of the most westerly point of Ero- manga—to 169° 45′ E.—the approximate longitude of the most easterly point of Anaiteum. Aniwa lies about twelve miles north- east of Tanna, and Futuna is about forty-eight miles as the crow flies directly east of the centre of this island. Eromanga, which is the largest of the five islands, is about thirty-five miles in length from north-west to south-east, and has an average breadth of twenty-five miles. Tanna is about twenty-three miles long at its greatest length, from north-north-west to south-south-east, and six or seven miles wide at its narrowest point. Futuna has an area of four square miles, and Aniwa is also very small. Aniwa is low-lying, but Futuna is a precipitous mass of rock rising abruptly from the sea.

Tanna has the only active volcano in the group. It is a fairly regular cone of volcanic ash rising from a plain of the same deposit. The eastern side has been broken away by some former outburst and irregular streams of lava have made their way to the sea. These are mainly covered now by a dense vegetation, except in the case of a fairly recent flow, which is not yet entirely overgrown. The volcano constantly sends up quantities of incandescent scoria from one or another of the several vents at the bottom of the crater, the intervals between the explosions being very irregular. There is a loud report at each outburst, varying more or less in intensity according to the direction of the wind. Sometimes these explosions occur at intervals of a few minutes for a day or two at a time; sometimes the volcano is practically quiescent for two or three days. The scoria leave a fine jet-like deposit on leaves and roofs to leeward of the crater for a distance of several miles, which, curiously, leaves no smudge if touched by the finger. Parts of the island remote from the crater are alone exempt from this visitation.

The Admiralty Chart of the islands gives the height of the volcano as only 600 feet above sea level, but it must be much higher, probably little less than 1000 feet. The highest point on the island, a mountain at the southern end, is given on the same chart as 3200 feet, but is probably higher as well. The shore line is a succession of coralline cliffs rising abruptly from the beach or directly from the sea. Outlying reefs are found only occasionally on the coast of the island, but there are no good harbours for sea-going craft. Those of Port Resolution and Sulphur Bay are exposed to the prevailing winds and are of no use to the infrequent mail steamer from Sydney. Port Resolution, though available at the time of Captain Cook's visit, is now so blocked at the entrance as to make it practically inaccessible. Several old tracks across the island have been widened into bridle paths and access from one part of the island to the other is easy and secure. Mission stations have been established for many years at Waisisi and Whitesands on the east coast and at Lenakel on the west. There were formerly other stations as well. Many of the inhabitants have been brought under Christian influence, but there are still numbers of bush people in the interior who are unconverted to Christianity. Except in modes of personal adornment there is no marked difference between these two groups. Fighting has been unknown since 1906 and the present population is believed to be a little under 6000 souls. The natives are, on the whole, a healthy folk, and fever and ague seem to be the only serious maladies. The population is on the increase and children are in evidence everywhere. There are eighteen or twenty whites on the island. These are the Government Agent, missionaries, planters, traders and their families.

The average annual rainfall for three years—1918, 1919, 1920 —was 6·94 inches, but the total rainfall for each year was very variable. In 1918, 17·68 inches of rain were recorded at White-sands on the easterly side of the island, where all the measurements were taken, but in the following year—1919—only ·64 inch. The average maximum temperature at Whitesands, taken at a point about 150 feet above the sea and perhaps 300 yards from it, was 79·0° for the same three years, and the average minimum temperature 69·1°. Both measurements were Fahrenheit.

Eromanga is one of the largest of the islands of the New Hebridean group, the coast line being about a hundred miles in length and the indentations, on the whole, not pronounced. There are two chains of mountains, one running in a general direction from north to south in the north part of the island, the other running more or less from east to west in the south-central part. The extreme eastern extremity, known as Traitor's Head, since Captain Cook's unfortunate experience at Polinia Bay, is an abrupt dual headland rising some 2400 feet above the sea. As in so many other places in the region of the trade winds, the eastern slope is fairly well watered by frequent rains, while the western side is subject to frequent periods of drought. The western slope consists of high tablelands, at an average elevation of from 500 to 700 feet, with a poor soil for agriculture, but carrying grass of an excellent quality for pasturage, so that sheep have been raised there successfully for a number of years.

The island is well watered, there being no less than five rivers of respectable length, two of which, Cook River, flowing into Cook's Bay on the east coast, and the Bunka, or Williams River, rising in the northern hills and flowing south and finally west into Dillon's Bay, are more than twelve miles in length; the former is navigable for several miles of its course, though the latter has barely a mile of smooth water at its mouth. In the south there are two rivers, only one of which bears a native name, the *Bunkil*, the other being now called South River by the Eromangans.

Traitor's Head separates two large bays from each other, Cook's Bay on the south of the promontory, and Polinia Bay to the north. Dillon's Bay, on the west coast, at the mouth of the Williams River, is the favoured anchorage for the steamers in their infrequent visits to the island, being sheltered from all save westerly winds.

A word about the native names for these islands may be appropriately inserted here. The native of an insular region of moderate size seems never to have a name for his own homeland until he has been a journey away from it. For instance, the proper native name for the island of Tanna is *Ipari*, which is given it by the natives of the other islands of the sub-group, all of which are in sight of it, when they point to it or mention it in any connection. The word *tanna* means "ground" or "earth" in the Waisisi dialect, and Captain Cook's mistake in thinking, when he pointed to the ground, that the native would give him the name of the island, and not of the object at which his finger pointed, was perfectly understandable from his point of view, but took no note of the workings of the native mind. This error on the part of so excellent an observer as Cook is, after all, of uncommon usefulness to the ethnologist of the present day. It is one of the "awful warnings" of the pitfalls that lie in the way of the unwary. Curiously enough, the name given by Cook has survived to this day, and there has never been any question of calling this island by the native name given it by its neighbours, or by any other. In this respect Tanna has been fortunate, for alternative names of islands in the Pacific have led to serious confusion in the past, particularly in Melanesia.

The native name for Eromanga is, reciprocally, that given it by the Tannese when they speak of it or point to it. Anaiteum— spelled Annatom by Cook—the island to the south of it, Futuna and Aniwa are also terms given to these islands by the Tannese. In return, the inhabitants of Futuna call Tanna *Ekiamo* when they point to it, but the tendency, in the two small islands at least, entirely Christianized as they have been for a long period, is to speak of all islands by their present geographical names.

The average rainfall for the eight years from 1916 to 1923 inclusive on the west coast of the island—the part most subject to drought—was 72·59 inches. During this period the largest annual rainfall was in 1917, when 107·67 inches are recorded, and the smallest annual amount in 1919, when the average recorded is 56·04 inches. During 1917, the year of the heaviest rainfall, the month of February, the record month for that year, had 18·91 inches to its credit, although the same month in 1923 exceeded it, with 27·80 inches. The smallest rainfall for any one month of the period is August, 1920, when only ·52 inch of rain fell. Unfortunately there is no record on the moist east coast, nor is any record extant of averages in wind velocity or wind direction.

Anaiteum is the most southerly of the entire group of the New Hebrides and is about one-third the size of its nearest neighbour, Tanna, to the north-west. It consists of a high central massif dividing the island into several deep valleys separated from each other by the buttress-like ridges running down to the sea. It will be seen later what influence this geographical condition has on the tribal life of the people. There is one good anchorage—Anelgahat—on the south-west coast, which is well sheltered from all winds save the south-westerly. During a hurricane this shelter is useless, but at all other times it affords a protection unknown elsewhere in the Southern New Hebrides. Of rainfall averages or any other meteorological data no records are available.

CHAPTER I

TANNA

PHYSICAL CHARACTERISTICS AND MEASUREMENTS

THE TANNESE is usually a fine specimen of the human animal, although of a less robust type than the native of some other parts of Melanesia, notably Fiji (Erskine, p. 16). The population of the island is increasing, and the latest census of the Government Agent shows something under 6000 souls. Whenever a ship arrives it is easy to believe that the population is dense, for the presence on the beach of large numbers of men and children, as well as women, suggests a thickly peopled area. Captain Cook found the island heavily populated in the part where he landed, and about the middle of the last century Erskine noted the large numbers that assembled when the arrival of a ship created general excitement (p. 303). In this particular Tanna is in strong contrast to its neighbouring islands, north and south, where one is impressed, even on steamer day, with the scarcity of natives on the beach.

The average height of 54 adult males on the east coast in the vicinity of Whitesands is 1638 mm. (min. 1518, max. 1803); 9·3 per cent. are of short stature[1], 64·8 per cent. are medium, 14·8 per cent. are tall, and 11·1 per cent. are very tall. On the west coast in the vicinity of Lenakel the average of 133 adult males is 1648 mm. (min. 1489, max. 1804); 13 per cent. are short, 55 per cent. medium, 21 per cent. tall, and 11 per cent. very tall. The measurements taken at Lenakel on the west coast are from men covering a larger territory than those taken at Whitesands on the east coast. The former cover a radius of about eight miles from Lenakel, the latter of perhaps five miles from Whitesands, though, in both cases, there are a few men from further afield. The differences between the east and west coasts do not appear to be significant, as there is a greater proportion of short as well as a greater proportion of tall and very

---

[1] Statures of 1480–1580 mm. are considered as short, 1580–1680 mm. as medium, 1680–1720 mm. as tall, and those over 1720 mm. as very tall.

tall men in the west. For the entire 187 the average height is 1645 mm.; 11·76 per cent. are short, 57·75 per cent. are medium, 19·25 per cent. are tall and 11·24 per cent. very tall.

The hair is woolly and often quite long. The coastal folk wear it sometimes closely cropped and there are evidences of wavy hair like that of the European on the east coast of the island. Captain Cook noted this on some Futunese whom he observed while he was ashore on Tanna (2nd ed. II. p. 78[1]), but this is found occasionally among the Tannese themselves. Curly or wavy hair is also found in several Melanesian islands, especially in the Loyalty Islands[2]. The hair of the Tannese is inclined to grow long and luxuriantly, if it is allowed to do so. The bushmen have an elaborate manner of dressing the hair, which is such an important part of Tannese culture that it will be described later in detail. Among the coastal folk it is often permitted to grow long on the top of the head and is sometimes dyed with lime to make it golden or blonde in colour. The normal colour is dark brown, never absolutely black, with variations through all the shades, from a very dark to a very light, dark brown. Gray (1899, p. 127) calls it sometimes chestnut brown, and says it is invariably woolly.

The eye is almost always dark and, among all the males measured, only two occur with very dark eyes. The eyes of all the others are very much alike in colour. No evidence of colour-blindness occurred among the 187 males examined, and the missionary on the east coast with twenty-five years of experience in looking after the health, as well as the souls, of the Tannese, has never had a case brought to his attention.

The skin colour has more variety, and of the 187 men examined, 13 per cent. have a skin colour that is very dark brown, 66·3 per cent. have a dark brown and 20·7 per cent. have a light brown, varying from a shade just one degree lighter than the average to extremely pale brown. This agrees with Gray's statement that no Tannese has a coal-black skin, but it is not

---

[1] In references to Captain Cook's Journal the 2nd ed. will be referred to unless otherwise indicated.

[2] See Finsch, O., "Die Rassenfrage in Oceanien," *Verh. d. Berliner Ges. f. Anthr., Ethn. u. Urgesch.*, bound with *Z. f. Eth.* 14, 1882, p. 164; see also Haddon, A. C., *The Races of Man*, Cambridge, 1924, p. 123.

possible to accept his definition of the skin colour of the darkest members of the community. "Sooty black" (1899, p. 127) they are not, most certainly. The skin is often soft and satiny and sometimes quite free from hair on the body; again, a man is covered, on the breast, under the arms, around the pubes and sometimes on the back, with short woolly hair or "down," as it is called by Erskine (p. 306). The proportion of smooth skin to extreme hairiness seems to be about the same as in European males.

Gray (1899, p. 128) detects a differentiation between the bodily odours of the males of different islands. With the continual visits on the east coast of canoes full of Aniwans it is a simple matter to test this question, but in spite of repeated attempts to discover a variation between Tannese and Aniwans in this strong characteristic of all Melanesians, it is impossible to report any differences at all.

The average cephalic index[1] of the 54 males measured on the east coast of the island is 79·1, which shows a tendency to the broad-headed Polynesian rather than to the primitive, long-headed Melanesian type. As stated above, these men come from an area not more than five miles from the mission station of Whitesands. But, as all are mission boys, this means that some at least must have come originally from villages further inland. Gray (1892, p. 648) found people in every district from all parts of the island, but there is no evidence now that those who came from the interior villages originally are more long-headed than their coastal fellow islanders. This tendency to brachycephalism is interesting and suggestive. Of the 54 men, one has an index of 86·1, and the lowest is 72·1.

Taking 77–82 as the range for mesocephaly, the percentages of cephalic index are:

	East Coast	West Coast	E. and W.
Dolichocephals	22·9	31·2	27·1
Mesocephals	57·5	47·8	52·6
Brachycephals	19·6	21	20·3
	100	100	100

On the other (west) side of the island the average index for the 133 adult males is only a little lower than on the east coast,

[1] See Keane, p. 137, footnote 4.

being 78·6. Here the highest is 89·1, and the lowest 69·9. The average for the total of 187 males measured is 78·7. The brachycephalism on the east coast is what one would expect, for there has always been a decided Polynesian influence there, but it is somewhat astonishing to find it stronger on the west coast. This bears out Speiser's statement that the culture of the entire island is almost pure Polynesian. Admitting that the outward appearance of the population would lead one to think otherwise, showing, as it does, so many Melanesian characteristics, he insists that it has little in common with the northern people of the group. He suggests (1912, p. 464) four elements in the inhabitants of Tanna, viz. smaller Melanesian type, typical Melanesian, early Polynesian, and late Polynesian. The probable explanation of the uniformity of the cephalic index on the two coasts is that, although the Polynesian influence came primarily from the north-east—Tonga and Samoa, where the brachycephalic type prevails in a marked manner[1]—the mixture with the original Melanesian elements was very general throughout the island, especially in the coastal areas. In an island no larger than Tanna it would be difficult for an aboriginal people to hide themselves as completely as they have been able to do in New Guinea and the larger islands of Indonesia and the Philippines.

Taking 79–84 as the range for euryprosophy, 84–88 for mesoprosophy and 88–93 for leptoprosophy, the percentages of facial index are:

	East Coast	West Coast	E. and W.
Hypereuryprosops	9·8	3·3	6·5
Euryprosops	21·2	18·3	19·8
Mesoprosops	33·3	32·5	32·9
Leptoprosops	21·3	31·1	26·2
Hyperleptoprosops	14·4	14·8	14·6
	100	100	100

The average facial index of the 54 males on the east coast is 85·8, which is almost the mean for mesoprosophy, the maximum being 98·2 and the minimum 73·1. On the west coast the average for the 133 males is 87·5, maximum 101·7, minimum 74·3. The total average for 187 males is 87·1.

The nasal index is also interesting, for the east coast average of the 54 males of whom measurements are recorded is 77·4

[1] See Dixon, p. 383.

with an individual maximum of 106·6 (excluding two cases of nasal deformity, 3 and 7), and a minimum of 52·2, while the 133 measurements taken on the west side show an average of 73·4, with a maximum of 99·1 and a minimum of 52·4.

Taking 70–85 as the range for mesorrhiny the percentages of nasal index are:

	East Coast	West Coast	E. and W.
Leptorrhines	27·4	32	29·7
Mesorrhines	46·2	56·2	51·2
Chamaerrhines	26·4	11·8	19·1
	100	100	100

As far as can be learned there is only one half-caste in the island, a boy, perhaps seven or eight years of age, rather poorly developed, but without noteworthy characteristics.

Tanna Measurements. All males over 18

East Coast. 1 to 54 inclusive

Name	Height	Head		Facial Height	Bi-zy. Breadth	Nasal		Indices		
		Length	Breadth			Height	Breadth	Cephalic	Facial	Nasal
1. NALAUAS	1663	190·4	143·5	99	132	45·7	45·7	75·3	75	100
2. JACK	1699	194·3	157·4	121·9	142·2	45·7	45·7	81	85·7	100
3. NANUA	1681	193	149·8	100·3	137·1	34·2	41·9	77·6	73·1	122·2
4. KUMELU	1600	185·4	142·2	111·7	134·6	38	40·6	76·7	83	106·6
5. PUSAI	1577	193	149·8	119·3	134·6	48·2	40·6	77·6	88·6	84·2
6. KAKO	1803	191·7	151·1	116·8	142·2	45·7	43·1	78·8	82·1	94·4
7. NAURA	1587	198·1	149·8	109·2	144·7	38	44·4	75·6	75·4	116·6
8. KAIUTI	1706	205·7	157·4	120·6	132	48·2	46·9	76·5	91·3	97·3
9. KUK	1727	200·6	162·5	119·3	154·9	55·8	43·1	81	77	77·2
10. LAPEAI	1701	203·1	149·8	116·8	147·3	50·7	45·7	73·7	79·3	90
11. LOHMANI	1635	193	152·3	121·9	139·6	53·3	48·2	78·9	87·2	90·4
12. NAHIET	1605	184·1	154·9	116·8	146	50·7	38	84·1	80	75
13. MAHU	1676	193	149·8	118·1	142·2	57·1	45·7	77·6	83	80
14. KURIN	1681	200·6	144·7	123·1	144·7	55·8	45·7	72·1	85·1	91·8
15. IAU	1732	185·4	152·3	126·9	134·6	50·7	38	82·1	94·3	75
16. IABATU	1612	187·9	142·2	121·9	139·6	63·4	41·9	75·6	87·2	66
17. NAKUALUMAN	1727	193	157·4	142·2	144·7	60·9	40·6	81·5	98·2	66·6
18. NOAL	1619	187·9	154·9	129·5	147·3	50·7	48·2	82·2	87·9	95
19. KOTIAMA	1574	198·1	154·9	111·7	144·7	71·1	48·2	78·2	77·1	67·8
20. NALAU	1752	193	157·4	137·1	152·3	60·9	40·6	81·5	90	66·6
21. NANUA	1587	193	147·3	121·9	142·2	58·4	38	76·3	85·7	65·2
22. NAMAKA	1720	196·8	154·9	126·9	144·7	53·3	38	78·7	87·7	71·4
23. REWA	1650	193	149·8	124·4	147·3	50·7	40·6	77·6	84·4	80
24. NAMUSI	1669	200·6	154·9	142·2	149·8	63·4	48·2	77·2	94·9	76

No.	Name										
25.	MOLIAKI	71·4	84·2	83	38	53·3	144·7	121·9	149·8	180·3	1606
26.	TARAWAI	66·6	85·9	75·3	40·6	60·9	144·7	124·4	147·3	195·5	1625·5
27.	IAKAVI	85	88·8	75	43·1	50·7	137·1	121·9	144·7	193	1581
28.	KUOKAREI	75·5	81·3	80·2	43·1	57·1	149·8	121·9	154·9	195·5	1657
29.	KATOA	66·6	85·7	77·2	38	57·1	142·2	120·9	151·1	185·4	1631
30.	POITA	64·3	86·3	84·9	31·7	58·4	139·6	120·6	157·4	180·3	1650
31.	KUONIAMUK	70·8	95·4	80·2	43·1	60·9	139·6	133·3	144·7	193	1600
32.	MAITI	73·9	94·7	84·2	43·1	58·4	144·7	137·1	162·5	187·9	1562
33.	WAMIHI	60·8	81·3	78·3	35·5	58·4	149·8	121·9	147·3	180·3	1600
34.	NILUA	77·2	83·9	80·2	43·1	55·8	142·2	119·3	144·7	182·8	1625·5
35.	KAMITI	75·5	91·6	83·2	43·1	55·8	152·3	139·6	157·4	189·2	1600
36.	IABUHU	82·6	86·7	79·1	48·2	58·4	134·6	116·8	144·7	182·8	1536
37.	MAIMAI	60	94·5	74·1	38	63·4	139·6	132	142·2	191·7	1625·5
38.	KAPUNEN	73·9	89·6	86·1	43·1	58·4	147·3	132	157·4	182·8	1581
39.	KAUKE	69·5	90·9	79·3	40·6	58·4	139·6	126·9	149·8	187·9	1612
40.	PUSI	83·3	87·2	77·3	44·4	53·3	139·6	121·9	147·3	190·4	1625·5
41.	IAKOLI	62	77·5	81	39·3	63·4	147·3	114·2	157·4	194·3	1581
42.	AMUA	67·3	84·6	81·3	39·3	58·4	140·9	119·3	149·8	184·1	1587
43.	IHIUA	72·7	89	81·3	40·6	55·8	139·6	124·4	154·9	190·4	1631
44.	NAIVA	60	83·9	77·7	29·2	58·4	142·2	119·3	146	187·9	1517·5
45.	NERUA	75	79	76·3	38	50·7	139·6	110·4	139·6	182·8	1644·5
46.	TIRU	84	89·2	77·7	46·9	55·8	142·2	126·9	151·1	194·3	1645
47.	NIAVIA	78·2	93·8	80·5	45·7	58·4	144·7	135·8	157·4	195·5	1638
48.	IAO	83·3	83·8	81·3	44·4	53·3	149·8	125·7	154·9	190·4	1706
49.	KALUATAV	52·2	84·8	77	29·2	55·8	142·2	120·6	144·7	187·9	1600
50.	NUMANAULA	64	88·1	81·5	40·6	63·4	149·8	132	157·4	193	1625·5
51.	NANUA	57·1	88·8	78·4	40·6	71·1	148·5	132	152·3	194·3	1676
52.	KAAS	70·4	84·4	76·6	39·3	55·8	162·9	124·4	149·8	195·5	1682
53.	NILAUS	82·5	83·3	83·1	41·9	50·7	152·3	126·9	156·2	187·9	1650
54.	POITA	62·5	84·1	83·5	38	60·9	152·3	128·2	154·9	185·4	1695

Tanna Measurements. All males over 18 (*continued*)

West Coast. 55 to 187 inclusive

Name	Height	Head		Facial Height	Bi-zy. Breadth	Nasal		Indices		
		Length	Breadth			Height	Breadth	Cephalic	Facial	Nasal
55. *Isaac	1730	191·2	149·2	129·6	136·8	59·5	41	78	94·7	68·9
56. Percy	1730	188·5	156·8	136·5	152·5	59·5	41	83·1	89·5	68·9
57. Captain ...	1641	178	155	135	144·5	63·8	39·5	87	93·4	61·9
58. Alec	1555	181	152	115·5	139·8	57·5	39·8	83·9	82·6	69·2
59. Jimmie... ...	1717	177·5	150	113·5	137·5	59·6	43·5	84·5	82·5	72·9
60. Kariko ...	1595	187	147·5	120·5	135	54·5	42	78·8	89·2	77
61. Bill	1598·5	182	160	107	138·5	55·5	41	87·9	77·2	73·8
62. Tom	1046·5	186	144·6	115·6	138	60	44	77·7	83·7	73·3
63. Charlie ...	1662·5	194·8	147·6	119·5	140·5	58	49·8	75·7	85	85·8
64. Sam	1715	186	146·6	113·5	140·5	50	41·5	78·8	80·7	83
65. Nalauas ...	1706	192·5	141	112·6	145·4	56·4	41·5	73·2	77·4	73·5
66. Kataina ...	1740	181·4	152	132	138·2	59·5	39	83·7	95·5	65·5
67. Tavo	1628·5	190·5	150·5	123·5	146·6	53	41	79	84·2	77·3
68. Lob	1706	194	154·6	123	142·8	60	46·5	79·6	86·1	77·5
69. Namel... ...	1646	191·7	148	113	139	62	45	77·2	81·3	72·5
70. Iama	1587	177·2	145·5	117	138·5	59·5	40	82·1	84·4	67·2
71. Kwarom ...	1617	191	149·5	125·5	139	61	32	78·2	90·2	52·4
72. Nauri	1686	198	149	113·2	136	54	39	75·2	83·2	72·2
73. Siaka	1636	183·6	148·5	122·5	140·5	60	39	80·8	87·1	65
74. Siaka (2) ...	1686	199	144·6	124	148	53·5	41	72·6	83·7	76·6
75. Iru	1628·5	180·5	146·6	119	146·5	59	37	81·2	81·2	62·7
76. Bukel	1560	189	152	131·6	141·5	62	44	80·4	93	70·9
77. Ialulu... ...	1611	188	155·4	124·4	156·5	62	53	82·6	79·4	85·4

* 55 to 64 nclusive all West Coast Tannese. Measurements taken on Eromanga.

78.	KOATA...	1489	197	152·5	110	148	54·5	41	77·4	74·3	75·2
79.	IATA ...	1710	195	155·2	128·5	147·4	55	45	79·5	87·1	81·8
80.	NAKOHMA	1667	197	149	127	145	63	47	75·6	87·5	74·6
81.	SIKUT ...	1684	195	145	113	137·5	50·5	40·5	74·3	82·1	80·1
82.	IASU ...	1662	193	145	117	135·5	52	40	75·1	86·3	76·9
83.	IAUS ...	1574·5	187	152	123·5	161·5	63	38·5	81·2	76·4	61·1
84.	KEKOB...	1616	186·5	153·4	121	146·4	61	38·5	82·2	82·6	63·1
85.	KAPABA	1691	193	145	115·5	140	55	45·5	75·1	82·5	82·7
86.	NATUMAN	1638	186	154	128·5	144	64	41	82·7	89·2	64
87.	NELBIN	1645	181·5	140	122	138·5	51	45·5	77·1	88	89·2
88.	LOAUA...	1645	193	143·4	122·4	137·5	57	45	74·3	89	78·9
89.	IARUEL...	1591	201	153	120	148	60	39	76·1	81	65
90.	KAIPAL	1587	194	156	126	147·5	60	47	80·4	85·4	78·3
91.	HARRY...	1641·5	190	153	126	149·5	61	49	80·5	84·2	80·3
92.	KIEL ...	1715	187·5	142	114	134	54	42	75·7	85	77·7
93.	TAVO ...	1676	193	153	122	147	56	45	79	82·9	80·3
94.	KAUT ...	1798	199·5	157·5	136·3	156	67	46	78·9	87·3	68·6
95.	MANGAU	1636	196·5	147	133·3	149	60	42	74·8	89·4	70
96.	IARAMANOK	1624·5	195	157	145·5	143	69	44	80·5	101·7	63·7
97.	IAUITUNG	1765·5	203	156	142	153	69	40·5	76·8	92·8	58·6
98.	IARUELI	1667	183·4	151	118	138·2	55	42	82·3	85·3	76·3
99.	IAUAK ...	1597	198	151	121	145	60	45	76·2	83·4	75
100.	KALIA ...	1720	185	143·5	124	139	55	44	77·5	89·2	80
101.	KAPALU	1804	195	138	126	137·5	57	44	70·7	91·6	77·1
102.	LAVA ...	1616	196	156·5	134	144	67	46	79·8	93	68·6
103.	IAMUS ...	1654·5	200	154	120	148	52·5	39	77	81	74·2
104.	IAUAI ...	1719	186	151	131	142	54	37	81·1	92·2	68·5
105.	IARUELI	1616	204	151	129·5	153	62	51	74	84·6	82·2
106.	IHUA ...	1681	187·5	150	124·5	145·5	55	49·5	80	85·5	90
107.	IAMONIK	1656	200	147	120	139	55	43	73·5	86·3	78·1
108.	TAMURO	1600·5	184	151	116	144	57	47	82	80·5	82·4
109.	IARUELA	1612·5	202	157	132	140	57·5	40	77·7	94·2	69·5

Tanna Measurements. All males over 18 (continued)

West Coast. 55 to 187 inclusive

Name	Height	Head Length	Head Breadth	Facial Height	Bi-zy. Breadth	Nasal Height	Nasal Breadth	Cephalic	Facial	Nasal
110. NERABO	1623	194	151	135	145	60	40	77·8	93·1	66·6
111. SAUDER	1656	190·5	160	124	147	60	44	83·9	84·3	73·3
112. IAVINIAU	1658·5	186	150	120·5	138·5	53·5	44	80·6	87	82·2
113. NOKLAUNG	1723	199	145	123	144	58·5	43	72·8	85·4	73·5
114. IATA	1641	190·5	141	123	136	60·5	47·5	74	90·4	78·5
115. SIUO	1565·5	188	153	133	145·5	62	41	81·3	91·4	66·1
116. KAPEN	1514	199	147	137	143·5	57	46	73·8	95·4	80·7
117. IAYAHA	1665	204	160	136	152	68	43	78·4	89·4	63·2
118. NILAU	1623	195	150·5	128·5	146	52	47	77·1	88	90·3
119. KASAOU	1600	179	148	136·5	142	68	44	82·6	96·1	64·7
120. IANUKEL	1622·5	199	151	123	139·5	57·5	40	75·8	88·1	69·5
121. IAMAAK	1596	195·5	150·5	120	150	60	46	76·9	80	76·6
122. NAMUL	1665	198	146	129·5	140	57	50	73·7	92·6	87·7
123. HEDOWET	1748	188	146	119	135	61	40	77·6	88·1	65·5
124. TAUIN	1590	200	148	126	141	59	45·5	74	89·3	77·1
125. NAGEBOK	1502·5	175	147	115	141	53·5	45	84	81·5	84·1
126. SIMON	1732	195·5	152	135	147·5	66	48	77·7	91·5	68·1
127. IAUNUM	1629	192·2	155	130	148	54	42	80·6	87·8	88·8
128. NIKOLO	1565·5	191	134	115	129·5	56·5	47	70·1	88·8	74·3
129. MALINO	1768	198	151	137·5	144·5	64	39	76·2	95·1	73·4
130. MAI	1616	187	147	123	142	55	44	78·6	86·6	70·9
131. IELAMI	1631·5	188	144·5	131·5	140·5	63	41	76·8	93·5	69·8
132. IAUS	1651·5	183·5	150	145	145	62	41	81·7	100	67·7
133. DEES	1715	191·5	151·5	140·5	144	65	47·5	79·1	97·5	73

134. IAUS ...	1690	184·5	156·5	132	154	63	45·5	84·8	85·7	72·2
135. IATIK OBA	1633	195	150	125·5	145·5	58·5	44	76·9	86·2	75·2
136. NALING	1660	190·5	142	117·5	135	60	41·5	74·5	87	69·1
137. IATELA...	1642	196	153	123	141·5	69	45·5	78	86·9	65·9
138. IALTEN...	1586·5	184	144	124·5	146	58·5	58	78·2	85·2	99·1
139. TUMAN	1632	184	151	144	151	64	43·5	82	95·4	67·9
140. NEMUK	1669	211	147·5	122·5	143	56	40·5	69·9	85·6	72·3
141. NOANKUM	1694·5	196	151	134	141	62	47	77	95	75·8
142. NOPUAT	1635	195	149·5	134·5	145	59·5	37·5	76·6	92·7	63
143. LOMATUK	1601·5	183	154	123	144	60	40	84·1	85·4	66·6
144. KASI ...	1613	188	157	127	152	54·5	39	83·5	83·5	71·5
145. KETAU ...	1571	190	152·5	123	139	60	43	80·2	88·4	71·6
146. IAO ...	1649	191	141	127	138	62	57	73·8	92	91·9
147. NOWEL	1716	206·5	156	135·5	157	56	46	75·5	86·3	82·1
148. IATIKDAION	1633	194	152	128	151·5	59	44	78·3	84·4	74·5
149. TAIGARIA	1576	190	143·5	122	134	53·5	40	75·5	91	74·7
150. KAURUDDA	1716	195	149	127	137	60	48	76·4	92·7	80
151. NOALUK	1675	179	159·5	124	149	57	43	89·1	83·2	75·4
152. NOAA ...	1689	200·5	147·5	135	138·5	60	40·5	73·5	97·4	67·5
153. IAOAU ...	1521	188	140	117·5	141·5	62	44	74·4	83	70·9
154. LOME ...	1667	183	146	114	140	51	44	79·7	81·4	86·2
155. IOAMIWAN	1565	189	150	126·5	144	60	42	79·3	87·8	70
156. NUMAKA	1689·5	177·5	146	124	144	63	40	82·2	86·1	63·4
157. AKUT ...	1667	191·4	153	138	147	64·5	36.	79·9	93·8	55·8
158. IAKOIAKO	1624	189	148	123	141·2	66	44	78·3	87·1	66·6
159. NOKALAON	1769	200·3	155	131·2	154	60·2	51·5	77·3	85·1	85·5
160. IAMET ...	1694·5	193·5	146·7	129·4	144·5	64	45	75·8	89·5	70·3
161. LOKMAN	1707	199	175	133·2	151·4	64	46	87·9	87·9	71·8
162. NAKO ...	1731	193	150·3	131	147	63	42	77·8	89·1	66·6
163. KATENA	1751·5	187·6	152	129·2	147	63	43	81	87·8	68·2
164. IOLU ...	1598	197·2	145	128·5	138·4	62	42	73·5	92·8	67·7
165. NUMISA	1682	181	141·5	122·5	152·5	57	41	78·1	81	71·9

Tanna Measurements. All males over 18 (continued)

West Coast. 55 to 187 inclusive

Name	Height	Head		Facial Height	Bi-zy. Breadth	Nasal		Indices		
		Length	Breadth			Height	Breadth	Cephalic	Facial	Nasal
166. IATI ...	1699	190·2	147·2	113·4	143·6	51	40	77·3	78·9	78·4
167. NOPUAT ...	1646·5	186·4	149·2	132	142	57	43	80	92·9	75·4
168. NIPIO ...	1668	205·4	158·3	128	149	56·5	47·5	77	85·9	84
169. IOMA ...	1625·5	196	161·2	144	143·2	63	45	82·2	100·5	71·4
170. JAMES ...	1632	190	147	128·5	142	64	37	77·3	90·4	57·8
171. CIRKOLOAO	1510	190·2	159	128·2	143	60	39	83·5	89·6	65
172. TOVI ...	1690	206	170·1	137	151	68	42	82·5	90·7	61·7
173. IAWA ...	1571	189	153·5	126	139	59	42	81·2	90·6	71·1
174. IATA ...	1692	199	152·3	128	151	57	45	76·5	84·7	78·9
175. KENTNA ...	1605	182	146	130·5	137	68	44	80·2	95·2	64·7
176. KAMUT ...	1572	191	153	131·5	149	56	45	80·4	88·2	80·3
177. MANHEV ...	1544	181	154·4	126	140	62	38	85·3	90	61·2
178. NABIKO ...	1664	186	162	133·2	144	60	42	87	92·5	70
179. NESIAN ...	1608	196	158	128	144	59	39	80·6	88·8	66·1
180. IOMA ...	1737	206	152	117·7	142	57	40	73·7	82·8	70·1
181. TOM ...	1696	194	147	138	150	66	41	75·7	92	62·1
182. IAKE ...	1632	182·4	156	127	146	57	44	85·5	86·9	77·1
183. JOE ...	1636	195	155	123	140	54	45	79·4	87·8	83·3
184. KAI ...	1559	190·5	141	125	140	60	50	74	89·2	83·3
185. NUBOIS ...	1710·5	196	147·5	123	145	52·5	46·5	75·2	84·8	88·5
186. NOK ...	1620	194	150	118	148·5	54	36	77·3	79·4	66·6
187. SERK ...	1700	179·6	142	117·5	137	50	43	79	85·7	86
188. VANI an Aniwan	1581	193	162·5	119·3	157·4	48·2	44·4	84·2	75·8	92·1

SOCIAL MORPHOLOGY

THE TRIBE. Tribal organization, as generally understood, exists in this island in a modified form only. The definition of a "Tribe," that perennial question, which has been the bane of ethnologists for many years, seems to be given best by Rivers. He says (1914, p. 15): "By the word 'tribe' I mean a group of a simple kind, always in Melanesia settled in a definite locality, which speaks a common language and is capable of uniting for common action as in warfare." In Tanna it is found generally that a group of villages, often five or six in number, is united by some common tie. This may be similarity of dialect or geographical position. Several villages in a small valley, enclosed by the same range of hills, have kindred interests in many cases, though this condition is not constant throughout the islands. Villages have been known to split into two or more factions through a disagreement concerning some local matter, the disgruntled members of the community removing in a body, with their wives and children, to found a new village elsewhere. It is possible that the tribe and village community may have been identical at one time and that the large number of villages today, speaking a common dialect, is the result of one disruption after another. There have been removals, also, of entire villages to a more healthful or otherwise advantageous site. In one case, in the village near Sulphur Bay, on the east side of the island, an old chief, KAWI (see Enophulus, Pedigrees I), lives on alone in his old home while his people have built a new village on a higher and more healthful spot more than a mile away. The women take a kindly interest in the old man and he seems to be plentifully supplied with food and constantly receives visits from the men and children of his village group.

Whether the tribe and the village community were co-existent originally is not material. According to Gray (1892, pp. 648-9) the geographical districts are not coincident with the tribal organization. There are two main groups in the island, the *Numrikwen*, covering the entire east and south-east section and part of the west and north-west; and the *Kauyamera*, living in the south-west only. These, as will be seen later, are linguistically quite distinct and their tribal grouping has nothing in common. The *Numrikwen*, numerically great and covering a large area, are divided into groups, sometimes large, sometimes small, with or without dialectic differences. In some cases separate tribal units have common dialects. There are also dialectic divisions in tribal units, though they are invariably large. On the whole the tribal units of the *Numrikwen* may be said to conform to the dialectic divisions of the people. Thus they fall into line with Rivers's definition. Of the *Kauyamera* tribal units little is known, and this linguistic group, remote, speaking a language quite un-Melanesian, though with certain Melanesian affinities, deserves further study before it is too late.

There is also a division of the people of this island, generally, into two groups, the *Kwatahren* or coastal folk and the *Nieli asolimin* or *Numata keiyiv*, the inland folk. Although these distinctions are said to go back to early days they are probably only geographical.

THE CLAN. Of clans, as usually understood, there is no direct evidence. Wherever one goes, however, one constantly finds unexpected evidences of what, in other parts of the world, would be called clan symbolism. Many of my informants believed that certain people are descended from certain birds. For example, the wagtail or flycatcher (*takaskisi*), the long-tailed tit (*garafi*), the hawk (*melikom*), the black hawk (*mianuhu*) are acknowledged to be birds from which people descended at one time, though the present knowledge of just who are these descendants of bird ancestors is entirely lacking. KUOKAREI told me of an instance where a group used to belong to the banana people and the eating of that fruit was taboo in a certain number of villages in the vicinity of the Mission at Whitesands. Today there is no sign of this prohibition. The banana is eaten freely by all people everywhere as far as is known and most certainly in this particular locality. KUOKAREI added that the people of the villages where the banana was taboo used to exchange the banana for a fruit which they might eat, making the exchange with villages where there was no prohibition against the fruit in question. This exchange form of totemism has no connection with the double form of the custom found in Fiji and elsewhere[1]. In Enophulus, a few miles from Whitesands, there is evidence that such things as bread-fruit, wind-and-rain and other natural phenomena have been used as clan symbols. More definite is the information as to fowls in this connection. Many natives bore testimony to this. There is reason to believe that fowls existed in the New Hebrides prior to the arrival of the Spaniards[2]. Indeed, Turner (p. 318) insists that they have always been there. More probably they came in from Indonesia with one of the many movements of people from that area[3]. In any event, the precise locality where fowls occurred as clan symbols is not known today nor if they might be eaten by the people who claimed them. It is curious that no evidence of clan symbolism can be found existing today. In making the inquiries on this point, it seems at first that, perhaps, the exact meaning of the question was not understood by the man then being questioned. But, when all the men interrogated insisted strenuously that there is no such thing nowadays, the testimony was too strong to be ignored. Nor can reticence about a matter which is of a very personal and private nature to the native entirely explain this denial. With the consensus of opinion given against clan symbolism by a large number of the more intelligent males in the community one must admit that it does not exist today. It is probable that the breaking down of old customs and traditions which is so evident in all Tannese culture has made particular havoc in the old clan organization[4]. Beyond the belief that at some time in the past a system of clan symbolism existed in this island, one dares not go. The opinion of Rivers (1909, p.172) that, of the Southern New Hebrides, in the island of Efate alone descent from a totem animal is found, bears out this contention.

FAMILY AND KINSHIP: KINSHIP TERMS. When we come to the question of the family we find a complex and difficult problem.

In dealing with the following relationships, it must be understood that, when the terms "father," "mother," "son,"

---

[1] de Marzan, B. J., "Le Totemisme aux Iles Fiji," *Anthropos*, ii. p. 400.
[2] See Codrington, p. 10.   [3] See Macmillan-Brown, p. 251.
[4] See Speiser, F., *Z. f. Eth.* xliv. p. 398.

"daughter," "brother," "sister," "husband," "wife" are used, it is always in the so-called classificatory sense and not in the sense to which we are accustomed in our civilization. When one of the above relationship terms is applied to the physical father or mother, son or daughter, of the person in question, this will be made clear by the context. By limiting the terms employed to the eight given above, a fairly clear statement of native relationships may be obtained and consequent confusion avoided. It is scarcely necessary to add that the native terms often have no counterpart in our social organization and, even when they have a kindred meaning, the same term may be used to express the relationship of a much larger circle of individuals than is possible in our system.

At this point a word in regard to pronunciation is important. Put in its simplest form, the following rules are adhered to throughout. The vowels are pronounced as usual in all Melanesia —"a" as in "father," "e" as "a" in "fate," "i" as "ee" in "seen," "o" as it is in English and "u" as "oo" in "soon." When two vowels occur together each must be accented separately. This is always true, although native elision may convey an opposite impression. In practice, the "e" is often spoken with the tongue more to the front of the palate than is possible in saying the word "fate." In some words this shorter pronunciation is imperative, but the distinction is so subtle that the difference can only be detected by the trained ear. The consonants are pronounced almost exactly as with us. "K" may always be used instead of "c" and a final "h" is sometimes added to prolong the sound of the last vowel in the word, as in the name of one of the old chiefs, IAMUH. The "g" is pronounced as the "ng" in the English "ing" when it occurs before "i," "o" and "u" and in some cases before "a" and "e." This "ng" sound is found in Maori but not in other Polynesian languages according to Macmillan-Brown (p. 88). In all native names the males are indicated by capitals, the females by small letters.

In Tanna, at present, the family consists of the true father and mother of the group of children forming the household. Sometimes more than one family group lives together under the same roof, but this arrangement seems to be temporary, in many cases, or a matter of convenience or loyalty towards blood relations in others. Under the British-French Condominium Government, which was established in the New Hebrides in 1906, no man may have more than one wife, whether he be a nominal Christian or a heathen. In the early days polygyny was common and there is always a desire on the part of some of the bush people to return to the old order. It cannot be practised openly at the present time and partakes more of the nature of concubinage when a man has more than one woman at his disposal. Before 1906 a man regarded all the wives of his brothers and the sisters of his wives as potential wives of his own, and as such these women were regarded by all the people of the community. In many cases these women were married to men other than their potential husbands, but on the death of their partner they became the property of the potential husband and might actually cohabit with him or be bestowed by him on another man. If the woman who became his property by the death of her husband was no longer young it was rare for the owner to insist on his marital rights. She was given to another, and often younger man. This tendency, in the old days, resulted in the custom of the older men to monopolize all the young and desirable women, by the power which they possessed under the classificatory system over the sisters of their wives and the wives of their brothers. As a result it was extremely difficult for the younger men to find compatible spouses when they reached puberty, so that they were forced to accept older women or not marry at all. This state of things in Tanna corresponds with the practice of gerontocracy in other parts of the New Hebrides.

Pedigrees

TANNA I. WHITESANDS

1. KUOKAREI

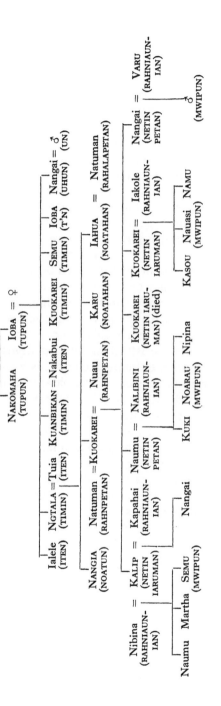

2. NALIBINI

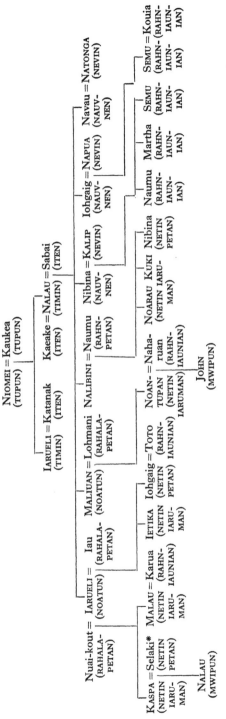

* Selaki is an irregular marriage under Christian influence. She was called NALIBINI's *netin petan* by everyone before she married KASPA. This is the only case noted in Tanna where the cross-cousin marriage regulation is not observed.

3. NATONGA

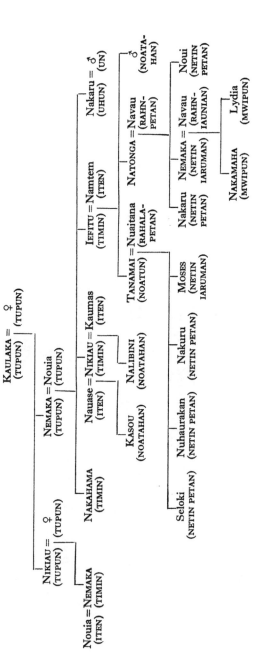

4. IAUILA

IOBA (TUPUN) = ♀ (TUPUN)

♀ (TUPUN) = SEMU (TUPUN) = Kaiva (TUPUN)   IETIKA (TUPUN) = ♀ (TUPUN)

♀-♀ = NAKUSAUKAI (ITEN) (TIMIN) — KOANELI = Maui (TIMIN) (ITEN) — IAKOLI = Wenai (TIMIN) (ITEN) — Nerevia = LAWAWA = Maui (ITEN) (TIMIN) (ITEN) — Navai = KALAGA (UHUN) (UN) — Nupaboga = NISIAN (UHUN) (UN) — Nesimu = SUUL (UHUN) (UN)

Navau = NAUVNEN (NAUVNEN) — Tauai = NAFENA (NAUVNEN) (NEVIN) — Ieris = NASE (NAUVNEN) (NEVIN) — NAPUA = Iohgaig (NOATUN) (RAHNPETAN) — KIANILI = Saloge (NOATUN) (RAHALAPETAN) — IAUILA = Nieri (RAHNPETAN) — SEMU = Kouia (NOATAHAN) (RAHALAPETAN)

Nasira = Noatira (RAHNIELI) (RAHNIAUNIAN) — Selaki = KASPA (RAHNIAUNIAN) (RAHNIELI) — Kaega = NALAU (RAHNIAUNIAN) (RAHNIELI) — SEMU (RAHNIELI) — Kapahai = LAMAI (NETIN PETAN) (RAHNIAUNIAN) — Navau = NATONGA (NETIN PETAN) (RAHNIAUNIAN)

5. Navau

NIHMEI = Kaukea
(TUPUN) (TUPUN)

IARUELI = Katanak   Kaeake = NALAU = Sabai
(TIMIN) (ITEN)   (ITEN) (TIMIN) (ITEN)

Nuai-kout = IARUELI = Iau   MALIUAN = Lohmani   NALIBINI = Naumu   Nibina = KALIP   Iohgaig = NAPUA   NATONGA = Navau
(NEWUN)   (NAMA-   (NEW-   (NAMA-   (NEWUN)   (NAMANIN) (NEWUN)   (NOA-   (RAHN-   (NOA-   (RAHN-   (RAHN-
          NIN)   UN)   NIN)   TUN)   IARU-   TUN)   IARU-   IARU-
                                                                                    MAN)   MAN)   MAN)

KASPA = Selaki   NALAU = Karua   IETIKA   Iohgaig = TOTO   NOARAU   KUKI   Nibina   Nauimu   Martha   SEMU   SEMU = Kouia   Nakaru
(NOEIN) (NOEIN) (NOEIN) (NETIN   (NOEIN)   (NOEIN) (NETIN   (NOEIN) (NOEIN) (NOEIN)   (NETIN   (NETIN   (NETIN (NETIN (NOEIN) (NETIN
                        PETAN)   IARUMAN)   PETAN)   PETAN)   IARU- IARU-   PETAN)
                                                                                                                  MAN)   MAN)

NALAU   NEMAKA = Navau   Nouia
(MWIPUN)   (NETIN   (NOEIN)   (NETIN
                                                                                                 IARUMAN)   PETAN)

                                                                                                 NAKOMAHA   Lydia
                                                                                                 (MWIPUN)   (MWIPUN)

6 A. KUKI

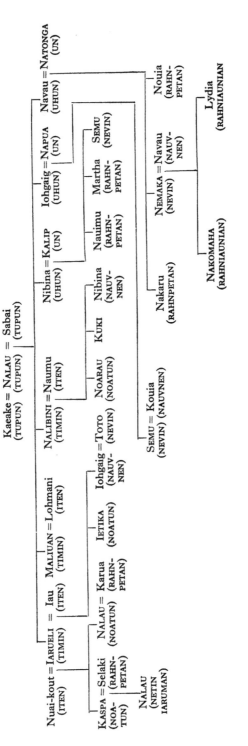

6 B. KUKI

```
                    NANGIA    Natuman = KUOKAREI = Nuau    KARU     IAHUA = Natuman
                    (TUPUN)   (TUPUN)   (TUPUN)   (TUPUN)  (TUPUN)  (TUPUN)  (TUPUN)

Nibina = KALIP = Kapahai              NALIBINI = Naumu        KUOKAREI    KUOKAREI = Iakoli    Nangai = VARU
(UHUN)   (UN)    (UHUN)               (TIMIN)    (TEN)        (UN)        (UN)      (UHUN)     (TEN)    (TIMEN)

        Nangai                                   Nibina                  KASOU       Nauasi       NAMU            ♀
Martha  (RAHNPETAN)                      KUKI    (NAUVNEN)               (NEVIN)     (RAHNPETAN)  (NEVIN)      (NAUVNEN)
(RAHN-
PETAN)
        SEMU
        (NEVIN)
Naumu
(RAHN-
PETAN)
```

TANNA II. ENOPHULUS

1. KAWI

RABAI = ♀   MARAU = ♀
(TUPUN) (TUPUN)   (TUPUN) (TUPUN)

MALIWAN = ♀   MAUIAKAN = ♀
(TUPUN) (TUPUN)   (TUPUN) (TUPUN)

NATUMAN = ♀   WAREWARE
(TUPUN) (TUPUN)   (TUPUN)

TAMEABEN = Kwanating   RAMAUHI = Kamiaua   Narua = NABUSIEN
(TUPUN) (TUPUN)   (TUPUN) (TUPUN)   (TUPUN) (TUPUN)

NAMBAS = Noanou   KILIMA = Nakit
(TIMIN) (ITEN)   (TIMIN) (ITEN)

(continued on next page)

1 KAWI (continued)

POITA (NOATUN) = Sabai (RAHNPETAN) Katenak (NAUVNEN) = IARUELI (NEVIN) Iagina (RAHNPETAN) = KAWI = Namtani (RAHNPETAN) Maui (RAHNPETAN) = NOUKOUT (NOATAHAN) = Issuela (RAHNPETAN)

Ialele (RAHN-IAUNIAN) NALIBINI (RAHN-IAUNIAN) Katenak (NETIN PETAN) Iagina = POITA (RAHN-IAUN-IAN) (NETIN IARU-MAN) Iagina = Nohlu (RAHN-IAUN-IAN) Katenak = NANGI (NETIN PETAN) (RAHN-IAUNIAN) KILIMA = Mohlu (NETIN IARU-MAN) (RAHN-IAUNIAN) Katanak = NIMETAU (NETIN PETAN) (RAHN-IAUNIAN)

MALIWAN (NETIN IARUMAN)

Katanak = IOUSI (MWI-PUN) NOUKOUT (MWI-PUN) KAWI (MWI-PUN) NIKIAU (MWI-PUN) POITA (MWI-PUN) LAWAWA (MWI-PUN) Ioa (MWI-PUN) Mavi (MWI-PUN) KOUTO (MWI-PUN) Ievis (MWI-PUN) WAKO (MWI-PUN) Numanohlu (MWI-PUN) Nanbre (MWI-PUN) PETER Wainui (MWI-PUN) ♂ (MWI-PUN)

Tau = IASUA (NETIN PETAN) (RAHN-IAUNIAN) NAMBAS = Ialele (NETIN IARUMAN) (RAHN-IAUNIAN) Rebecca = IAHIBE (NETIN PETAN) (RAHN-IAUNIAN)

Makaru (MWIPUN) TIRU (MWIPUN) Nakit (MWIPUN) Nohlu (MWIPUN)

2 A. Katanak

KILIMA = Nakit
(TUPUN) (TUPUN)

POITA = Sabai   Katanak = IARUELI   Iagina = KAWI = Namtani   Maui = NOUKOUT = Iasuela
(TIMIN) (ITEN)   (UHUN) (UN)   (ITEN) (TIMIN) (ITEN)   (ITEN) (TIMIN) (ITEN)

MALIWAN (NAMANIN)   Ialele (NEWUN)   NALIBINI (RAHN-IAUNTAN)   Katanak (NOATUN)   Iagina = POITA = Nohlu (NEW-UN) (NAMA-NIN) (NEW-UN)   Katanak = NANGI (NOATA-HAN) (RAHN-IARUMAN)   KILIMA = Nohlu (NAMA-NIN) (NEWUN)   Katanak = NIMETAU (RAHN-IARUMAN)

Katanak = IOUSI (NOEIN) (NETIN IARU-MAN)   NOUK-OUT (NOEIN)   KAWI (NOEIN)   NIKIAU (NOEIN)   POITA (NOEIN)   LAWAWA (NOEIN)   Koa (NETIN PETAN)   Mavi (NETIN PETAN)   KOUTO (NOEIN)   Ievis (NOEIN)   WAKO (NETIN IARU-MAN)   Numan-ohlu (NETIN PETAN)   Nanbre (NETIN PETAN)   PETER (NETIN IARU-MAN)   Wainuri (NETIN PETAN)   ♂ (NETIN IARU-MAN)

Tau = IASUA (NOATA-HAN) (RAHN-IARUMAN)   NAMBAS = Ialele (NAMANIN) (NEWUN)   Rebecca = IAHIBE (NOATAHAN) (RAHN-IARUMAN)

Makaru (NETIN PETAN)   TIRU (NOEIN)   Nakit (NOEIN)   Nohlu (NETIN PETAN)

2 B. Katanak

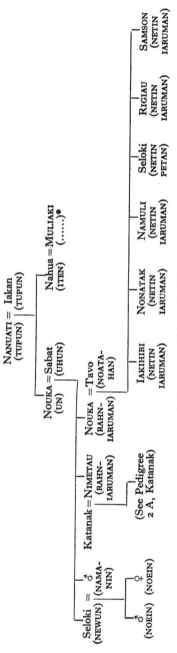

* No one could give this kinship term.

2 C. Katanak

Koupa = Matu = Nakabui
(TUPUN) (TUPUN) (TUPUN)

Kuras (UN)

Koaneli = Selogi (UN) (UHUN)

Lawawa = Tuia (UN) (UHUN)

Maui = Noukout (ITEN) (TIMIN)

Nupapoga = ♂ (ITEN) (TIMIN)

Nasi = Kavianu (NAMA-NIN) (NEWUN)

♂ (RAHNIARU-MAN)

♀ (PIAN)

Katanak = Nimetau (RAHNIARU-MAN)
(See Pedi-gree 2 A, Katanak)

♂ (NAMANIN) = ♀ (NEWUN)

♀ (NOATA-HAN)

= ♂ (RAHNIARU-MAN)

Natuman (NOEIN)

Kuk (NOEIN)

♂ (NOEIN)

♀ (NOEIN)

♂ (NETIN IARUMAN)

♀ (NETIN PETAN)

Relationship Terms

English Relationship terms of men in roman; of women in italics.
All native names in capitals, in the tables, in the text in italics. All
native terms in third person singular.

WHITESANDS DISTRICT. TANNA.

	Term	Reciprocal	
Father	TIMIN	NETIN IARUMAN	Son
Mother	ITEN	NETIN PETAN	Daughter
Elder Brother	NOATUN	NOATUN	Younger Brother
Elder Sister	NAUVNEN	NAMANIN	*Younger Brother*
Younger Sister	NAUVNEN	NAMANIN	*Elder Brother*
Elder Sister	NOATUN	NOATAHAN	*Younger Sister*
Father's Sister	UHUN	NOEIN	*Brother's Son*
„ „	UHUN	NOEIN	*Brother's Daughter*
Father's Sister's Husband	UN	RAHNIAUNIAN	Wife's Brother's Son
„ „ „	UN	RAHNIAUNIAN	Wife's Brother's Daughter
Father's Sister's Son „	NEVIN	NEVIN	Mother's Brother's Son
„ „ „ „	NEVIN	RAHNPETAN	Mother's Brother's Daughter
Father's Sister's Daughter	RAHNPETAN	RAHNIARUMAN	*Mother's Brother's Son*
„ „ „	RAHNPETAN	NEWUN	*Mother's Brother's Daughter*
Mother's Brother	UN	RAHNIAUNIAN	Sister's Son
„ „	UN	RAHNIAUNIAN	Sister's Daughter
Mother's Brother's Wife	UHUN	NOEIN	*Husband's Sister's Son*
„ „ „	UHUN	NOEIN	*Husband's Sister's Daughter*
Father's Father	TUPUN	MWIPUN	Son's Son
„ „	TUPUN	MWIPUN	Son's Daughter
Father's Mother	TUPUN	MWIPUN	*Son's Son*
„ „	TUPUN	MWIPUN	*Son's Daughter*
Mother's Father	TUPUN	MWIPUN	Daughter's Son
„ „	TUPUN	MWIPUN	Daughter's Daughter
Mother's Mother	TUPUN	MWIPUN	*Daughter's Son*
„ „	TUPUN	MWIPUN	*Daughter's Daughter*
Wife's Father	UN	RAHNIAUNIAN	Daughter's Husband
Wife's Mother	UHUN	RAHNIAUNIAN	„ „
Husband's Father	UN	RAHNIAUNIAN	Son's Wife „
Husband's Mother	UHUN	RAHNIAUNIAN	„ „
Wife	RAHNPETAN	RAHNIARUMAN	*Husband*
Wife's Sister	RAHNPETAN	RAHNIARUMAN	*Sister's Husband*
Brother's Wife	RAHNPETAN	RAHNIARUMAN	*Husband's Brother*
Wife's Brother	NEVIN	NEVIN	Sister's Husband
Brother's Wife	NEWUN	NEWUN	*Husband's Sister*

All father's brothers and mother's sisters have the same relationship term as the father and
mother respectively, their children, the same as brother and sister.

Relationship Terms

SOUTH TANNA.

	Term	Reciprocal	
Father	RIMINI	NERIN IARUMAN	Son
Mother	REHNI	NERIN PERAN	Daughter
Elder Brother	P'RENI	P'RISINI	Younger Brother
Elder Sister	PINI	PUMANI	*Younger Brother*
Younger Sister	PINI	PUMANI	*Elder Brother*
Elder Sister	P'RENI	P'RISINI	*Younger Sister*
Father's Sister	KUSI	—	Brother's Son
			Brother's Daughter
Father's Sister's Husband	M'RENI	KAFUKWANIAN	Wife's Brother's Son
	M'RENI	KAFUKWANIAN	Wife's Brother's Daughter
Father's Sister's Son ,,	—	—	Mother's Brother's Son
	—	SAVANIPERAN	Mother's Brother's Daughter
Father's Sister's Daughter	SAVANIPERAN	SAVANIIARUMAN	*Mother's Brother's Son*
	SAVANIPERAN	—	*Mother's Brother's Daughter*
Mother's Brother ,, ,,	M'RENI	KAFUKWANIAN	Sister's Son
	M'RENI	KAFUKWANIAN	Sister's Daughter
Mother's Brother's Wife	KUSI	—	*Husband's Sister's Son*
,, ,, ,,	KUSI	—	*Husband's Sister's Daughter*
Father's Father	RUPUNI	MWIPUNI	Son's Son
	RUPUNI	MWIPUNI	Son's Daughter
Father's Mother ,,	RUPUNI	MWIPUNI	*Son's Son*
	RUPUNI	MWIPUNI	*Son's Daughter*
Mother's Father ,,	RUPUNI	MWIPUNI	Daughter's Son
	RUPUNI	MWIPUNI	Daughter's Daughter
Mother's Mother ,,	RUPUNI	MWIPUNI	*Daughter's Son*
,, ,,	RUPUNI	MWIPUNI	*Daughter's Daughter*
Wife's Father	M'RENI	KAFUKWANIAN	Daughter's Husband
Wife's Mother	KUSI	KAFUKWANIAN	
Husband's Father	M'RENI	KAFUKWANIAN	Son's Wife ,,
Husband's Mother	KUSI	KAFUKWANIAN	,, ,,
Wife	SAVANIPERAN	SAVANIIARUMAN	*Husband*
Wife's Sister	SAVANIPERAN	SAVANIIARUMAN	*Sister's Husband*
Brother's Wife	SAVANIPERAN	SAVANIIARUMAN	*Husband's Brother*
Wife's Brother	—	—	Sister's Husband
Brother's Wife	—	—	*Husband's Sister*

Relationship Terms

KWAMERA DISTRICT.   TANNA.

	Term	Reciprocal	
Father	RIMINI	TINI	Son
Mother	RINI	TINI	Daughter
Elder Brother	BREIANI	BRASINI	Younger Brother
Elder Sister	PIVINI	POMANI	*Younger Brother*
Younger Sister	PIVINI	POMANI	*Elder Brother*
Elder Sister	BREIANI	BRASINI	*Younger Sister*
Father's Sister	GUSUII	BRASINI	*Brother's Son*
	GUSUII	BRASINI	*Brother's Daughter*
Father's Sister's Husband	MERANI	KUNKWANIEN	Wife's Brother's Son
„ „ „	MERANI	KUNKWANIEN	Wife's Brother's Daughter
Father's Sister's Son	IAFUNI	IAFUNI	Mother's Brother's Son
	IAFUNI	—	Mother's Brother's Daughter
Father's Sister's Daughter	—	—	*Mother's Brother's Son*
	—	RUKWEINI	*Mother's Brother's Daughter*
Mother's Brother „	MERANI	KUNKWANIEN	Sister's Son
	MERANI	KUNKWANIEN	Sister's Daughter
Mother's Brother's Wife	GUSUII	BRASINI	*Husband's Sister's Son*
„ „ „	GUSUII	BRASINI	*Husband's Sister's Daughter*
Father's Father	RUPUNI	MIPONI	Son's Son
	RUPUNI	MIPONI	Son's Daughter
Father's Mother	RUPUNI	MIPONI	*Son's Son*
	RUPUNI	MIPONI	*Son's Daughter*
Mother's Father	RUPUNI	MIPONI	Daughter's Son
	RUPUNI	MIPONI	Daughter's Daughter
Mother's Mother	RUPUNI	MIPONI	*Daughter's Son*
„ „	RUPUNI	MIPONI	*Daughter's Daughter*
Wife's Father	MERANI	KUNKWANIEN	Daughter's Husband
Wife's Mother	GUSUII	KUNKWANIEN	„ „
Husband's Father	MERANI	KUNKWANIEN	Son's Wife
Husband's Mother	GUSUII	KUNKWANIEN	„ „
Wife	—	—	*Husband*
Wife's Sister	—	—	*Sister's Husband*
Brother's Wife	—	—	*Husband's Brother*
Wife's Brother	IAFUNI	IAFUNI	Sister's Husband
Brother's Wife	RUKWEINI	RUKWEINI	*Husband's Sister*

An explanation of the pedigrees will throw some light on the system of relationship prevailing in Tanna. The terms in brackets below each name express that person's relationship to the subject of the pedigree. This term would not be used by the man or woman concerned, but would be used by a third person in speaking of them. For example, suppose a man wishes to say "KALIP is KUOKAREI's son." He expresses himself as follows: *KALIP netin iaruman KUOKAREI*, or simply *Netin iaruman KUOKAREI*, indicating KALIP by a gesture. When a man speaks of his own son to another man he uses an entirely different form. In this case KUOKAREI says of KALIP, *KALIP netaku iaruman* or "KALIP is my son," or, as the jargon-English has so literally translated it "KALIP son-belong-me."

In Pedigree I (Whitesands) we find a marked regularity of kinship terms throughout. KUOKAREI has an older brother NANGIA. This man is always spoken of by a third person as KUOKAREI's *noatun*. His younger brother is his *noatahan*. His wife Nuau was his *rahnpetan*. She died many years ago. Also, his wife Natuman, whom he took to himself after the death of his brother IAHUA, is spoken of as his *rahnpetan*. This later wife, while she was still living with her first husband IAHUA, was called the *rahalapetan* of KUOKAREI. These two words have the same meaning in Tannese but *rahnpetan* seems to have a more intimate meaning than *rahalapetan*.

Again, his father NGTALA is called his *timin*. The brother of his father KUANBIKAN is also his *timin*. His mother Tuia is spoken of as his *iten*, as is also Ialele, the sister of his father. In the line of the descendants of this same KUOKAREI his son KALIP is called, as we have seen above, his *netin iaruman*. This term is used in speaking of all his sons, TAMAS, the KUOKAREI who died, and the other KUOKAREI still living. His daughter Naumu is called his *netin petan*, as is his younger daughter Nangai. NALIBINI and VARU, the husbands of these two women, are always spoken of as his *rahniaunian*, as are the wives of his sons, Nibina, Kapahai and Iakole, *rahniaunian* being a term applicable to either sex. The children of his sons and daughters are all spoken of as his *mwipun*, without regard to the sex of the child. Thus it will be seen we have in this pedigree of KUOKAREI an excellent example of all those taken on Tanna. It is an extremely regular system of relationship[1] containing nothing in the least unusual. An examination of the other pedigrees in the tables will convince the reader that there are no special terms for a particular relative, such as the mother's brother or the father's sister, found in some other parts of the Western Pacific, and that the relationship system of Tanna is one of the most simple in the New Hebrides. In passing it must be noted that calling the father and all his brothers the father of the child does not in the least signify "any looseness in the actual view of proper paternity and maternity" (Codrington, 1891, p. 36).

There is no present evidence of a dual organization of society with matrilineal descent in the island, and the present descent is purely patrilineal, but a gradual change from matrilineal to patrilineal descent may have been in progress for some time[2], and one cannot help thinking that a state of exogamy and matrilineal descent existed in the past.

ADOPTION. This custom is common even at the present time and has been so always. Its method seems to be entirely free and if anyone takes a fancy to a child and its true parents do not object the matter is considered as settled without further ceremony. The child inherits from his adopted parent equally with the latter's own children and becomes one of the tribe of his adopted father. In the old days, in the event of a declaration of war, he was expected to fight on the side of his adopted parents, even if the hostilities were being conducted against the tribe of his true parents. KUOKAREI is an adopted son, having been taken by NGTALA when he was very young, so young that he remembers nothing of his life before that event.

CHIEFTAINSHIP. Turner, an early observer of Tannese life, found more than one chief in village groups of from eighty to one hundred people (p. 315), but each village community in the island has only its own chief today. It is a question if the word explains precisely the status of this leader in village life.

[1] This is noted by Fison, L., pp. 156-7.
[2] This is noted by Lang, A., "The Origin of totem names and beliefs," *Folklore*, XIII. 1902, p. 351.

A chief, ethnologically speaking, is the man in whom the government of a fairly large body of people is vested. Although the term "head man of the village" expresses better, perhaps, the sort of man a Tannese chief really is, the latter term will be adhered to as being shorter and more concise than any other. In the old days, the power of this chief was considerable, nor is it now insignificant. For example, no fighting was allowed to begin unless all the chiefs of all the villages constituting the tribe agreed to it. The control of a chief over the people of his village was, in those days, practically absolute. No marriage of any member of the village group could take place without his consent and all women eligible as wives were at his disposal. In the case of any delinquency among his people, the chief dealt with the offender, pronounced judgement and ordered punishment. Even if death was the penalty commanded, his prerogative seems to have been absolute. When the matter concerned the other villages of the tribe as well, the chiefs met in council and after a long discussion came to an agreement as to the manner of punishment. On the east coast of the island there seems to have been no suzerain chief with power of final decision over the village chiefs. On the west coast, on the other hand, there is direct evidence that a chief IAMUH, now long dead, but remembered by the older men, was suzerain over eight villages and wore a *qeria*, or head-dress, higher than that of the village chiefs. A chief of the type of IAMUH had also certain privileges at certain feasts. If a turtle was caught, he took the head secretly and cooked and ate it in private, unseen by his people. The following day the remainder of the turtle was eaten by all.

On the east coast, where any chief with superior powers over the village chiefs of his group seems to be entirely lacking, the relation of the village chiefs to each other in common council is curious, and so distinctly different from that found in most parts of Melanesia that one is inclined to regard it as one of the evidences of the breaking down of old traditions, and to believe that in the past there was a suzerain chief over every group of villages in this part of the island as well. It is curious, if this be true, why there is no recollection of some kind of suzerain chief among the older men of this region. KAWI and

3–2

KUOKAREI insist that no man was endowed with superior powers in that vicinity even when they were children. If a neighbouring group of chiefs was called into consultation, there was no one in the council with superior powers. Matters were discussed freely and frankly, various opinions were expressed as to the method of procedure; if disagreements occurred, a postponement of the gathering might take place, but, at the final meeting, some definite decision was reached by general agreement. This agreement was not reached by a vote of those present, but by a kind of general groping in the dark of uncertainty toward the light of a final decision. It seems to have been a good deal like the general discussion in any board of governors today, with the intimate opinion of the group decided in the end by instinctive feeling and not by a definite vote. In these discussions, today as formerly, other males of the chiefly class may take part freely and express frankly their opinion, but the final decision today rests with the Government Agent who presides at these meetings and seems to take the place of the suzerain chief in other parts of the island in the old days. It is said that any old man of the tribe who was of the chiefly class might, in the old days, attend these councils without being asked and express his opinion freely. While no objection to this appears to have been made by the chiefs present, the final decision rested with the highest chief present (except on the east coast of the island), independent of any remarks made by the uninvited members of the community.

When a chief dies he is succeeded by one of his sons, in the classificatory sense[1]. In the old days, when polygyny was common, the son of a favourite wife had no especial claim to the succession. Nowadays, there is no evidence that the dying man names his successor. Rather, the men of the village, of the chiefly class, meet together and name the youth who is to become chief. If the eldest son of the late chief is not considered a proper person to rule, he is never chosen. On this everyone insists. This practice of selection of the best man seems to be common in the Pacific[2]. Even if there is only one male who

[1] Speiser, F., *Z. f. Eth.* XLVI. p. 464, says that the office of chief may be inherited directly, without conditions.
[2] This is found on Saa by Codrington, 1891, p. 50.

may be regarded as son to the deceased chief, he is not chosen if he is considered undesirable by the council of old men, but some male member of the group fitted for the duties of chieftainship is chosen in his place. In some cases adoption, which we have seen is a simple process with these people, precedes this choice.

Without any doubt, there were special insignia for each chief in the old days. We have seen that a certain man (IAMUH) wore a head-dress higher than his fellows. This was, evidently, something quite apart from the clan symbol, for no one can be induced to admit that there is now any such thing. It is admitted that the common design of tapa belt, a sort of lozenge pattern, of which one is now in the Ethnological Museum at Cambridge, was worn only by the family of the chief in the old days, although the prerogative is not exclusively adhered to now. Belts of this design are still very common in the bush, and a more elaborate design is also found, but this is said to have been introduced from another island.

On the whole, there seems ground for believing that there was a suzerain chief over every group of villages in the old days in all parts of the island, and that the lack of this group head on the east coast is due to some outside influence, which weakened the local council. This accounts for the fact that the people of the west coast near Lenakel regard IAVIS (now a ruling elder of the Presbyterian mission in that part) as one who was formerly a suzerain chief, worthy to wear the high head-dress of his office. But KUOKAREI (an elder in good standing on the east coast) is thought by his people never to have been a chief of higher standing than the others in his part of the island. It is significant that KUOKAREI is regarded by IAVIS's people as one who was a suzerain chief in the old days, though his own people know nothing about any such office.

TRIBAL LIFE

DOMESTIC CONDITIONS. The clothing of the Tannese is extremely scant. The men wear a belt made of tapa not more than half an inch wide, drawn tightly around the waist and pressing tightly on the hip bones. This and the penis case constitute the entire clothing of the male. The women wear a grass skirt reaching to a little above the ankles and that is all. The children wear nothing before puberty, although young girls sometimes wear a double apron made of grasses[1]. Under Christian influence the men have adopted the *lavalava* now general in Melanesia, which consists of a long piece of cotton cloth, usually brightly coloured, of regulation length and width, being perhaps two yards long and half a yard wide, worn around the loins, held by an adroit twist at the navel, the surplus part hanging down in front. The Christianized women wear some sort of garment over the grass skirt, often the ubiquitous "mother-hubbard" of the Pacific. There is a decided tendency now to reduce the amount of clothing worn rather than to increase it. Older women sometimes wear a cap made of a plantain leaf fitting quite closely to the head. This seems to be most common at feasts, when a freshly made cap is worn looking very trim and neat[2].

Concealment of the penis is found with a wide distribution in the Pacific[3], and this custom is one of the strongest in Tannese culture today. The delicacy of a man in this respect, even when bathing in a group of his own sex, is remarkable. The penis case is made of fibre, cloth, or leaves, over an inner case of leaves. Around this is wound a twine made of plaited fibre, from the base outward, leaving the outer end knotted so that it may be loosened easily. This article of dress is worn invariably under the *lavalava* by the Christianized natives. The free end of the penis case is tucked into the belt in front.

The native method of hair-dressing is remarkable. A curved wooden frame is used for supporting the neck of the victim, who lies on the ground on his back while the hair-dresser does his work. Beginning at the forehead, strands of hair are plaited with a twine made of fibre from the inner bark of a certain tree. The hair is pulled so tight that a headache lasting for several days often results from a dressing. The whole process is a

[1] See Gray, 1892, p. 647.   [2] See Forster, p. 280.
[3] See Krusenstern, A. J. von, *A Voyage round the World*, London, 1813, p. 156, for remarks on this custom on Nukahiva in the Marquesas.

lengthy one, for, as the hair grows, additional strands of fibre are added. Colour is now seldom used, but in earlier days these wisps would be coloured red or black[1]. When the work is finished, all the plaits are drawn back from the forehead and a band is passed over the head from ear to ear, to hold the dressed hair in place. The band is made of leaves, of tapa, or of imported cloth, and has no design or ornamentation on it nowadays. The hair behind the fillet is very long in many cases, and being woolly, sticks out in a great mass. Most of the Christianized natives now clip the hair fairly short in the manner of the American negro, but among the bush people the native method is almost universal, though occasionally it is dyed a light colour with lime and worn long in a great mop on the head, as one sees it in Fiji, thus adding another element to the strong resemblances between the islands[2].

No scarification or tattooing exists today, though the former is still to be seen on Aniwa.

The women make their skirts of grass or of the leaves of pandanus or sugar cane. These are plaited on to a band of tapa cloth and the workmanship is sometimes extremely good and suggests what is commonly called "smocking" by women of our civilization. Skirts are worn longer as the years go by, but never so long in Tanna as in Eromanga.

The men often wear an arm band just above the elbow, in which they carry a clay pipe at the present time. These arm bands are made of coconut shell, or of one of the many kinds of sea shells found on the beaches[3]. The pipe is an innovation since the first coming of the white man, introduced, according to Erskine, about 1849[4]. Some of the younger men and an occasional woman wear white or coloured beads or shark's teeth around the neck in the form of necklaces[5]. Earrings in the shape of a three-pronged fork are often worn in the pierced ear lobe and this perforation is almost universal among the males. There is now no evidence of boring the septum of the nose, although it was noted in the island in the middle of the last century[6].

[1] Cf. Turner, p. 309. He counted 700 separate wisps of hair on one head.
[2] Williams, pp. 136 et seq.
[3] Cook, p. 80. [4] Cook, p. 312; Codrington, 1891, p. 352.
[5] Turner, p. 311. [6] Turner, p. 310.

Face painting is still resorted to, especially at important feasts. The most common design consists of narrow lines of green drawn horizontally across the face. In the old days, a common form of face decoration seems to have been a plastering of red ochrous earth over a layer of black[1]. A special red earth used in making this pigment was brought formerly from Anaiteum[2], but this commerce is now extinct.

Houses are generally scattered at random, although, in the newer Christian villages, there are evidences of symmetrical arrangement. The Tanna house nowadays is rectangular, with gable roof. The uprights, cross beams, gable poles and ridge poles are made of the peeled trunks of trees of the proper length and thickness. These are said to be made of different kinds of wood in different parts of the island. The inner wall is of nicely plaited reeds of the *nameli* plant in symmetrical pattern. A certain number of strands are plaited together horizontally and an equal number vertically, each group being carried below the other at regular intervals. The result is a diaper pattern which is extremely neat and agreeable to the eye. The thatching of the roof and the outer wall is usually of dried wild sugar cane, laid on very thick. Sometimes these outer walls, and also the ridge pole, are reinforced along the top with "weather strips" of dried coconut leaves. A house well made in this way will be dry in the heaviest tropical downpour. In some cases the ridge pole is protected by a flat plaited strip of coconut leaves laid lengthwise, half covering the roof on each side. One modern native house is oval in shape, with a sort of verandah carried round the apsidal end. This is the only evidence of a round house in the island and no one can tell why it is built in this way or whence the builder derived his inspiration. Certainly no round house has ever been heard of there.

The house of the olden time, the only type found by the first white visitors to the island[3], is quite a different affair. Some are still seen in the bush. They are more like a tent with a ridge pole and the gable sides sloping to the ground, while the open ends are often closed by a thatching of sugar cane to keep out the rain. The women do their part in building the houses, for

[1] Erskine, p. 306.   [2] Brenchley, p. 207.   [3] Erskine, p. 318.

they gather all the reeds used for thatch and make it up into
bunches of the required size. The rest of the work is done by
the men and there do not seem to be any special carpenters:
all men know how to build a house, and fall to when one is
about to be erected, a common custom in other islands[1]. All
the houses, except in a few cases where certain articles of white
man's furniture have been acquired, are practically empty.
Plaited grass mats on the ground seem to be almost the only
furnishings and sometimes even these are lacking. A house is
usually put up in a few hours without undue exertion, for the
physical power of the men in performing manual labour is
great[2].

In an island rich in fruits of all kinds, where there is ample
food for everyone, the preparation of food does not seem to be
as important a matter as in some less favoured parts of the
world, and no attempt at preservation of fruit like the *madrai*
of Fiji is found here[3]. Whenever a native feast is in prospect,
however, the activity of the housewife gives ample evidence
that the women are able to prepare food whenever the need is
urgent. The principal article at a native feast is the pudding,
which is made from a wide variety of ingredients, though the
coconut is usually common to them all. Tanna is particularly
rich in coconut palms[4], and they are, as is usual in the Pacific,
largely distributed along the beaches, though there is a tendency
now to plant further inland[5]. The preparation of this article of
food is as follows: a certain kind of banana is peeled and left
in the sun to dry, the dried fruit is grated over a banana leaf
by rubbing up and down on a stick of tree fern, the thorn-like
projections of which make a perfect grater. Coconut kernel is
grated in the same manner, and the two ingredients are mixed
together, with a little water, until a dough-like substance is
formed which, after being moulded by hand into a large round
mass, is wrapped in banana leaves. The permanent oven, which
forms a part of every village and which is used only once a day,
as in Fiji and elsewhere[6], consists of a large round hole in the

[1] See Coombe, F., p. 7.   [2] See Gray, J. A. I. p. 128.
[3] Cf. Codrington, 1891, p. 319.
[4] This was noted by Forster, p. 260.
[5] Guppy, II. 1903, p. 436.   [6] See Williams, p. 139.

ground, perhaps two or three feet deep, in a place convenient to a group of houses but not too near any of them. A fire is made near the oven, to heat the stones used in cooking. All fire-making on Tanna is by means of a grooved stick. An exact picture of the method employed is given by Hutchinson (I. p. 85), which is in agreement with the only method observed by Codrington (1891, p. 320). A layer of the hot stones is placed in the bottom of the oven and upon these a number of puddings wrapped in their covers are laid, another layer of hot stones being placed on these. A covering of earth and a plentiful scattering of dried leaves is placed on the upper layer of hot stones and the whole is left for several hours. No water is poured in at all and steam has no place in the process, which seems to be unlike the usual custom in the New Hebrides[1]. The women have an instinctive feeling when the right moment for opening the oven arrives, for when the earth, the leaves and the upper layer of stones are removed, the pudding is found invariably to be neither over- nor under-done. The pudding is lifted out carefully and set on the ground at one side. This manner of cooking is common to the Pacific, though water and consequent steam are more generally employed than not, but a general uniformity in the process is found as widely scattered as the Society Islands[2] and Torres Straits[3].

On one occasion, when a number of visiting Aniwans arrived unexpectedly and it was necessary to prepare food for an unusual number of people, a pudding was made at least three feet in diameter, requiring the united efforts of three men and three women to lift it from the oven. Tough fibres were worked under the pudding diametrically across in three directions, so that each person had a good hold on the cord. The smaller puddings are removed by women who protect the hands by a piece of banana leaf.

Pigs are cooked, wrapped in leaves, in the same manner. If the pig is small (and the little ones are considered a great delicacy), it is cooked in the same oven with the puddings, and the pork is excellent. A large pig often needs an oven to itself,

---

[1] Noted in Tahiti by Ellis, I. p. 352.   [2] *Ibid.*
[3] Haddon, IV. 1912, p. 132.

but, being a rare treat, is usually cooked only on festive occasions. While we have every reason to believe that the pig was introduced into the Pacific, the natives themselves have no remembrance of a time when it did not form a staple article of diet, particularly at feasts. Pigs were noted by Captain Cook's party (Forster, p. 328), and Erskine (p. 321) found them plentiful at the time of his visit.

The cooking is done usually in the early evening and the men sit in groups by themselves and often eat far into the night. The women, too, form groups by themselves. This seems to be the usual plan at the ordinary evening meal[1], and Codrington has shown how general this custom is in the Pacific (1891, pp. 232–3).

The usual evening meal is eaten in the open space in the centre of the village and does not take place at a regular time, for various circumstances, such as the return of the men from their hunting or from working in their gardens, govern the hour. It is a common sight to see a group of men eating together and being waited on by some women who are busy cooking the yams or taro prepared directly in the ashes of the common fire on ordinary occasions, while others from the same village group chat with them but show no desire to eat. To make a noise with the mouth while eating is regarded as a compliment to the cook, and at feasts the audible evidence of the appreciation of the food set before the guests is very great. This is not in accord with the observations of Forster (p. 288), but the polite native he observed may have been a sporadic case.

Formerly each village is said to have had its own dancing ground, where all feasts were held[2]. The great number of deserted dancing grounds today testifies to the large number of villages in the old days, but it seems unlikely that a dancing ground existed in each village, in spite of the word of Turner on the subject and the testimony of the older men. Gray says that the common public square or dancing ground was, in his day, the centre of a tribe and that where there was a "square" there was also a chief (1892, p. 648). The native name for this dancing place is *imeium*, which is the word applied to the men's

---

[1] Wharton, p. 91. [2] Turner, p. 316.

house in each village as well, so that some connection between the two may have existed in the past. In the vicinity of White-sands each village site, whether deserted or still occupied, has its own dancing ground just as it has its own men's house, while on the west side of the island the *imeium* is sometimes shared by a group of villages.

Even today, when in the act of eating, no native will receive food from the bare hand of another, for it is taboo to do so, and no Tannese would think of offering anything eatable to another unless he wrapped it in a leaf. The native does not know now why this is so, but there is an instinctive aversion to do otherwise throughout the community. Any woman may cook except during her menstrual periods, when she is restricted to preparing food for herself. No one else may cook for her or even offer her food at this time.

SEX AND MARRIAGE. This subject, in a record of any people, is a far-reaching one and may be treated most conveniently under the following subdivisions: Adultery, The *Iowhanan* Perversions, Avoidance, Marriage Regulations.

Adultery. In the old days adultery was not punished by the village chief, but he allowed the man who had been wronged to settle the matter by a trial of arms with his wife's paramour, fought with clubs. Other men of the clan of the combatants took part in the scrimmage which led to a general mêlée, though fatal results were practically unknown. No penalty for the man beyond a more or less perfunctory fight is common in parts of Australia[1], which is in decided contrast to the custom prevailing in the Northern New Hebrides and Banks' Islands, where the man is shot or clubbed and the woman beaten or scolded[2].

The more general manifestation of adultery is the seduction of a woman of a village by a man of some other tribe or group, in which case the woman is induced as a rule to run away with her lover. The economic aspect of the case makes the offence a serious matter. The woman is an important asset to the man who owns her as well as to the tribe to which she belongs.

[1] Howitt, pp. 257–8.   [2] Codrington, 1891, p. 243.

As a bearer of children, a worker in the gardens and a cook she is a distinct economic loss to her tribe and at the same time a gain to the one she joins. All sorts of complications arise in this case, and one of the most common cases brought before the Government Agent nowadays concerns this form of adultery. In the old days, war between the two groups involved was very common. Sometimes a division arose in the village where the woman lived, the people taking sides with or against the injured man. Very often some of the people of a village would belong to the clan or group of another tribe and their sympathies were invariably with their own people though, if it came to actual hostilities, these people fought always on the side of their adopted group. One distinction was always observed: if the dispute about the woman was between villages of the same group, the fighting was done with clubs and was really performed for the sake of appearances, with no fatal results; whereas, if it involved two distinct groups, the usual rules of warfare were adhered to. Since the introduction of firearms it is common for the injured man to take the law into his own hands, the man who has wronged him being ambushed and shot. It is only since 1906 that jurisdiction in the matter has passed to the Government Agent with the advice and counsel of the chiefs of the groups interested.

The Iowhanan. All villages have special houses where all unmarried circumcised males live[1]. With the exception of those under Christian influence no man may contract a marriage who has not been initiated into sexual matters by the *iowhanan*, and a man may not be betrothed until he has been touched by her. There is no special ceremonial act in the touching and it is admitted that it is generally the prelude to connection with the woman. There is no payment made to the woman for this service, but the village or tribe which furnishes her receives compensation. A young woman is sometimes given by her parents to be an *iowhanan*; but the parents seem to receive no compensation for this. The woman is painted in a special manner as a sign of her profession and wears turtle-shell earrings and other ornaments, while a shorter skirt distinguishes her from

---

[1] This agrees with Gray, 1892, p. 647. See also Webster, p. 6.

other women. After a circumcision ceremony the *iowhanan* is sent to a village to initiate the young men who have reached man's estate into the mysteries of sexual intercourse. She lives in the bachelors' house with the unmarried men, and the payment for her services is made in pigs. After her services are no longer required she returns to her native village and later makes a good marriage, and there seems to be no feeling against her on account of her former life[1]. While she is living in the bachelors' house, the mothers of the young men living with her take food to their sons, but the sisters of the youths, who are still unmarried, are most rigorously kept away. In case the *iowhanan* bears a child as a result of this visit, any man living in the *imeium* may adopt the child and become responsible for its upbringing, or it may be cared for by the inmates acting in common, though one of the men is declared to be the father of the child in order to establish its status in the community. A similar provision exists among some of the Australian tribes[2]. In the old days, a youth who was still living in his mother's house was put to death by his father if he was found to have had connection with the *iowhanan*, and he is still reprimanded severely. The unmarried men in the *imeium* make use of the *iowhanan* while she is living with them, but when she is absent a period of abstinence prevails, and very little indulgence in sexual intercourse takes place at this time. The visits of the *iowhanan* occur at the close of the circumcision ceremonial, which takes place as a rule once a year.

Perversions. Perversions of the sexual act are uncommon and, when they occur, are blamed upon the white man, though it is admitted that certain acts have crept in from islands, such as Pentecost, where such practices are resorted to on account of the scarcity of women. On the whole, Tanna has a fairly clean record and Cook, before he left the island, discovered his error in thinking the Tannese guilty of unnatural vice (2nd ed. II. pp. 66–7).

Avoidance. Avoidance was common in the past, doubtless, but there is not very much evidence of it today, though a woman

---

[1] Codrington, 1891, p. 235.   [2] Thomas, p. 106.

will never pass a man on the tracks through the bush, but will turn aside and wait for him to pass. Gray (1892, p. 674) mentions the fact that no liberties may be taken with the wife's brother by a man's sister, but careful observance of the behaviour of persons of this relationship betrays no evidence of this today. There is the same companionship between brothers and sisters, both among the bush folk and the Christianized people, as among children in our own civilization, but, after the circumcision ceremonial, there is a decided tendency to keep them apart, though the fact that the youth lives in the *imeium* may have a good deal to do with this. In the centre of the island some interesting evidence of avoidance exists, so that a certain woman may not be spoken to by a man on the track unless she is one who is spoken of by all as his *nauvnen*, which, as we have seen, means "his sister." This custom has been found in the Banks' Islands[1].

Marriage Regulations. Of marriage regulations cross-cousin marriage is the first precept that one notes everywhere and no case occurs of a marriage between the children of two sisters or the children of two brothers, while the marriage of a man with the daughter of his mother's brother or of his father's sister is common[2]. No present evidence of marriage with the daughter of the mother's brother's daughter or with the wife of the mother's brother is found here, though it still exists in the northern part of the group (Rivers, 1915, p. 85). No reason is forthcoming for the existence of the cross-cousin marriage and endless questionings on this point in different parts of the island never failed to yield the same response, that it has been so always. The Levirate still prevails in this island and Codrington is right, probably, in thinking it common to all Melanesia (1891, p. 244). The woman, as we have seen already, is at the disposal of her husband's brother, directly she is a widow. No other prohibitions survive today, though the marriage between near blood relatives is never allowed, according to the testimony of several chiefs. Among the Christian portion of the population several prohibitions are found that are not necessarily enforced by the heathen portion

[1] Rivers, *Folk-Lore*, 1910, p. 50.   [2] Thomson, p. 195.

of the Tannese. One Christian native insists that he cannot marry his sister, his mother, his brother's daughter, his mother's sister, the wife of his father's brother, or his mother's sister's daughter. All these terms are used in the Christian sense of relationship. Sometimes a Christian marriage is consummated when there is known to be a distant blood relationship on the ground that the connection is too remote to matter. No evidence of any caste restrictions of marriage are found anywhere. In fact, if we except the division of people into two classes, chiefly and common[1], no caste distinctions of any sort are discovered anywhere. The daughter of a chief, whether Christian or heathen, may marry anyone not a commoner not proscribed by the above prohibitions.

Marriages are usually arranged, at present, as in the past, by the chief of the village, and female children, at birth or soon after, are set apart for a definite alliance. The father of the youth about to be married pays in pigs for the wife of his son, but this act has nothing in common with marriage by purchase as suggested by Hobhouse (pp. 200–1). A man, on his marriage, usually remains in his native village and his bride comes to live with him and there is no memory of a time when this was otherwise. There is no evidence whatever of any special rights of the mother's brother or of the father's sister over the young man, in connection with the arrangements for or the consummation of his marriage. No woman ever makes any advances for the hand of a wife for her own son or for that of a brother. She may talk with the mother of the boy about the desirability of a match, but she has no official prerogatives in the matter as she has in some parts of Melanesia. If a man has a married sister, the child of this sister belongs to the sister's husband exclusively and not to him. He has no special jurisdiction over them, even after the death of their true father. It is a common custom that the daughters of a woman must be given to her brother's sons as wives (whether the marriages be monogamous or polygynous), at the request of the woman's brother, the father of the boys.

Let us take some concrete examples of these marriage pro-

[1] Gray, 1899, p. 130.

hibitions. If we look at Whitesands Pedigrees I we find that KUKI may marry Nangai, his mother Naumu being a sister of KALIP, the father of Nangai, which, of course, is an example of a pure cross-cousin marriage. KUKI cannot marry a daughter of Nangai (the elder of that name) and her husband VARU, had they one, for this female child would be the daughter of his mother's sister; nor can Naumu, daughter of KALIP, marry KASOU who is son of the younger KUOKAREI and her father's brother's son. This example suffices to show the method employed, and it is confidently asserted that the rule will be found to be invariable if it is applied at random in any part of the pedigrees recorded, for numberless cases were tested, always with uniform results.

Although the pedigrees recorded are from the east side of the island exclusively, the same prohibitions are found on the west coast as well as in many other parts. The ability of certain men and women, notably the latter, to remember family relationships with great accuracy, is marked. One, Katanak, of Sulphur Bay (see Enophulus, Pedigrees 2, A, B, C), has a really remarkable memory and, even if she failed occasionally, her mother Maui supplied the missing name without a moment's hesitation. Old KAWI (see Enophulus, Pedigrees 1) is almost phenomenal in his memory of these matters, considering his age and infirmities. In his case his accuracy is tested by reference to other pedigrees. Reference to his pedigree will show that he gives names of five generations of direct ancestors before his time as well as having a marvellously accurate knowledge of all his descendants. This skill in remembering relatives has often been noted in dealing with people of rude culture[1].

At Lenakel a tradition exists still that, in warfare, in the old days, a man did not shoot his sister's husband, even if he were a member of the group with which his own people were at war. In other words, friendship is possible between different tribes, where there are marriage ties, though it may be doubted if it exists where there are none. Friendship between males is shown publicly on many occasions but never

[1] Rivers, *Soc. Rev.* 1910, p. 1.

between the sexes, except between an occasional Christianized couple[1].

Among the bush people there is no special marriage ceremony. A woman may not marry before puberty, that is, before the breasts have fallen. Intercourse between those who are betrothed, before they have a home together, while not approved of officially, is condoned, and sexual laxity before marriage is not frowned upon, although it is generally ignored. Codrington shows how widely regarded chastity is in the New Hebrides (1891, p. 235). It is customary for the young man to provide a house for his wife, but sometimes it is not a convenient season to build, or for some reason a new house is not possible at the moment. In this case the couple live with the husband's father, but any such arrangement is regarded always as of a temporary nature.

There is no definite evidence of polyandry in the island, a fact confirmed by Codrington (1891, p. 245). KUOKAREI recalls one case where a woman was shared by two men, but it was not approved of, led to trouble, and one of the men was killed.

There is ample evidence how many different forms of infanticide existed in Melanesia in the old days[2], and it seems to have been a common practice in this area, sometimes however tending more to abortion, as in Fiji[3]. Female children were sometimes buried alive by the father if sons had been hoped for and not daughters. KUOKAREI never saw this done, but remembers hearing in his youth of a female child being buried alive as soon as born. In another part of the island an angry father is reported, only a few years ago, to have dashed out the brains of a female infant, but the story lacks corroboration.

There is no evidence of couvade or any traces of it in the southern part of the New Hebrides, although there is no doubt of its existence in the north[4].

CHILDHOOD GAMES. As is usual with primitive people, one is impressed in Tanna with the similarity between the children in the island and those in our own lands. Childhood seems to have its joys and sorrows in common in whatever part of the

---

[1] This was noted by Williams, 1. p. 137.   [2] Codrington, 1891, p. 229.
[3] Lawry, p. 134.   [4] Codrington, 1888, p. 844.

world we examine it. A few games played by the children are recorded. They are played at almost any time during the day, and on moonlight nights it is very common to hear the laughter of the children at play.

(1) *No name given.* This game is played with a reed of some kind. The players are divided into two groups of equal number. The boy chosen to run first for his side takes the reed in both hands and runs for the goal on the opposite side of the field. The goals are made of two uprights with a cross piece, like those used in our game of football. He tries to pass under the opposite goal before the reed is taken from him by one of the boys on the other side. The tactics are somewhat like those in our game, but no special duties are assigned to any particular player and any player in a good position for overthrowing his adversary may tackle him. At first it appears that this game must be a late introduction into the island, perhaps by some of the returned Tannese from the Queensland plantations, but several old men assert that this is not the case. It has been played as long as the oldest inhabitant can remember.

(2) *No native name ascertained.* This game seems to be played exactly as "Tag" in Europe and America. One is chosen to begin and he pursues the rest until he catches, or rather touches, another boy, when it becomes that boy's turn to pursue. This game is old, going back to before the days of the white man.

(3) *A game like our "marbles." No native name ascertained.* This is played with the operculum ("cat's eye") of a gasteropod. One is set up and another thrown at it from a given distance away. Those that miss belong to the boy that sets up the target. A hit gives the target as well as the operculum thrown to the thrower. The boy to whom the target belonged has to set up again.

(4) *Noaniberiba.* This is a variant of the above (3) but is played with black beads instead of the operculum. Very likely the same name applies to (3), although it is stated by some that such is not the case.

(5) *Musukmusuk.* This is a guessing game and is played as follows: one player is chosen and he shuts his eyes and turns his back on the other children. Someone touches the back of

the blind player, who has to guess who it is who is touching him. If he guesses correctly, the player who touched him must be blinded. Otherwise he has to continue until he has made a correct guess. The name comes from the words which the other children chant during the play. It has no meaning at the present time as far as can be learned, and seems to be only a jingle and no more. A diligent search to find some meaning for the words yielded no result.

(6) *No native name ascertained.* In this game the company is divided into two groups each with a leader. One of the players on one side is then enveloped in a big cloth or a grass mat. The entire group of the shrouded player moves out of sight and in a moment the shrouded player reappears. Often a rapid change has been made. Sometimes it has not been attempted. The other side guesses who the concealed player is. If the guess is correct the cloth goes to the opposite side. If no one guesses correctly the cloth remains with the side which commences the game. The game is finished if no one is able to identify the concealed player after all the players on the guessing side have had one chance. This seems to be a variant of (5). It is said to be a very ancient game.

There was little evidence of any knowledge of Cat's Cradle in the islands. One form called *kumhal* is practised, but it is recognized as an introduction from Efate. Considering the frequency of this pastime in Papuasia[1] and the Solomons, and its rarity in the Northern New Hebrides, its absence in this area is not unexpected[2].

NATIVE EMOTIONS. The native emotions observed and recorded are picked up at random whenever any occurrence throws light on this side of the character of the Tannese, and here, as elsewhere, notwithstanding the doubts of some observers[3], they seem to show a greater similarity to our own than is usually admitted.

One day a baby died in its mother's arms at the Mission clinic. As soon as the woman realized that the child was dead, she let

[1] See *British Museum Handbook to the Ethnological Collections*, London, 1910, p. 135.
[2] Codrington, 1891, p. 341.   [3] See Williams, I. pp. 134–5.

someone else take the body and moved away very quietly. When she was clear of the group, and before anyone suspected what she was about, she darted away towards the abrupt cliff at the top of which the Mission station stands, as if to throw herself into the sea. One of the men succeeded in overtaking and restraining her. She broke away again, however, and climbed a coconut tree hard by, and a man climbed up after her, lest she should throw herself down, though she did not attempt it. She was helped down finally, and led to her village by some of her neighbours. In the evening the missionary who had been trying to save the child at the time of its death went to see the mother, and found her moaning and being watched by some women neighbours. He gave her a hypodermic injection of morphine which put her to sleep at once. In the morning she had returned to her usual life and appeared to be normal thenceforward. Suicide among these people is generally induced by grief (Gray, 1899, p. 132), and devotion to children is a strong and pleasing characteristic[1].

A tall, commanding woman in Tanna took a fancy to a baby of about one year. She had no children of her own, and the parents of the baby had no other child. It was not a case of adoption, and no attempt toward this end was made by the woman, nor could it be learned that she was a relative of any kind. She assumed an interest in and a care of the child while it remained in the possession of the father and mother and this interference was not resented by the true parents. When the child was ill it was the foster mother who carried it to the Mission for treatment each day but, as its own mother was regarded as rather young and inexperienced by the community, this may have explained the easy acquiescence with which she permitted this interference in her domestic affairs. Evidently the foster mother thought that the baby was not properly looked after, for she was heard on one occasion roundly scolding the mother for her neglect. Later the child died. One expected a dramatic scene between the two women, but nothing happened, for when the foster mother was told of the death she took it very quietly

---

[1] See Forster, pp. 325–6; also Jackson, J. R., "Des arts et inventions de la vie sauvage," *Mem. Soc. Eth.* O.S. I. i, Paris, 1841, p. 288.

and, as far as one could observe, had forgotten the matter entirely in a couple of days.

Practical joking is very common and the Tannese are a jovial and talkative people, not, in this particular, in the least like some other Melanesians[1]. A bush boy came to the Mission one day to procure a remedy for toothache, and it was necessary to extract the tooth. He howled lustily when he felt the pain as the pincers were pressed down on the tooth. Although the pain was over in a moment, he continued to howl for some time. He did not seem to realize that the pain had ceased. Meanwhile, his companions rolled on the ground with mirth at his discomfiture. After he realized that the pain had stopped, he sat still a moment, then smiled feebly and ended by laughing as heartily as his friends, thereby only adding to their infectious mirth.

In spite of the tributes of Forster (p. 319) and Gray (1899, p. 128) to the musical voices of the natives, singing is not one of the accomplishments of the Tannese, and the hymns in which the Christian people join at a service are rendered with a great amount of enthusiasm but little melody. On the other hand, the rhythmic chant that accompanies the native dances of the bush people is soft and not unmelodious, while the sense of rhythm is perfect. Crooning over babies is heard but rarely, and always from Christian mothers. Still, it cannot be claimed that the bush women have no lullabies at all, though it is odd that none was heard when they were seen nursing their young children.

Two heathen old men of the neighbourhood accompanied a planter to a cave on the west coast of the island to remove some bones that had been discovered there. One of the men made no objection when he saw the bones being stowed in a rice sack, but the other wanted to know why they were being removed, as well as where they were to be carried. When it was explained that the bones were to be taken to a country far away so that people in that country could look at them, it made little impression. He did not appear to object to their removal and could not define his fears. He murmured something about the

[1] See Pfeil, Graf von, *Rep. Brit. Assoc.* Liverpool, 1896, pp. 939–40.

eramus—evil spirit—but made no further objection as the bones were borne away. Permission to keep the bones was asked of the chief of the village nearest the cave, and was granted without the least hesitation. The chief said that the man who objected was not a chief at all but only a *nahaknatak*, that is, not of the chiefly class, a word best translated by the jargon-English term "rubbish man[1]." The bones were placed in the store of the planter by whom the cave was explored, until such time as they could be sent across the island to be ready for shipment. The news that the bones were in the store soon spread to the native women in the planter's kitchen, and, although no objection to their removal from the cave was expressed or implied, a decided reluctance to enter the store was manifested by the entire household staff. It transpired that the chief who gave permission for the removal of the bones was a Christian, and the man who objected to their removal a heathen, but this was probably pure chance, for superstition seems as rife among the Christian people as among the heathen.

When finally the bones were sent across the island, they were wrapped carefully in paper and packed in a box, so that all evidence of the nature of the contents was destroyed, and the boy who carried the box had no idea what it contained, for, had he known, he might not have taken it so willingly.

Kissing, which is not indigenous certainly in the New Hebrides (Codrington, 1891, p. 354), seems to be unknown, and no special form of salutation is used, rubbing of noses being entirely unknown, even among Aniwans (Codrington, *loc. cit.*). Assent by a lifting of the eyebrows is very common, but this is not a custom confined to the island of Tanna[2], as it extends throughout the New Hebrides, and is found in the Solomons[3].

LAW. ENFORCEMENT OF RULES. All legal questions in the days prior to 1906, when the British-French Condominium Government was established, seem to have been decided by the chief of the village or, if the matter concerned more than one village of the tribe, by the chiefs concerned. These councils were held with or without the assistance of the older men in

[1] See Turner, pp. 320–1.
[2] See Gray, 1899, p. 130.   [3] See Guppy, 1887, p. 126.

the village, at the discretion of the chief or chiefs. If the dispute concerned one village only, it seems to have been settled by the local chief without consulting with his brother chiefs in the tribe. The procedure was as follows. The injured person, on complaint to the chief, was granted a hearing and the chief heard the evidence, gave judgement, and ordered punishment. If the chief himself was the offender, one whom he would call brother in the classificatory sense would consider the matter and consult with the other male members of the village, and even death could be ordered in this case if the acting judge and the old men agreed that it was deserved. This temporary judge might not order the death penalty without consulting the older men, but in other cases the chief himself might do so without any consultation at all.

In cases where the dispute or crime involved more than one village of the tribe, the chiefs of all the villages met in council and passed judgement. It is not clear whether judgement was pronounced if there was a disagreement between the chiefs gathered together, nor what steps were taken if one of the chiefs was judged by his fellow councillors.

Sometimes, if a man of a certain tribe was accused of witchcraft or black magic, the chief of the village to which the accused belonged, or the group of chiefs of the tribe, would ask the people of a neighbouring tribe to carry out the punishment which had been ordered. It was stated that this happened only when there had been a division among the chiefs of the culprit's tribe as to the mode of punishment, for, if the other tribe was willing to act, the use of some of the land belonging to the culprit's tribe for garden purposes was granted to the tribe whose assistance was asked.

The force of public opinion still seems to be the motive power behind the enforcement of obedience to the unwritten laws of the community.

WARFARE. In the old days, fighting was generally the result of disputes over women or land, and the trouble was inter-tribal. When one tribe decided to go to war with another, a branch of the banyan tree was sent to friendly tribes as a sign of the impending hostilities, and to ask for help in the fighting. It was sent as secretly as possible to friends and allies by both tribes about to fight, each hoping to be ready for the conflict before its enemy, so as to become the aggressor. Of course it happened often enough that one tribe only sent out the signal for war, those about to be attacked knowing nothing of the matter. The branch of the banyan was broken into small pieces by the messenger as he went along, and a piece was left at each village of the friendly tribes visited. The messengers were always young men who had recently been circumcised. On receiving the pieces of the banyan a deliberation was held by the chiefs of the friendly tribes, in which all male members seem to have taken part, but it could not be learned whether the final decision for or against war rested with the chiefs or with the entire male suffrage of the tribes. A tribe has been known to refuse to go to the assistance of its neighbours.

Sometimes a man in one of the tribes about to go to the assistance of its ally had a friend in the tribe to be attacked and, through him, a warning was sent, so that the latter was found to be prepared and fully armed when the attack began. Again, if a man had a friend in one of the groups to be attacked, it was his prerogative to refuse to fight with his own tribe. The exact meaning of this "friend" is not known, and any attempts to establish a connection between this person and a clan relative in another tribe are futile. This prerogative to remain neutral did not apply to members of the tribe beginning the hostilities, but only to those friendly tribes which agreed to come to its aid. In the one case all males over puberty were bound to fight, and any refusal to do so was regarded as treason, which was punished by death; while, in the other, if a man elected not to join the expedition, he had a perfect right to do so, and no question as to his bravery was involved.

The weapons used were the sling, by which throwing stones were despatched, these being in use in Erskine's time (p. 319), the bow, used with the sharp arrow in warfare (blunt arrows are used for killing birds), the spear and the club, the three last being seen by Cook's party[1]. Poisoned arrows, apart from

[1] Seen by Forster, p. 262.

those magically treated, seem to be unknown in this part of Melanesia[1].

Even the oldest chief interviewed did not remember the days before firearms were used in warfare, for white men have been in communication with the island since the latter part of the eighteenth century; but two or three old men remembered the flint-lock musket, which must have been one of the earliest in use. Of shields used in war there is no recollection whatever, and of killing stones careful search does not reveal one now extant. Although they were seen as recently as during the visit of Speiser in 1912, and figured by him (1923, Pl. 59), the natives persistently profess to know nothing whatever about their use.

The introduction of firearms modified the tactics of fighting to a considerable extent. In the old days, the fighting parties sometimes cleared away the bush for a clearer vision, though bush-skirmishing was the usual form of mass fighting[2], but, with the advent of firearms the bush was allowed to become as thick as possible, in order to afford protection from picketeers. Also, in the old days before the introduction of firearms, youths did not fight until hair had begun to grow on their faces, but with the use of firearms came the custom for youths to begin to fight at puberty.

Kava was prepared before leaving the village for the tribal rendezvous, and it was drunk just outside the village on this occasion, and not in the kava house. The bowls used in this ceremony were always made of coconut shell and were left in a pile by the warriors as they took the war pàth, and were not used again.

The actual fighting was more or less perfunctory[3], for when the first man was killed on either side, the man who killed him became the hero of the hour and the fighting was generally given over for the day, and a special demonstration given the successful warrior by his tribe and its allies. This meant that the next day a man must be killed on the other side in return, which is akin to rules of combat in many remote parts of the world, in early as well as late historic times[4]. Fighting was a

[1] Codrington, 1891, pp. 306–7.   [2] See Turner, p. 313.
[3] Erskine, p. 304.   [4] This agrees with Gray, 1892, p. 649.

matter of single combat in this case as it was with the Hellenes to such a great extent, and may be compared to a series of duels, as is so well pointed out by Codrington (1891, p. 305), though there is reason to believe that single combat went hand in hand with a general skirmish on certain occasions (Ellis, II. p. 487). As a rule the casualties in massed fighting were rare (Turner, p. 313).

KUOKAREI recalls an incident in his youth in North Tanna when fighting took place on one of the many small peninsulas extending a short distance into the sea, so that many of the warriors of the defeated side attempted to swim across to another point of land but were prevented from landing by the victors, who spread themselves along the shore and despatched those who came ashore in their desperation, while those who tried to remain afloat at a distance from the shore were finally drowned. This seems to be an unusual incident, for the Tannese are excellent swimmers, though less expert than the pure Polynesian peoples of the Eastern Pacific; Cook notes the ease with which the people near Port Resolution swam out to his ship when he arrived off the island (2nd ed. II. p. 51).

When fighting was the order of the day, and it seems to have been going on pretty constantly in the old days, there was no distinction between the two geographical divisions of the people and the *Numrikwen* and *Kauyamera* were allies or enemies indiscriminately. This is in accord with Gray (1892, p. 649), though there is no present evidence that cannibalism might only be indulged in when the fighting was between these two groups, as he suggests.

The signal that hostilities were over seems to have been green fronds of the coconut palm carried out between the combatants. This agrees with Cook's account, some of the natives being so armed when he landed at Port Resolution[1]. After the fighting was over, looting the villages and gardens of the vanquished was in order but, as the women and children of the latter always fled as soon as the news of defeat was spread abroad, there was never any murder or rapine following in the train of war as is

[1] Reported by Forster, p. 265.

common in so many other parts of the world. The women and children took shelter with their allies, and the villages of these people were never molested. After an interval, when feeling which ran high at first had subsided, the inhabitants of the ravaged villages returned to them and were allowed to do so without interference though, if the village had been utterly destroyed in the absence of the refugees, this occasion was chosen to found the new village in a more convenient or salubrious spot. The peaceful periods between warlike activities were short, and all the old men agree that warfare was more or less continuous in the old days. This is confirmed by the observations of Turner (p. 312) and Paton (p. 89). Holding captured land for more than a few days seems to be unheard of and the native aversion to disposing of any land belonging to the tribe is almost as strong today as it seems to have been before. This aversion is not confined to the New Hebrides[1]. The victors were too intent on the feast which was to be theirs by virtue of their prowess to bother to remain long in the villages of their conquered enemies, for, after their return a great feast was given by the aggressive tribe to all its allies, and there was great preparation and killing of pigs. At this feast, parts of the bodies of those of the enemy who had been captured after they were slain were eaten, but only the chiefs of the tribal hegemony and the warriors who had killed a man partook of this luxury. Of this latter point there seems to be some doubt, but it is very hard to make even a bush man talk frankly on these matters today. Cannibalism, as a ceremonial rite, did undoubtedly exist. It is quite likely that it was finally discontinued in very recent times.

ECONOMICS

HORTICULTURE. The question of horticulture is one of the most perplexing of the many problems in the culture of the Tannese, and it seems to resolve itself into the following statement of conditions. The land is not owned by the individual but by the tribal group, although there are indications that in some cases the chief of a village has some rights of disposal of

[1] Lawry, p. 214.

land to his heirs after his death. Whether all the land belonging to the tribe is vested in the chiefs, with the privilege of bestowing certain tracts on their successors, or whether this right now exercised is an assumed one of recent introduction, is a moot question. Land leased by planters for a term of years is paid for and the chief (or chiefs as the case may be) receives the money. That the trees on the land are owned by the individual with the right of bestowal on his heirs there can be no doubt (Woodford, p. 33), and this rule applies in all cases whether the trees are on certain parcels of land that have been inherited from a former chief or not. In some cases land is inherited with the trees on it, especially on the west coast. Coconut trees belonging to an individual are chopped down after his death, but all other trees are transmitted to his heirs together with his other possessions. This custom is common in Melanesia as observed by Codrington (1891, pp. 255, 263, 285). The son of the chief, if he succeeds his father, receives the largest share of the trees of the deceased. This rule of inheritance applies also to pigs and personal effects, although the other sons are not neglected, for they receive a share of trees, pigs and other possessions as well.

If specific instructions are left by a man as to the bestowal of his personal property, they are invariably carried out. In this, as in other matters, a high sense of honesty prevails, petty thieving being very rare[1]. Sometimes a quarrel results from the distribution of property, and this has been known to lead to bloodshed, and the breaking up of a village into two factions. The inheritance goes to the sons only, as remarked by Hobhouse (pp. 268-9), though trees are bequeathed occasionally to women. An unmarried daughter inherits nothing from her father, but she must be cared for by her eldest brother until her marriage, when he receives the bride price.

Formerly, when the population of the island was very great, and more land had to be cultivated than is necessary at present, trees were owned by a large number of people. Sometimes not more than one or two branches would belong to an individual, and the accurate knowledge of the exact location of each branch

---

[1] This is noted by Forster, p. 304. But see also Paton, p. 99.

was remarkable. At the present time, with the reduced though still large population, the rotation of garden sites for all is possible, with the result that the crops are abundant in a normal year, everyone is well fed, and the Tannese present every evidence of *bien-être*, a fact noted by Cook a century and a half ago[1].

After two or three years' use garden sites are allowed to lie fallow for some years, and one is constantly coming across overgrown and neglected gardens in the bush. If yams have been planted, the garden is often allowed to lie fallow for seven years after one year of use, so as time goes on the garden making moves further afield and sometimes the gardens are found a long distance from the village to which they belong. If virgin forest is cleared for a new set of gardens, the whole tract is fired, but if the new garden site is a spot that has been used years before, the old fruit trees are allowed to remain and are protected from the fire as far as possible. The boundaries of the individual plots are very irregular and intricate, but there is never any question in the mind of the owner just where the line of demarcation lies. The unfailing accuracy of the native in matters of this sort has been noted by ethnologists in various parts of the world.

The crops are planted in rotation. The chief ones on Tanna are taro, manioc, sweet potato, sugar, some maize and, last but not least, the yam. Yam cultivation is as follows. In August and September the land is cleared for the new gardens. First the ground must be burned over as in all garden preparation, then a certain amount of wood ashes is required for fertilization, though in the vicinity of the volcano this is hardly necessary[2]. Then the yam mounds are built up by the men. At present this is usually done with shovels bought from the white traders, but digging sticks were used formerly, although none is ever seen in use now. The mounds are about three feet in height and perhaps a yard and a half in diameter at the base, and when they are erected they are smoothed over by the women with their hands. Sometimes the actual planting is delayed as late as December, although the mounds seem to be prepared not

[1] Forster, p. 266.   [2] See Ella, ii. p. 562.

later than the end of September (Gunn, p. 197). The date of planting seems to have some connection with the amount of rainfall during the cool season—April to October or November. The appearance of Achernar in the east is the first sign of the coming of the harvest, at the end of the hot weather, from early March to late May, in the month called *Iati*, though some varieties ripen later (Gray, 1892, pp. 667–9). A shelter is built in the yam gardens of dried reeds or sugar cane and a piece of yam is placed inside, an act certain to ensure a good harvest. After one year of yam culture the gardens may be used for other produce for a year or two more, and it is very common to see old yam mounds in gardens given over to manioc, sugar, or even taro. A new yam site may be chosen a year or two before it is used, in which case, perhaps, bananas will be planted at first. Often, the chance fall of a big tree in the bush is enough to suggest a garden site to the watchful agriculturalist, and a few bananas are planted at once before the entire tract is cleared. With the big array of fruit trees with which the island is overgrown, bread-fruit, pawpaw, rose-apple, coconut, orange, mandarin, wild lemon, to mention only some of those having the most general distribution, abundant food for the population is practically guaranteed without the tuberous foods which, in their seasons, add to the variety and excellence of the diet.

Before leaving the subject of horticulture, two other matters may be mentioned. One is the amount of time spent by the native in caring for his garden. The other is the pig fences, which are built to protect the cultivated land from the bush, where the pigs run at will. One of the astonishing things to an observer of the labour in the gardens is the short amount of time spent by a man and his wife in working in them and the excellence of the results. In one case a man and his wife habitually give about four hours a week (one long afternoon) to the care of their garden, which is one of moderate size. In this case the couple have a garden of their own, and not a part of a general garden belonging to the village group. In another case, two men are able, in one full day a week, to do all that is necessary for the maximum of results from a fairly large portion of a garden site. Of course this has nothing to do with the clearing of new sites, for then all the men of the village fall to and work together, and it is plain why "man Tanna" used to be in demand for work on the Queensland plantations (Woodford, p. 10). It is said that one full day's work a week by two people will keep a garden in the best of condition so that it will supply a family of six.

The pig fences are built of stones, logs, bamboo, reeds, or of a combination of these. Sometimes they are very massive and high and form a barrier over which a man has some difficulty in climbing; sometimes they are nothing more than bamboo palings, but nicely woven reed or bamboo, five or six stems together, is the common form. In riding about the island on horseback over the less travelled bridle-tracks that have been constructed from the old native tracks through the bush since 1906, one has to dismount frequently and remove some of the upper parts of the pig fences that bar the way. One way to insure respect in the native mind is to be careful to restore the removed palings after passing through.

FISHING. Fishing on the reef with a spear, and occasionally with the bow and arrow, is common and the patient fisherman never seems to be discouraged, though the results of his labour are usually very small[1]; Cook (p. 56), however, records one large catch. In calm weather, which, on an island like Tanna, where there are few harbours and consequently little shelter from the strong winds, is rare, the natives put to sea in the outrigger canoes and fish with a line. Then also the results are disappointing, although the number of smooth, calm days is too few to prove the deep-sea fishing abilities of the Tannese[2]. Nowadays fishing from the reefs and rocks with a pole and line is common but, here again, the results seem to be meagre and, on the whole, "man Tanna" is not a gifted and expert fisherman, although a very patient one. Perhaps if fruit and tuberous foods were less abundant he might pay more attention to the art of fishing.

HUNTING. Since there is no mammalian fauna on the island, if we except the introduced pig and rat, there is no hunting in

[1] This agrees with Gray, 1899, p. 131.   [2] See Ella, p. 571.

the usual sense. A native almost always has his bow and blunt arrow with him when he is going through the bush, but it seems to be unusual for him to bring down a bird. The bow is exceedingly well made, of mangrove wood, well shaped and polished, permanently strung at one end and tied at the other, but not noosed. A strong fibre, made of a twisted native vine, is used for the string and no bow is strung with any imported material, although one trader has stout cord in his store which, according to his own account, he sometimes sells to the natives for bow string. The bow has tapering ends which are not ungraceful. There was no variation of the model in any part of the island, and it is said to be made today as it always has been.

The arrow is of *nameli* wood, well made, with bell-shaped, blunt end if for shooting birds, or with a sharpened end to the arrow itself, but in neither case is there a separate arrow head of any material attached to the shaft. It seems that the arrow as a weapon, except for killing birds with the blunt end, has ceased to be an article of practical use, and repeated inquiries fail to elicit any evidence of heads attached to shafts, or of the use of poison in any form.

In the old days wild pigs were hunted by groups of men, although these affairs could hardly be called hunting expeditions such as are conducted by some peoples of rude culture in different parts of the world. Dogs and horses are fairly common nowadays, but both are of fairly recent introduction.

HANDICRAFT. The building of houses and fences, and the making of bows and arrows, have been described already. The loom never existed. The rough plaiting of grasses into mats and the beating of tapa, from which belts worn by the men and a few other articles of apparel are made, are constant industries, but the workmanship, in the tapa-making at least, is of a decidedly inferior quality, when one compares it with that of the more northerly islands of the group, or even with Aniwan and Futunese workmanship.

It seems odd, the evidence of pottery on Efate being clear, that there is no indication that it ever formed a part of Tannese culture. The contention of Miklucho-Maclay (p. 576) that, although the Efatians do not now make pottery they have not lost the art of doing so, may be open to serious doubt, but he is quite right in stating that there is no manufacture at all now in the New Hebrides, if we except the curious anomaly in Santo. It is difficult to see how it could have disappeared so completely on Tanna, where there is no evidence of potsherds as far as is known, if it ever formed a part of Tannese culture (Macmillan-Brown, p. 150).

There is no megalithic work whatever. There is no art beyond the crudest tracing of a design on the tapa belts, as is noted elsewhere, and an occasional face marking with colour, and it is difficult to account for the inclusion by Pain (p. 103) of the Tannese with the Tongans and Samoans, in speaking of aboriginal art. There is no evidence of the boomerang in the south-eastern portion of the group, although it was found in a limited area in Santo by Rivers (1915, § 59). The *kasaua*, or native head rest, is still made, but the examples now extant are of very crude workmanship and have no carving whatsoever. It seems odd that no really well made one can now be found on the island. The same remark applies to the tapa beaters of the old days, which were often decorated in rather primitive fashion, the native today being content with a roughly-hewn wooden beater which accomplishes his purpose but has no artistic value. The club-handled paddle, the spear of one piece of wood, the pandean pipe or flute, the light drum, the bamboo comb, so common in Eromanga, and the spear thrower, all mentioned by Speiser (1923, pp. 449–50), are now conspicuous by their absence[1].

[1] Speiser gives excellent plates of various articles of Tannese handicraft, of which the following are of special interest and importance:

Head rest ...	...	Table 19, No. 2
Kava bowl...	...	Table 19, No. 10
Stone axe ...	...	Table 33, No. 13
Bamboo comb	...	Table 34, Nos. 53–4
Nose ornament	...	Table 38, No. 26
Ear ornaments	...	Table 39, Nos. 1, 2, 3, 4, 6, 7, 8
Breast ornaments ...		Table 39, Nos. 14, 15, 16, 18, 27, 28
		(Nos. 27, 28 are for women)
		Table 40, Nos. 1, 3, 4, 5, 6, 7, 11, 15
Arm bands	...	Table 40, Nos. 19, 20, 21, 22, 23
		Table 41, No. 1

CANOES AND NAVIGATION. The canoes built by the Tannese
are not to be compared with the elaborate affairs in some parts
of Polynesia, for they are distinctly more clumsy and heavy
than those of the neighbouring Polynesian islands of Samoa
and Tonga[1], nor have they anything in common with the fine
examples of canoe craft produced formerly by the Malekulans.
The Tannese canoe is exclusively of the single outrigger type,
and is said to be built today on the same lines as the ancient
model. It is always a dugout, scooped out from the trunk of
a tree by the aid of a knife or by burning, exactly as made
today in parts of the Loyalty Islands[2]. European knives, bought
from the traders, are now used, but in Cook's time the Tannese
were found using "hatchets" with blades of black stone or
broken shell, exactly like those which his ship's company had
noted in the Friendly and Society Islands (Forster, p. 313).
The canoe has several athwartship, outrigger booms, cut to fit
into grooves in either gunwale, extending, on one side to the
float, which is modelled more or less like the canoe on a small
scale, though it is not dug out, the top being left flat. The end
of each boom is attached to the float by small sticks, the ends
being, in one case, inserted into holes made for them in the
flat surface of the float, in the other, crossed over the boom and
securely lashed to it by woven strands of native fibre. The

[1] Cf. Erskine, p. 306.
[2] In Eni and S. W. Mare, cf. Sarasin, F., p. 228.

booms are not evenly distributed across the canoe but there seems to be no uniformity in this irregularity, when different craft are compared, and the man at the paddle (or men, if there are two or more) seems never to sit in any special space between these booms. As many as eight to ten persons generally occupy the large canoes. The bread-fruit tree is generally used for canoe-making and the best quality is said to be found on the west side of the island. The paddles are spade-shaped and about two feet long on an average, though longer ones are occasionally used. Heavy and shapeless forms prevail throughout the New Hebrides[1] and these show no decoration whatever, nor was it customary at any time to add any ornamentation.

Canoes were usually made by the people living nearest to the places where the best material for their manufacture was known to grow. It did not follow that these places were always near the coast and inland people have been found expert in making canoes as well as fishing materials[2]. The descent of the craft from father to son, though widely distributed in the Pacific[3], appears to be unknown here, nor are there guilds or anything resembling them in connection with canoe building. Many attempts were made to discover if any traces of ceremonies connected with canoe building still existed, but all recollection of them seems to have died out.

In the old days, skilled weapon makers were in demand, but these seem to have been, like the canoe makers, those who had developed a special proficiency in this direction, for there is no evidence of the craft descending from father to son, or from craftsman to apprentice. In the same way certain women become proficient in the making of native skirts, and are in great demand, especially before some ceremonial occasion.

The plaiting of native baskets and mats is crude, and Tannese basketry cannot compare with Aniwan and Futunese work.

Navigation seems to have played an unimportant part in the life of the Tannese. Today there is a constant intercourse by means of small cutters, manned entirely by natives, between

---

[1] This agrees with Codrington, 1891, p. 287.
[2] Paton, p. 178, makes the same observation.
[3] See O'Ferrall, p. 225.

Aniwa and Tanna, but it is significant that the boats are owned exclusively by Aniwans, so that the voyages originate from that island, which is almost purely Polynesian. Nevertheless, there are always sporadic voyages in canoes from Tanna to the other four islands of the southern portion of the New Hebrides which we are considering in the present work. In most cases, the voyaging is accomplished during the daylight hours and when it is necessary to navigate at night, the steering is done always by the land outlines and not by the stars. This latter method of navigation seems to be unheard of, for the constellations are practically unnoted by the Tannese[1]. When asked what happens when the land outlines are blotted out by mist, the answer is invariably that one creeps cautiously along until it clears.

A tradition is extant that some Aniwans and Tannese, who were together in a canoe, once, long ago, were blown far away to the north by bad weather, an accident not uncommon in the Pacific[2]. They were at last given up as lost, the coconuts belonging to the Tannese portion of the ship's company were cut down, and the usual division of their property was made. The men were not drowned but finally landed safely on the small island of Emai about 130 miles to the north-north-west. Here they stayed for some time until they had built a new canoe, in which they succeeded eventually in reaching their own islands again. There is no record that any inhabitants of Emai came with them on this occasion, neither is there any recollection in the memory of living man of the arrival of any immigrants from other islands, if we except the four nearest neighbours of Tanna referred to already. There is now a certain amount of intercourse by the inter-island steamer but it is of too recent a character to be of any ethnological importance.

CURRENCY. As far as can be learned, the only medium of exchange in the old days was the pig. Mats were never used here, as they were in many of the northern islands of the group, and although mats and belts were sometimes exchanged for other commodities, this could hardly be considered as currency, the

---

[1] This is in agreement with Turner, p. 319.
[2] See Sittig, pp. 529 et seq.

exchange being more in the nature of barter. No chief consulted remembers the use of any medium of exchange besides the pig, and no one can explain what happened before the pig was introduced. The natives believe that pigs have always been common in the islands, and certainly they were observed as early as 1774.

MAGICO-RELIGIOUS IDEAS AND PRACTICES

SPIRITS, GHOSTS, SUPERIOR BEINGS. The distinction between spirits and ghosts made by Codrington (1891, pp. 120–1) is followed in this account of the Tannese. A spirit is a being not human, which never had human shape (pp. 122–3), and is not necessarily a god[1]. Certain people on Tanna are believed to have the power of divination, and it is thought that they have intercourse with some spirit and, by its aid, are able to forecast future events. *Narumin* is the native name given to these people, and Gray contends that they firmly believe in their own powers (1892, p. 655). In the old days, if a man disappeared in warfare the *Narumin* was consulted and usually told what had happened to him. Often his divinations were incorrect, but most people continued to have faith in him. And today, if he proves to be wrong, he always has some excuse at hand, and does not suffer loss of reputation on account of the error in his prophecy. No evidence of the use of animal entrails or of any instruments of divination is found although magic stones are used. Divination may be regarded as pertaining more to magic than to belief in a spirit, but several old men insist that it is the power derived from a spirit which has never been a human being that enables the *Narumin* to see into the future. It seems to be one of the manifestations of *mana* which are so common throughout the Pacific, and is moreover the only evidence found in Tanna of a definite belief in any being endowed with supernatural powers, which never had a human existence.

When we turn to the subject of ghosts we find little more to enlighten us. It is admitted that ghosts of the dead wander about, at least for a certain period after death, and that the

[1] Cf. Hubert, H., and Mauss, M., pp. 108 *et seq.*

ghost is the soul of the deceased[1]. Nothing definite can be learned as to the length of the wandering. This may be because the natives dislike to speak of this dangerous subject, or because they have really outgrown any fear of the supernatural powers of the dead, but a strong belief in ghosts undoubtedly exists today[2]. There is still a fear of the *eramus*. In the dark this being may seize you, and several women employed about the Mission were attacked by him. It is admitted that the *eramus* was once a man, so that the belief suggests a ghostly rather than a spirit influence, and Turner's statement that "spirits" of departed ancestors are deified is open to serious doubt (pp. 318–19). The distinction in the native mind between those supernatural beings which have and those which have never had human shape is too vague to build any hypothesis upon, and it seems clear that prior to Codrington's masterly analysis of the Pacific region the terms "spirit" and "ghost" were very loosely used in records of native beliefs in supernatural powers.

The natives have some vague idea of a superior being named *Ungen* who exists alone and who made and rules over all things. The interrogation on this abstruse subject was with Christianized natives, and he would be an intrepid ethnologist who claimed to distinguish between the primitive belief in a supreme being and the superimposed idea, however vague, of the Christian deity: moreover, as Gray says (1892, p. 651), no inquiries into religion can be satisfactorily made without accurate knowledge of the native language.

The use of magical stones is still very common in the island. Stones suggesting the shape of certain fruits or vegetables, called *navuetinuh* or *narak*[3], are placed in gardens with the idea of making the harvest of the real fruits as large as possible. This simple form of magic does no harm. With the more hurtful forms, or what is commonly called black magic, it is different. Stones are used to compass the hurt or death of an enemy, and the procedure is as follows: the man, who wishes to injure his enemy, must first obtain something that has been in contact

[1] This is in agreement with the findings of Rivers in other parts of the New Hebrides, *Folk-Lore*, XXXI. 1920, p. 62.

[2] Gray, 1892, p. 650.

[3] This is given by Gray, 1892, p. 653.

with him. A skin of banana recently eaten, excrement, or anything belonging to him will suffice. Great care is therefore taken that nothing discarded be thrown away where it may be found and recognized. When the material is obtained it is ground to a powder, if that is possible, or broken into pieces, though sometimes left in its original state. Great care is taken not to wash the substance, or even to place it in the vicinity of any water. The *Nuruker* then mixes the leaves of certain trees with this and the whole is buried in the ground, whence it is disinterred after a proper interval, and special stones which have been selected by the *Nuruker* are rubbed with the mixture. The stones are suspended over a fire, on reeds, from which the leaves have been removed, which have been rubbed with the root of the *tubahan*, the reeds being bound at the top by native fibre to which the fibre sustaining the stones is attached (Gray, 1892, p. 652). Sometimes the stones are selected at random, sometimes they resemble a part of the human anatomy (Gray, 1892, p. 653). They may also suggest by their shape some piece of property of the individual against whom the magic is to be used, but they must, in any event, become properly imbued with the necessary power before they are efficacious against their victim. If only a minor injury is desired, the mixture with which the stones have been smeared is allowed to burn only partially; if complete destruction of the mixture is allowed, leaving the stones quite clean, the result will be death. This black magic succeeds in terrorizing the native mind almost invariably, even today[1]. The *Nuruker* should be one of the chiefly class, though it seems that men not of this class have been very successful in the practice of magical arts. If a man showed ability in this direction it is not likely that he would be disallowed because he was not of the proper social condition (Gray, 1892, p. 656). It is interesting that the *Nuruker* of the east part of the island becomes *Netuker* on the west side and *Nahaker* at Kwamera, which is in accord with Gray[2].

This power is in certain persons and not in others. If a man who does not possess it wishes to injure an enemy or cause his death, he must find a *Nuruker* to act for him. The stones

[1] Cf. Deane, p. 162.   [2] Ray, *Int. Arch. f. Eth.* p. 234.

used are collected by the *Nuruker* and are held by him or placed by him where they will have the most injurious effect on the victim. During my stay in the island the Government Agent seized some magic stones which were said to have compassed the death of three men, but fear of incurring the displeasure of the Government representative restrained the *Nuruker* from revealing the means employed for this purpose. This fear is always an insuperable barrier in any attempt to gain knowledge of magical practices at the present time. Talismanic stones are still seen, but are now uncommon[1].

In the old days, discussion of magic and witchcraft was general but was always secret. The old men would talk over these matters with the young men who had just reached puberty. Some time ago an old man of Weasisi came to talk about magical matters with the old men of Whitesands and afterwards several old and young men went into a house and tried to perform some magical rites. The chief who recounted this to me was a young lad at the time and could not recall just what was done on this occasion, but he said that there was no special house where it took place, and that it was not done in the bachelors' house of the village, but in a house belonging to the chief. He insisted, however, that it might be done in any house. The magical experiments were entirely in connection with rain-making, wind-making and food supply, stones being used freely to alter the course of nature (Gray, 1892, p. 653). All attempts to connect this with a survival of secret societies failed utterly. The same informant recalled other occasions where he was not present, but of which he heard others speak, where rites were performed to bring down rain when the crops of an enemy tribe needed sun, or wind when an enemy was on the point of embarking in canoes for a voyage to another part of the island; and here, as elsewhere, failure to make good aroused no suspicion of the powers of the *Nuruker*[2]. Repeated attempts to obtain fuller information about these practices failed, and no taboo of certain houses, such as was observed by Paton (p. 87), was discoverable.

[1] They were noted in Gray's time, 1892, p. 651.
[2] Cf. Woodford, p. 26.

There is no evidence of the bull-roarer or of the boomerang. When one of the missionaries first came to the island many years ago he brought a bull-roarer from Australia, but when he showed it to several of the older men, no one exhibited the least sign of ever having seen one before or of knowing its use. It seems that strange sounds of any description were never employed to frighten away women and children from special places, as was customary with the *Werewere*[1] of the Northern New Hebrides. There is no special evidence of the use of nail parings in connection with magical practices, though finger nails are mentioned as "idols" by Paton (p. 73).

CEREMONIAL LIFE

Circumcision, which, according to Codrington (1891, p. 234) came to the Southern New Hebrides from the east, plays a very important part in the life of the Tanna male. There is a ceremony practically every year and all youths who are considered ready to enter man's estate submit to the operation, which is still retained as a compulsory puberty rite[2]. Young boys may be circumcised at the same time, and even infants, but this does not seem to be common. Gray (1892, p. 646) says that the average age in his time was from five to eight. Special houses are built in the bush for this ceremony, with a small compartment for each boy. The house is made large or small according to the number of boys to be cared for, but it must be built in one day and is more or less a makeshift affair, the reeds being gathered and all the work done between sunrise and sunset, everyone falling to to help. On the day when the ceremony is to be performed the boys are called "before the fowls are off the trees," but until this moment there has been no isolation or special preparation of any sort. All males already circumcised may attend the ceremony and may visit the boys at any time during their seclusion. After all the eligible males have proceeded with the boys to the new house, each boy is taken a short distance into the bush and here the act is performed. No special

---

[1] See Rivers, 1914, pp. 96–8.
[2] This agrees with Ray, quoting Gray, 1892, p. 229.

words are used, nor is any ritual employed during the operation, but it is very important that the cutter holds a leaf in his left hand so that his fingers do not come in direct contact with the boy whose penis he holds[1].

During the operation one or more men hold the boy and the cutter performs his duties, in the old days, with a bamboo knife, but now, usually, with an ordinary knife purchased from the trader, there being, apparently, no objection to the use of iron for this purpose. Certain men have the prerogative of the circumcision and those who become very proficient are in great demand on the day when the ceremony is performed in a tribe or village. When the cutting is finished the boy stops in the bush until all have been attended to, the men who have held him remaining by him, though no special relative has any special rights or duties during the operation. All those employed in holding the lad make loud cries while the cutting is being done, partly to drown any noise the boy may make, strict fortitude being enjoined on the victim during the operation.

The foreskin is held by the fingers, the incision being made by the knife on the upper side, at the top and carried as far as the base of the glans. The finger is then inserted under the foreskin which is removed close to the base until the under-point is nearly reached, when the knife is deflected a bit and continues its cutting, from the base, outward, to a point on the under side of the foreskin, opposite the point of beginning. The other half is then removed in precisely the same manner. In the old days the foreskin was left under the glans and formed a large growth there, and even today the father of the boy may have this done if he wishes, although the complete removal as in the modern European method is much more common. The foreskins of all the boys are gathered together and wrapped in taro leaves, which are hung up in the special house during the seclusion, after which they are buried and, sometimes, coconut trees are planted to mark the spot, to which the boys may point in after life as a kind of proof that the rite was performed and, as the age of the trees is always known, they become a record of the year when it took place.

[1] Cf. Gray, 1892, p. 659.

This development from a kind of incision to pure circumcision is interesting and suggestive. Brewster (p. 313) records two kinds of circumcision-incision in the interior of Fiji, the *noemalu*, in which the foreskin is cut but not removed, and the *noikoro*, in which case it is entirely cut off. The size of the lump remaining, in the performance of the *noemalu*, is the determining factor, and this may well have been the case in the Tannese custom in the old days, leading, finally, to complete circumcision for all, as it exists, with a few exceptions today.

After the operation, the man who has performed it touches the blood of the boy and anoints the tip of his nose with it, after which he dresses the penis in a temporary case of dried banana leaves, applying first some soft, moist, tender leaves, with the dry leaves for the outer cover. On the third day after the operation all the cases are removed, the boys having been carried from the spot where the cutting was done before nightfall on the day of the operation to a compartment in the temporary house and here they remain, each in the care of two men, one of whom is always on duty while the other sleeps. This is in direct disagreement with Gray, who maintains that, in his day, virgin youths were detailed to care for the boys during their seclusion (1892, p. 659). He also maintains that the food for the boys must be prepared by a virgin girl, but there is no evidence of this today and there seems to be no prohibition in regard to the food the boy may eat. The food for the boys, however, must be cooked in a special oven and not with that for the other members of the village, and special ovens are usually made near the seclusion house, for the food for each boy must be prepared at a special fire, but as these fires are almost invariably in the vicinity of the seclusion house, it seems very unlikely that a virgin girl would have been allowed to go to that spot even to cook food for the boys. During the three days before the temporary dressings are removed the boys must not walk at all, and when it is necessary for them to go outside the house, they must be carried by one of the men set to wait on them. On the morning of the fourth day the boys go together down to the sea and they leave the special house in the order in which the operation was performed. At the beach they

all enter the sea where the temporary dressing is removed, in
each case by the man who did the cutting, and the boys bathe.
The dressing is changed whenever the boys go to the sea and the
leaves of a different tree or shrub must be used each time. There
seems to be no order in which the different leaves are used, nor
are the same varieties used during every ceremony. No belt
is yet given to the boy, for if he cannot hold the penis himself
during his walks to and fro to the sea, this must be done for
him by his father or some near relative. Here again all effort
to discover a special prerogative of a special relative, as of the
mother's brother, failed utterly. The bathing is continued each
morning and evening, but the change of dressing takes place
at the morning bath only and, after the period of bathing
begins, the boys must go to a special place to eat their food,
usually near the special oven. There is no evidence of covering
to protect the body from the sun during the morning or evening
walk. Each boy must lie, face downward, while eating, on a
stick covered with leaves, so that his belly rests on the stick.
This is said to prevent distention of the belly and while a boy
eats he must not speak, neither must he cough nor choke, for
if he does any of these things he may have nothing further to
eat at that meal. Often boys will forget this rule and will have
to go without food for several meals until the necessity of complete silence has been impressed on them. They drink through
a hollow reed. There are three feeding times daily, this being
continued as long as the penis of any member of the group is
unhealed. If a boy dies during the ceremony the body is removed of course but the ceremony is not interrupted.

During all this time women and children are not allowed to
see the boys at all, this exclusion from all ceremonials being
very common in Melanesia[1]. Conch shells are blown when the
boys go to the sea for their morning and evening baths to warn
the women and children to keep out of the way, no other means
of warning being used, but conch shells have no other part in
Tannese culture today[2]. No penalty exists for a "peeping
Tom," and it is insisted that any such act is unknown, and
that the force of public opinion would condemn it utterly.

[1] See Whitehouse, p. 147.   [2] See Turner, p. 321.

This exclusion of women bears some relation to the "close time" of the Banks' Islands (Codrington, 1891, p. 85).

When all are recovered, a belt of tapa cloth is given to each boy and a great feast is held. The belts are pulled very tight and the penis, still in its leaf dressing, is placed under the belt in front, in the same position in which it is worn by all men. On the day of the feast itself a proper penis case is given each boy and this he continues to wear thereafter. He is shown how to adjust it at first by the man who has acted as his mentor throughout the ceremonial, but the boy must do the actual adjusting himself. After it is once adjusted, the penis must never be exhibited to another man (Gray, 1892, p. 360). Indeed, the delicacy of the native in matters of this sort is most astonishing to a European (Gray, 1899, p. 129), and concealment of the penis gland is one of the customs that has survived in its original force to the present day among the Tannese. A group of native males bathing is most circumspect in this particular and no exception to the rule was ever observed. It is hardly possible to regard this as a matter of good breeding in the Tannese, and Captain Cook and his company were probably led somewhat astray by this custom into crediting the Tannese with points of good breeding which they do not possess. For example, Forster (p. 284) tells us that the men were polite enough to excuse themselves when they wanted to sleep, a form of courtesy that has now disappeared entirely.

As in many other parts of the Pacific, the circumcision ceremonial is the occasion for adopting manly dress and "putting away childish things[1]." The boys, when the last stubborn case is healed, are prepared for the feast that is to take place. They are rubbed with coconut oil until they shine and the face is painted, usually with narrow green stripes horizontally across the cheeks, although, in the old days, other colours and different patterns were used. When all is ready the boys proceed to the village in a group and the women and children see them for the first time since they went into seclusion. Since sporadic cases sometimes take two, or even three, months to heal, the feast is delayed, in this case, for a considerable period after the

[1] See Codrington, 1891, p. 231.

operation has been performed. In such a case, if another
ceremonial of any kind takes place during the confinement of
the boys, no one is released to attend, and the circumcision
feast takes place hard upon the other. While it is quite likely
that initiation into elaborate secrets at the time of the seclusion
used to be the custom, as it is still in some parts of the New
Hebrides and in Australia[1], all the old men stoutly insist that
such is not the case today. A single boy may be circumcised
but this is rare, and usually, where there are one or two only
in a certain year, they will wait over till the next year, but never
longer than that (Gray, 1892, p. 659). There is no evidence today
that an operation is performed on girls, although Gray (1892,
p. 660) insists that this was done in his time for the purpose of
making coition more easy. That circumcision-incision in the
male was first resorted to for this reason is the opinion of one
ethnologist, Webster (p. 37), who says of it, "Losing its once
practical character as a primitive effort to assist nature it now
serves in the puberty rites as a mere badge or evidence of in-
corporation into the tribal community." Codrington (1891,
p. 234) calls the rite a "social distinction," and it seems that,
whatever the original incentive for its performance, it is today
more concerned with the admission of the youth to a place in
the community than with any idea of procreation. Forster
(p. 277) noted sporadic cases of incision in his time but, as we
have seen, circumcision is the common form today. Perhaps
the adoption of the latter in its pure form made it unnecessary
to perform the act on the young girls any longer.

When the boys make their appearance at the feast, their
mothers and sisters have not seen them for some time and they
find them much changed, for they have grown in stature and,
being well fed during the seclusion, are usually fat and sleek,
so much so that it is usual for the women to surround the boys
and exclaim about their good health and fine appearance; indeed,
this enthusiasm is enjoined by custom and is usually done, even
if, as sometimes happens, the boy has changed very little.

Occasionally a very young child, not yet weaned, is circumcised with the rest, in which case the mother cannot see her

[1] See Spencer, B., and Gillen, F. J., pp. 142 *et seq.*

child at all, but is conducted with her eyes shut, by one of the male members of her family, to the special house and the sustenance is given the child by inserting her nipple through a hole made in the wall, the temporary nature of the building permitting this quite readily. The child is held on the inside by one of the men delegated to care for him. The woman is not blindfolded and the force of public opinion is relied on to restrain her from opening her eyes. Here again all efforts to find a special relative employed to lead the mother to the seclusion house fails. It will of course be one of her brothers or her husband as no woman may walk with a man of any other relationship, but it is impossible to find any special prerogative of a mother's brother in the action.

Men from all parts of the island may visit the boys during confinement, but no man who has had intercourse with the *iowhanan* since the inauguration of the circumcision ceremonial of that year may go near them. All the men who care for the boys during the period of seclusion must take their own food in a leaf from the hands of another man. This seems to apply to the period of seclusion only, for all return to the usual mode of eating directly the ceremony is finished, taking food in the bare hand at will for personal consumption. It is tempting to see in this a survival of two distinct groups of society caused by the conquest of an earlier people by a later folk. The ethnologist, however, must be very guarded in matters like this. It is so easy to be misled by slight but attractive facts for the construction of hypotheses, for it may be only a special taboo that had its inception in the remote past, the reason for which is lost in the complex cultures that have had a part in producing the social order of the Melanesian today.

When it was asked how the people in the middle of the island manage about taking the boys to the sea for bathing purposes twice a day, my informants insisted that this is done, even if the tribe or village performing the ceremonial is at a distance from the coast. They denied emphatically that the special houses built for the reception of the boys of an inland village are put up far away from that village so as to be nearer to the sea. Sometimes the boys of a group of friendly tribes are circumcised together and few villages or tribes in the interior have no allies near the sea. A village near the sea is chosen, in this case, and a convenient spot not too far from the beach is found for the building of the special house for general use.

Ear-boring is very common and is done just after birth, when the lobe of the ear of all males is pierced by a sharp instrument, usually a bit of shell properly shaped and smoothed. A small, thin, wooden stick, neatly rounded, is inserted in the hole and left for a few days, when another piece, slightly larger, is put in its stead, until the required size is obtained. There is no special ceremonial in this act as far as can be learned.

Of distention of the ear lobe, as usually understood in many parts of the world, there is no evidence whatever. The lobe of the ear seems, at times and in certain males, larger than the normal size, but it cannot be properly called distention.

A word in regard to the prevalence of venereal disease may be introduced at this point. It is not more common on Tanna than on other islands of the group, which is somewhat surprising when one considers how much in demand the Tannese male is for work in other islands or on inter-island craft. Perhaps it was introduced by the first white visitors, but it is suggested by some observers that it was indigenous[1].

Kava is prepared in two ways in the island. In one process, root of the wild pepper—*Piper methysticum*—is chewed by the old men and, when the mass is well mixed with the saliva, is expectorated into a wooden trough or bowl, or, more commonly, into a coconut shell; by the other, which conforms to the Fijian custom with modifications (Williams, I. p. 141), the chewing is done by the youths instead of the old men and this is the more common form. The root only is used and it is divided into pieces about the size of a mutton chop[2]. In both processes the rest of the performance is identical. A virgin youth pours water over the expectorated mixture and works it with his hands until it forms a pulpy substance, which he strains by a wringing process, through the mid-rib of a banana leaf, beaten to a white condition, looking not unlike a fresh

[1] See Guppy, 1887, pp. 177–8.
[2] This agrees with Gray, 1892, p. 661.

towel, into a coconut bowl. About twenty ounces are drunk at a time and may be taken directly from the bowl or poured into a banana leaf held in cup fashion in the hand and taken from that.

Chewing the root of the *Piper methysticum* is not easy, and it may be that the young men are called to do the chewing as the teeth of the older men begin to fail, though the virgin youth who does the mixing in the bowl is a constant factor. There is no evidence of the pounding process in Tanna, although it has a wide distribution in the Pacific. The chewing process is the more common and the vigour with which it is performed reminds one of the energy employed by the Tannese in working his jaws at a feast, and the description by Radiguet (p. 64) of the Marquesans: "Tous se livraient à une mastication acharnée."

The youths who have assisted in the making are never allowed to drink the kava, but some food is usually provided for them, the drinking being an exclusive prerogative of the old men. As each man drinks he rises and expectorates with great violence afterwards, though he manages to swallow a good share of the mixture. Although this is now done purely as a matter of form, it had a certain significance in the old days, before warfare ceased, and the expectoration was always in the direction of some known enemy, of whom every man seems to have had a few at all times. Kava tossed to the ghosts of the dead is common in Melanesia (Codrington, 1891, p. 128), but there is no evidence of this in the present form of the custom in Tanna. There is, however, a peculiar shout which each man gives just before he drinks, and the noise of each individual seems to be quite different from that of his fellows[1]. After drinking, some food is usually taken and then everyone goes to sleep. The effect is not at all uniform in different individuals, although it seems never to have had the effect on the brain that excessive drinking of spirituous or mixed liquors may have with us. It is said that the power of the concoction may be increased by mixing the leaves of other plants with the *Piper methysticum*, notably the flowers of the rose-apple, which are said to add a certain potency

[1] This was also observed by Gray, 1892, pp. 661–2.

to the drink (Gray, 1892, pp. 661–2). In its most powerful form it seems to have no effect on the brain beyond a certain over-stimulation, while it often affects the legs very much indeed[1]. Drinking is usually done late in the evening, although there is no rule about the matter, and all agree that it may be done at any time as it is in Tonga (Mariner, II. p. 184). As the men usually sleep in the kava house till the morning, the choice of the evening for drinking may have a quite simple explanation. It goes without saying that no women are allowed in the vicinity of the kava house at any time.

Each village has its kava house, usually not far from the *imeium* where all the feasts are held, although it is occasionally somewhat further removed from the centre of village life. This house has nothing to distinguish it from the ordinary houses of the villagers. Remains of these kava houses are found in some of the newer Christian villages, where they have been allowed to fall to pieces gradually, the use of the beverage being forbidden by the missionaries.

The custom of drinking kava in this island partakes of both the Melanesian and the Polynesian manner. Making the drink in large quantities and drinking it in the company of a con-siderable number of men has more affinity with the manner employed in the latter region than in the former, but the use of small bowls and a larger trough interchangeably suggests a combination of both methods in this form of culture.

Before considering the native feasts and dances which occur at different seasons of the year, a word must be said in regard to cannibalism in the old days[2]. It was still carried on as a common rite when most of the early voyagers reached the island, and until fairly recently there are stories, mostly false one thinks, of an occasional occurrence; but it must be remem-bered that this custom, in Tanna at least, was the prerogative of the chiefly class alone[3], and was at all times a ceremonial rite in connection with warfare, whereby the chiefs of the conquering tribes thought to receive strength and prowess from the physical consumption of part of the captured enemy's body,

---

[1] Cf. Clavel, p. 122.
[2] See Erskine, pp. 320–1.
[3] Gray agrees in this, 1892, p. 663.

by a sort of "contagious magic." Abuses must be admitted, but it is rare to find a case of cannibalism recorded without this *raison d'être*.

NATIVE FEASTS AND DANCES. Some festivals have no exact calendar date, as, for example, that following the circumcision ceremony, which depends, as we have seen, on the length of the period of seclusion. Others, such as the yam-planting ceremony, when there is a special festival of elaborate proportions, are at fixed seasons, and it was a matter of great regret that none of these occurred during my sojourn on the island. One festival, however, which had been held shortly before my arrival, was specially and faithfully reproduced in my honour.

Two days before the time appointed for the feast, a large gathering of the chiefs of the villages belonging to the tribe which made it was held. As it was during a period of drought, it was decided unanimously to ask the rain-makers to cease their efforts to induce rainfall until the ceremony was over. But the day of the feast was, unfortunately, a decidedly wet one, with alternating sun and shadow which interfered most effectually with all photographic efforts.

The festival took place at the village of Lepagalis, about three miles inland from Lenakel, a Mission station on the west side of the island. The dancing ground was just like all these places in the island. It consisted of a big stretch of bare ground, perfectly level, in the midst of the tropical bush, shadowed by a banyan tree of enormous proportions, with a kava house at one side. At this time special attempts were made to solve the vexed question of the kava house and secret societies, but all inquiries failed, as in the case of the bachelors' house in the villages. Everyone insists that no secret societies ever existed on the island and no more information on this subject was forthcoming. It seems necessary to accept the native statements and to believe that, if secret societies or anything like them ever did exist, all memory of them has actually passed away. Perhaps the increased power of the chiefs is responsible for the decay in secret societies, as suggested by Codrington (1891, pp. 54 *et seq.*).

The people assembled for the festival soon after noon. The

people of the village making the feast piled a high mound of
food in the middle of the dancing ground, and native puddings,
yams, coconuts, pigs and fowls were heaped together in great
quantities. After the invited guests had assembled and greetings
had been exchanged, the men retired to the bush, the old men,
the women and children remaining sitting in groups around the
edge of the dancing ground, the women always by themselves.
After an interval, the men came from the bush in a single line
and marched in a circle until the leader reached the very centre
of the spiral. Suddenly there was a great cry from one of the
men and the dance began. Dancing is here always a movement of
the feet, not of the body with the feet rooted to one spot[1]. The
first movement was a rush to the centre of the circle by all. This
was accompanied by a cry that was not unmelodious and a step
that suggested the hop-skip of European children. Then all
dashed back again to the very edge of the dancing ground where
one big circle was formed, this movement being repeated three
times. Then, at another shout, the men began to jog around in
a great circle in single file, chanting a cadence that had a decidedly musical sound. No musical instruments appeared at
this time and no pandean pipe was ever observed[2]. The rhythm
was in perfect accord with the quick steps taken by the men
and the sounds suggested an endless repetition of words, but
all attempts to find out if they had any meaning were unavailing.
It may be that they were words that had been used in this
special dance until their meaning had been quite forgotten. The
dancing step became more and more intricate as the affair progressed and the excitement increased. Finally it resembled what
is commonly known as an African "break down," although much
less impetuous than that practised by the negro in America
at the present time. Heels and toes came into play alternately
and the movement consisted in throwing the balance rapidly
from one to the other. It was said that constant practice and
infinite patience are necessary to perform these steps well. At
no time did the excitement become particularly intense. Even
at the end there was a certain measured decorum. After dancing

[1] See Langsdorff, p. 158.
[2] It was seen in Erskine's time, p. 319, and noted by Turner, p. 312.

around the circle a goodly number of times the leader disappeared into the bush followed by all the dancers.

The men now seated themselves in groups around the edge of the open space, each village group sitting together[1]. The women sat outside, but not in village groups. The people giving the feast then distributed the food piled in the middle of the dancing ground and all began to eat. The yams, some of which were of enormous size, were set on one side to be taken back to the villages from which the guests came. This applied also in part to fowls and pigs, but native puddings were eaten on the spot. Each one of the villages represented at this feast must give a feast in return to their hosts on this occasion, unless, indeed, this feast was in payment of former hospitality. Return feasts between tribes are found widely distributed in Melanesia (Haddon, 1912, p. 311). On this occasion the native puddings were made mostly of coconut and banana, eaten by removing the wrapper of leaves and cutting off a generous slice with a knife. A great noise was made with the mouth by all in eating, this being an appreciation of the hospitality shown the guests, as noted above. A stew made of fowls and rice seemed to be the most popular viand and it was consumed with much appreciative noise. The white man's contribution to the feast of some tins of biscuit seemed to be enjoyed also, the biscuits being dipped in the stew and eaten with much gusto. At first the visitors seemed loth to begin to eat, and one chief said that this is a necessary display of good breeding, for when the guests conquered their diffidence the food disappeared rapidly enough.

After all had finished with the feast the men again retired to the bush for the next dance. This was a movement in a big circle, in formations of three or four, accompanied by the clapping of hands, in perfect rhythm. In this some of the women joined, dancing around outside the circle of men, in formations of two, three or four. Although this participation of the women is recorded by Paton (p. 135), it seems to be an innovation (Codrington, 1880, p. 133). The step this time was less difficult than the first and was almost exactly a skipping step such as children use in games among ourselves.

[1] This is not in agreement with Paton, p. 136.

The women had their faces stained with colour, mostly orange, but not laid on in any particular design. They wore the usual grass skirt and, with the exception of an occasional bead necklace, nothing else. One elderly woman had a small, tight-fitting cap made of a banana leaf.

Some of the young men were fancifully dressed. A few had a scant petticoat of grass around the loins, but most of them had only the penis case and tapa belt. A bit of green vine about eighteen inches long attached to one elbow, with the other end hanging loose, seemed to be a popular method of adornment. Necklaces, armlets and hair-dressing were as described above. It might be added that this was entirely a heathen festival and there was only one Christian native present, whose interest in the proceedings proved how novel they were to him.

After another interval two more dances were performed. Both resembled the first, except that in the fourth and last the men rushed from the centre instead of towards it, at a given signal from one of the dancers. It seems never to be the leader who gives the signals, and special reasons for a certain man being chosen to do so do not appear.

All attempts to learn the meaning of the dances are entirely futile. The chiefs, questioned again and again, as tactfully as is possible, always shake the head and say they do not know. Whether it is because they think the white man would not approve if he knew, or whether they have forgotten the significance, must remain a mystery. Even the dance at the time of planting the yams seems to have lost its original meaning. Yet this special group of dances must have received much attention, for the manner in which all perform the rather complicated steps, particularly of the first, is sufficient evidence of that.

A report of an obscene dance seen by one of the planters on the island some years before added to the confusion in the mind concerning native dances. Certainly there is nothing in the least suggestive in those described above, yet it is quite possible that the people see meaning in the dances quite unintelligible to the white man. The missionaries' disapproval of the native dances is recognized all over the island and, although at this special dance no Christians were present, with the one exception noted above, it is quite possible that the heathen mind considers that all whites object to the dances, and will not speak frankly about them on that account. In the old days, it is admitted, promiscuity and general licence occurred after a native feast on certain occasions, as in Fiji and elsewhere[1]. All those present insisted, however, that after the dances witnessed on this occasion, no licence was allowed.

Meagre accounts of one or two other ceremonies were given by native chiefs at different times. Sometimes there is a special ceremony when a young child sits on the ground for the first time, or when it cuts its first tooth, the parents presenting pigs or making a feast, but it does not appear if this custom applies to both male and female children.

Inquiry made as to any trace of certain other ceremonials in the island revealed no evidence of any in connection with disposal of the afterbirth, umbilical cord, birth of a first child, twins, sterility, or finger-nail parings, to mention some of them. There is no evidence of trepanning, in spite of its presence in Northern Melanesia, especially in New Ireland and New Britain[2], no totemism, at least of the kind defined by Rivers (1909, pp. 156–63), no true potlatch, which seems curious in consideration of its prevalence in other parts of Melanesia[3], and nothing that may be called true scarification, although the ridges appearing on the face and body are indicative of a survival of the custom, which probably was common in the old days. There is no tattooing, which is odd in an island that has had as much Polynesian influence as Tanna. If it is true, as Keane observes (p. 143), of scarification and tattooing, that the former is characteristic of darker skinned people and the latter of the lighter, one is surprised at the absence of both, for with the evident mixture of the Melanesian type overlaid with a filtration of Polynesian influence, one would expect the two customs to exist side by side.

---

[1] See Thomson, p. 154.
[2] See Crump, p. 168.
[3] *L'Anthropologie*, xxx. 1920, pp. 396–7.

DEATH AND BURIAL. Disposal of the dead in Tanna resolves itself, on the whole, into one form with variants; that is, extended burial, in the ground, on the back, with or without the knees flexed, precisely the same form that is found in the Loyalties, notably in Lifu, where it seems to be done to prevent, by flexing the knees of the deceased, the ghost of the departed from wandering about (Ray, 1917, p. 288). There are sporadic examples of other forms in the islands, but hardly enough to be considered proof of migratory wanderings as a marked variety of modes of disposal might suggest[1]. In the bush, extended burial, on the back, with the legs straight, seems to be more common than in the coastal regions; and the south-east part of the island, even on the coast, has more of this form of burial than the neighbouring coastal districts. By the people of the Ianikahi ridge, to the north-west of the volcano, and most of the people just to the south-west of it, however, the usual form, with legs flexed, is almost exclusively practised, and in some of the bush villages this form prevails alone. In this latter case the body is wrapped in a mat of pandanus or other fibre and the grave is made just long enough to take the body with legs flexed. Some say that economy of labour is the reason for this.

Of the sporadic cases of burial noted the following are the most significant. In the north part of the island, where the coralline strata are in some cases far above sea level, as also in Eromanga and Efate[2], cave disposal, in the extended position, on the back, with the legs straight, is still practised, but the reason given is the coralline nature of the country and the impossibility of digging a grave.

Across Siwe, the fresh-water lake at the foot of the volcano, a case is recalled by the chief of a village, where the body was interred in the ground, but in a sitting position with the knees flexed. This chief also remembered a case, long ago, where the deceased requested that he be buried in the sea. In this case it was said that heavy stones were attached to the feet of the corpse and it was taken out in a canoe and dropped into the

[1] See Rivers, *Contact of Peoples*, 1913, p. 480.
[2] See Guppy, 1887, p. 66.

sea. Paton (p. 191) observed cases of sea burial at Kwamera in his time. A man who loved the sea once asked to be buried in sight of it and was placed in a sitting position in the back of a cave with his eyes toward the sea, which was visible from that point, in this case the legs being straight. One case of recess burial is cited by Turner (p. 324) in his time. One case of cremation is recalled, of a man accused of black magic, who was killed and his body burned to destroy all evil influences that might have attached to the corpse had it been buried. This is not a true form of cremation, perhaps, but it is hard to assign any other term to it. In none of these special cases can it be learned whether the deceased was a native of Tanna or an immigrant or visitor from one of the other islands.

Some special forms of mourning are practised. If a married person dies, the surviving husband or wife puts black charcoal on the forehead, a very common form in the New Hebrides (Codrington, 1891, p. 282). Women sometimes wear cowrie-shell necklaces as a sign of mourning and a new grass skirt is made somewhat longer than the common one, but of the usual materials. All these evidences of mourning among women are worn until remarriage. A case is recalled by the chief of one village when the widow of a man was strangled at the burial of her husband and put in the same grave with him, a frequent feature of Melanesian funerals in the old days[1]. It is said to have been at her request, and was a long time ago[2]. Sometimes a woman who is a widow wears some of her husband's hair attached to a fibre around her neck.

The graves are dug by four persons in two shifts of two each and are lined with coconut leaves. Two of the gravediggers are always in the grave until the interment has taken place, when they all go to the sea to bathe after their labour, to remove the dirt which they have acquired. Whether there is any ceremonial rite connected with removing the defilement of grave making is not known, but gravediggers even from the centre of the island always go to the sea to bathe. These men receive compensation for their services, but in what form this is given is

[1] See *Brit. Mus. Handbook*, p. 135.
[2] Turner (p. 324) records this in his time.

not known. After the interment and the filling in of the grave it is usually marked with dracaenas or other plants, and a handful of ashes is put on the grave, just over the spot where the head of the deceased lies, so that the footprints of the ghost of the departed will be detected if it walks about. If the deceased has died a violent death the scattering of ashes is on no account omitted, for if tracks are found in the ashes they will lead invariably to the abode of the person who is responsible for his death. This way of determining the identity of the murderer was a constant source of fighting between tribes, or sometimes between members of the same tribe.

On the death of a man, in addition to the cutting down of his coconut trees already referred to, sometimes one or more of his bread-fruit trees is cut down as well and a branch is cut from the banyan tree nearest to his house. This branch is laid against the banyan tree and a kava bowl belonging to the deceased is set beside it. In the old days, if the deceased had been murdered, these emblems were removed only after the murderer of the deceased had been discovered and the murder avenged. In cutting down coconut trees they were cut in multiples of five, but a final group of under ten would be left standing. For example, of thirty-three trees, twenty-five would be cut; of thirty-eight, thirty; of forty-four, thirty-five and so on. When plants grow of their own accord on the grave of a deceased, a feast is held but, before this, nothing seems to be done except that on the day after his death the relatives burn the mat on which the deceased used to lie in his house. At this time women from other villages of the tribe come to weep and presents are made to them by the women of the deceased's village. When the women return to their own village these presents must not be given to children on any account.

The people of the Ianikahi ridge, a fairly recent lava flow from the volcano, now covered with a rich vegetation, believe that the entrance to the future home of the deceased is through the vent of the volcano, where there is a beautiful country, like their own, but more luxuriant and fertile. This belief, where there is an active volcano, and in some cases, a quiescent one, is not uncommon and is noted by Codrington (1891, p. 273) in the Banks' Islands. In most cases the people in other parts of the island believe that the future home is beneath the surface of the earth, but the entrance to this unknown land is never, seemingly, thought to be through the volcano vent. That idea seems to be held only by the people in the immediate vicinity of the volcano inhabiting the more recent lava flows now covered with vegetation. In one of the folk tales (6) we find the home of the dead in the sky, but this is a sporadic example, and no other evidence of any such belief appears. Perhaps it is not really a home of the dead in the tale, although it is called so in the narrative.

MYTHS AND TRADITIONS

The following tales are from the west coast of the island, although the second is a story of the volcano and must have some connection with the east coast. No record of tales on the east coast was ever made. In recording those offered here the greatest care is observed to retain the native idiom by using the nearest English equivalent to the native expression. The planter who translated the tales from the native dialect has lived many years in the island and has always been interested in the folk lore of the people in his vicinity, a most fortunate circumstance for the field worker, whose hearty thanks and appreciation are offered here for his unfailing interest in and accurate knowledge of native legends. Just as far as possible the language of the translator is used.

1. *The Origin of Things*

On Tanna a snake stole a woman and took her for his wife, and she bore him a son. He held her captive in the jungle against her will. She made several attempts on his life and at last succeeded in poisoning him. While he was dying he told her to be sure to remember the place where he was buried, because his two eyes would grow into trees which would provide very good food for her people. She remembered the words of the snake and watched the place where he was buried and eventually saw two green shoots sprouting just above the spot where his head lay. In due time these shoots grew to be high trees, the fruit of which proved to be very palatable. Besides the trees, a spring of very sweet water gushed forth over the place where the snake's body lay, around which the woman built a strong stone wall. She forbade her son to tell anyone of these trees or of this water, which, she said, were to be for their own use only. The boy soon outstripped his playmates and became strong and finely developed, being fed with coconuts and anointing his body with the oil and bathing in the spring. While playing one day with other boys they asked him how it was that his body was so fat and clean and shiny. He said it was because of the food which his mother gave him and the water in which he bathed. They asked him to take them and show them where this food was. Forgetting his mother's injunctions, he took the boys to the enclosure and gave them some of the fruit and they bathed in the spring, much to their delight. By and by his mother came home and noticing something amiss asked her son at once who had stirred up the water in the spring. He told her he had brought some boys to bathe. In anger at his disobedience, the woman threw down the stone wall surrounding the spring and the waters gushed forth in a great stream, which, the natives say, eventually formed the sea. Where the water poured out, on the south-east coast of Tanna, there is a valley today in which all the trees have a leaning toward the sea. With the rush of the waters many people were swept away into the newly formed sea. These people became, eventually, the inhabitants of other islands. The natives today think this was the origin of the white people in the world as well. The trees which sprouted from the snake's head were the coconut, of which the name today on the west coast is *nien*. On the face of the waters a number of coconuts were carried also, which were washed up on various islands, there to take root and grow. That is the reason, according to the natives, that the islands of the Pacific have, so often, a fringe of coconut palms around their coasts and very few in the interior.

2. *Sabai and Manga*

These two women were cooking at an oven when the pudding began to burn. One brought a section of bamboo full of water (a common way of carrying water, to this day) to put out the spreading flame, but it only spread the more. Suddenly there was a big explosion and the women were blown to pieces and were never seen again. The destroyed oven continued to burn and to explode at frequent intervals. The volcano on the island is the ancient oven still burning.

3. *How the Yams came to Tanna*

One day a man was out shooting and he saw a beautiful bird in a tree. Just as he stretched his bow the bird spoke and said, "Don't shoot!" and turned into a woman. The man took this woman for his wife. Previous to this time the people of the island had lived entirely on nuts and native fruits. The woman introduced the yam into Tanna and the people found it a very good food. The woman's name was Masineruk. By and by she had a son of whom she became very fond. One day a neighbouring tribe was making a *niel*—a festival of bread-fruits—for the tribe of Masineruk's husband. As it was a long way to go the parents left the child with its grandmother—the father's mother. The couple went to the *niel* and got their share of bread-fruit. On the way home they were travelling in the usual Tanna fashion, the man in front, with his weapons, the woman following with the load tied to her back with creepers[1]. Suddenly she dropped her load and dashed past her husband, who cried out to know where she was going. "Someone is beating my child!" she cried, as she rushed on. On reaching the village she found the child in tears. The grandmother had been beating him. Masineruk was very angry and said, "Why have you been beating my child? Haven't I given you yams and taught you how to grow them? Before I came you lived like pigs. I will not stop here any longer. I will go away!" Catching up her son she ran toward the beach. Just as the husband, who had run after his wife, reached the beach, the sea parted and the

---

[1] See Cook, 2nd ed. II. p. 79.

woman and her child walked away on the bed of the ocean. When the husband tried to follow the water closed behind them. He stood on the shore, wringing his hands and calling for Masineruk to come back, but there was no answer. He is standing there now—on the north-east coast of Tanna—in stone, shaped like a man and can be seen to this day.

4. *Semsem*

SEMSEM was a devil who devoured all the people of Tanna. A woman working in her garden, to save her child, hid the little girl beneath a shrub which had a juicy root, thus saving her daughter's life, after the mother, as well as all the other people of the island had been eaten. The child sucked the root, which gave her sufficient sustenance to live and, eventually, she grew to be a woman. On the west side of the island, north of Lenakel, near a fresh-water spring, is a soft stone, which the natives believe to this day has special properties in inducing conception in sterile women. Nepkalam, for this was the woman's name, ate of this stone and in due time conceived and bore twin sons, whom she named KASASAOU and KANIAPNIN. When these boys had grown to young manhood she taught them to use spears and the bow and arrow. She knew that SEMSEM would visit Tanna again and decided to be prepared for him. So she and the boys passed most of their time in making spears and bows and arrows to defend themselves with. The spears were made of the *niel* tree—ironwood. After sufficient preparations for defence had been made, Nepkalam lit a fire. It was the first time a fire had been kindled on Tanna since the destruction of the inhabitants. SEMSEM, whose abode was in Anaiteum, an island to the south, on observing the smoke from Nepkalam's fire, exclaimed, "I thought I had eaten all the people there. Who is making this smoke? I must go and see." With a few giant strokes he swam across and landed at Kwamera, on the south coast. The mother and her two sons were expecting him and were fully prepared. They had planted spears and bows at intervals on the main track leading from south to north, on the west side of the island and were waiting for SEMSEM on the beach. As he approached the land, the boys called to him and warned him not to come ashore, else they would kill him. He said, "What do you want to kill me for? I am your friend." The boys replied, "You are not our friend. We know you. You are SEMSEM the devil and will eat us." SEMSEM proceeded to land and, as he was advancing up the beach, one of the boys shot an arrow which hit him in the arm. With a roar, SEMSEM charged them, crying out, "Now I will eat you!" As he advanced upon them they retired along the north track, preceded by their mother, who kept them supplied with the weapons placed there previously for the purpose. Many of the spears hit SEMSEM and many did not. The latter are the iron trees which may be seen at intervals along the track today. By the time they had reached Lenakel SEMSEM's body was pierced with many spears and he was seen to be very weak. He staggered and the smaller of the twins rushed at him and gashed his side with a spear, so that his liver fell out. It may be seen to this day in stone which, the natives say, resembles the shape of a man's liver. SEMSEM staggered on for a short distance and fell on the top of a bit of rising ground. The mother and the boys, fearing that he might not be dead, asked some small birds to go close to the body and see if life were really extinct. One bird touched the body of SEMSEM with its head and flew away in terror. This is a bird that has red feathers on the top of its head today. Another bird, more venturesome, put its head and shoulders into a wound. This is a bird that has red feathers on its head and shoulders today. A third bird went directly through the body entering at one wound and coming out by another. This bird is almost entirely red today. The first and second birds are honey eaters, the third a variety of parrot. When the third bird came out of the body of SEMSEM the victors were certain that the giant was dead. They were delighted and cut the body into numberless small pieces, to ensure complete destruction. The boys, in jubilation, blew blasts on the conch shell and immediately the pieces of the body changed into the people of Tanna whom SEMSEM had eaten. On the north-west coast of the island, in a limestone cave, two stalactites and two stalagmites, may be seen today, each of the former shaped like a woman's breast, with a nipple from which water drips regularly. These two water drippings have formed the stalagmites below, which the natives say are KANIAPNIN and KASASAOU being fed from the breasts of their mother above.

5. *How Rejuvenation was Lost*

An elderly woman, who had given birth to a son late in life, was on the beach one day with the child, whom she left on the shore while she went for a swim in the sea. While in the water her old and withered skin fell from her and she came out a young woman with soft skin. She went to the boy and said, "Come, my son!" But he cried and said, "I don't know you!" She replied, "I am your mother." But he said, "No! You are not my mother. I don't want you." In vain she tried to convince him, but he cried and rejected her, saying, "You are not my mother." Finally, in anger and despair, she went back into the sea and sank to the bottom where she may be seen in stone to this day. The natives say, if the son had acknowledged the young woman as his mother, he and all future generations would have lived for ever[1]. To this day the natives cast sticks and stones, in derision, at a rock, which they say is the boy. This rock, as well as the one beneath the sea, may still be seen on the south-west coast of the island.

6. *Masineruk and the Child*

Two women and a little girl were clearing their garden and burning the dry leaves. The child was warned not to go near the fire but, with childlike curiosity, she went close to it and was caught into the draught and carried up, with the smoke, to heaven. Here she saw a blind woman feeding a large number of pigs. Feeling very hungry the child began to eat the pigs' food. The pigs, in fright, made a disturbance, which caused the blind woman, whose name was Masineruk, to cry out, "Who is there?" The child replied, "It is I." Masineruk asked, "Where did you come from?" The child replied, "I came up with the smoke from the earth." Masineruk begged the child to live

[1] This agrees with a tale told by Ray, in an abstract of Gray, with some minor exceptions, 1901, p. 151. It was found almost intact in Saa and the Banks' Islands, Codrington, 1891, p. 265.

with her and told her she might go about anywhere she liked, with the exception of one spot, which was a sort of door or gate in the ground. The little girl told Masineruk she thought she could cure her of her blindness. So they went together to the sea shore and the child made a mixture of fruit and leaves of trees growing close to the beach. Then she told the blind woman to dive into a pool in the reef and while she was below the surface poured the mixture into the water. On coming out of the pool Masineruk found her sight restored and was delighted. One day Masineruk was away from the house and the child, yielding to her curiosity, went to examine the door in the ground, which she finally succeeded in opening. She saw the earth below her and her home and her people at their usual tasks. The sight made her very homesick, but she closed the door and went back to the house. On Masineruk's return she found the child in tears and asked what was the matter. The child, not wanting to confess her disobedience, said there was nothing wrong. On going outside the old woman noticed that the door in the ground was not perfectly closed and concluded that the child must have opened it and seen her home below. She asked the child if she would like to go back to her own people again and the child answered, "Yes!" Masineruk was very disappointed for she wanted the child to stop with her, but she prepared a long line made of creepers, to which she fastened the child and lowered her through the door in the floor of heaven. When the child was nearing the earth a strong wind began to blow her to and fro. Her sister, on the earth, saw her and cried out in delight, "Oh! Here is my sister!" and ran and told her mother. But, by the time the mother came out of the house, the child had swung out of view and she exclaimed, "I can't see her!" Eventually the child swung back again and was gently lowered to the earth, much to the delight of herself and her people. The line to which the child had been attached was seen to ascend to the sky again and, later, returned at intervals, each time with a pig fastened to the end. These pigs were a present to the child and her people from Masineruk. The dark place in the sky, close to the Southern Cross, now known as the Coal Sack, is said by the

Tannese to be the opening through which the child and the pigs were lowered.

7. RAMSUMAS *and* MATIKTIK

RAMSUMAS, the devil, had eaten all the people of Tanna, except a number of the young boys. These he kept to fatten for future feasts. He put them in an enclosure surrounded by a stone wall and told them to stop there while he went to fetch some taro for their food. In his absence, MATIKTIK[1], the good spirit, who had assumed human form, appeared to the boys and asked what they were doing inside the stone wall. They replied, "Our father put us here and told us to remain here while he went to fetch us some food." MATIKTIK said, "He is 'gammoning[2].' He is not your father. He is a devil and is only keeping you here to fatten you so that he may eat you by and by." With these words he broke down the stone wall and told the boys to follow him and he would save them. He led them along a track into the bush, until they came to a high tree. MATIKTIK spoke to the tree and it immediately shrank so that he and the boys were able to climb into the branches. As soon as they were safely lodged the tree returned to its original height. RAMSUMAS, on returning to the enclosure, was very angry to find the stone wall broken down and the boys gone. He exclaimed, "Here is all my food lost! I must go and look for it." Being gifted with a sense of smell like a dog, he soon got on the boys' track. He went along with the fury of a storm, his feet making a noise like thunder as they touched the ground. The roaring of his voice made the boys very much afraid. MATIKTIK told them not to be frightened and assured them they were quite safe. His keen sense of smell at last brought RAMSUMAS to the foot of the tree, where there was a clear pool of water which reflected the boys in the branches. RAMSUMAS, thinking he had run his quarry to earth, dived into the pool to secure it. On rising to the surface he was greeted by a shout of derisive laughter and on looking up into the tree he beheld MATIKTIK and the boys well beyond his reach. He cried out, "Hello! How did you

---

[1] MATIKTIK is known throughout the Pacific with slight variations in spelling. See Gray, 1892, p. 656.

[2] The jargon-English word used by the narrator.

get up there?" They told him that they came up on their knees. He tried to go up that way but only succeeded in taking the skin off his knees, so that he soon gave up. Then RAMSUMAS cried out to them, "You are only 'gammoning.' You could not go up that way. How did you get up?" They replied, "We came up on our backs." He tried this with the same result as with his knees. By this time RAMSUMAS was beginning to be very angry but had cunning enough not to show it until he had secured the boys, so he pleaded with them again to tell him how they got up. In reply, MATIKTIK lowered a strong creeper that grew on the tree and called out to RAMSUMAS that they climbed up by it. The devil seized the creeper as soon as he could reach it and commenced to climb. As he neared the lower branches of the tree his anger got the better of his cunning and he cried out, "Now I have got you and I will eat you all!" He had no sooner said this than MATIKTIK severed the creeper, with a sharp knife, above the head of RAMSUMAS and the latter fell with a great crash on the rocks below and was killed. A long stone, not unlike the body of a man, on the south coast of Tanna is pointed to today as the body of RAMSUMAS.

The final passages of the story of SEMSEM are also told by some at the close of this tale. The episodes of the three birds, the cutting of the body in pieces and the blowing on the conch shell thereby bringing all the inhabitants of the islands to life, enter into both tales.

KNOWLEDGE AND ART

The general knowledge of the Tannese is very limited in its scope, but accurate information on this subject is difficult to obtain, even with the most intelligent of witnesses during a visit of not more than five months.

Of anatomy and physiology the natives seem to know nothing, nor can repeated inquiries produce any information. Of the stars, again, almost nothing is known and it is a most astonishing fact that even the most brilliant constellations seem never to have made any particular impression on the native mind. The Milky Way is sometimes called "Ashes" and the constellation of Orion the "canoe with outrigger," or the "belt with outrigger," and there are distinct words for the morning and evening star. The former is called *Fatukai* or *Iaiubama* and the latter *Nonunalibini*, while one informant says the Southern Cross is called *Mahauianateni*, or "Star over the land."

Counting is done on the fingers and toes, in fives, up to twenty, and the numbers above twenty are obtained by saying "one twenty," "two twenties" and so on. The left hand is used first, then the right hand, then the left foot and the right foot. The fingers are held down, not up, and it is the number of fingers bent down and not those erect, that indicate the desired number.

Decorative art is practically non-existent. Kava bowls are sometimes inscribed with a simple pattern and the finishing of bows and arrows shows a certain amount of attention to grace in outline. The checker-board pattern on the side walls of some houses has been referred to already, as well as the designs on some of the tapa belts worn by the men. With these exceptions there is no art of any kind. This is to be regretted, for an inquiry into the sociology of the subject would be greatly facilitated by examples of native handicraft to be studied as expressive of native thought and feeling.

No evidence of caution in ordinary life to reduce disease to a minimum or of any sort of prevention except that assisted by magical means is found anywhere, and an epidemic of measles swept away one-third of the population in 1860[1].

No megaliths have been found in the island, nor is there any recollection that any ever existed, which confirms Rivers's contention (1913, *B. A. Rep.* p. 634) that they usually exist with secret societies and not without them.

LANGUAGE

The question of language on Tanna must be dismissed with a few words. Tannese belongs to the Melanesian branch of the Oceanic languages, with strong Polynesian affinities (McDonald, p. 464). For a linguist the complications of the

---

[1] See Paton, pp. 160–1, and Brenchley, p. 206.

language are great, but for one who like myself has no linguistic attainments they are insuperable. It may be that for this reason the study of the language, beyond a simple knowledge of some common forms of expression, was postponed until all the other information recorded had been collected, when the arrival of the Government yacht and the opportunity to leave the island put an end to all work. The small amount gleaned is here offered with a considerable amount of trepidation, for it can do little more than suggest a few grammatical rules that may be of interest.

There are two distinct dialects in the island, so different in fact as to lead one to think that they may be really distinct languages. One group is in the region around Kwamera, on the south-west coast, and this form is spoken by upwards of 2000 people, while about the same number speak the Waisisi dialect on the central east coast. The entire north part of the island speak a dialect akin to that of Waisisi, but practically unintelligible to the people of Kwamera. The west coast dialect seems to be a cross between the Waisisi dialect and that of Kwamera, but with strong characterizations of its own[1]. In some cases a distinct dialect extends for only a short distance. For instance, in the region south of Lenakel on the west coast there are four distinct dialects, all with certain affinities, within a coast line not more than ten miles long. Still, the Polynesian influence, which seems to be much stronger on the east coast (that is, wherever the Waisisi dialect prevails), has not affected the language to such an extent that it may not still be called a part of the Melanesian branch of the Oceanic tongue, in spite of the evident differences between it and the languages of Northern and Central Melanesia[2]. Most natives understand more than one dialect and some understand almost any dialect of the general Waisisi form, though it is rare to find a native who understands dialects of the two contrasted forms of Waisisi and Kwamera (Gray, 1899, p. 131).

As has been stated by ethnologists for many years, linguistics are an unreliable test of racial movement, but there must be

[1] Cf. Gray, 1892, p. 647.
[2] See Ray, 1901, p. 147.

some reason to account for the existence of two such distinct dialectic forms of the Melanesian branch of the Oceanic languages.

Some of the variations between the dialects are very constant. For example, the *r* at Waisisi on the east coast becomes *t* at Lenakel on the west, the *ng* at Waisisi becomes *k* at Lenakel, the *p* at the former is *b* at the latter place. Between Lenakel and Kwamera, too, there is a certain agreement between certain letters in one place and the other, though the root of the word itself in the two instances may be quite different. Thus, the *r* at Waisisi which we have seen becomes *t* at Lenakel, is invariably *t* as well at Kwamera.

We find the *ian* or *ien* at Kwamera added to the verb in all parts of the island to make it a verbal noun. Thus, the *rahniaunian* of Waisisi becomes *tahniaunian* at Lenakel, but the word for this relationship at Kwamera is *kunkwanien*. The name for the volcano, *Iahoi* at Waisisi and *Iasur* in the Kwamera district[1], does not follow this rule.

The native word for "skirt" is the same both at Lenakel and Waisisi. In fact it is used in every part of Tanna except in Kwamera. *Niaua* is the general form, *rous* is that used at Kwamera. It is hard to think of a word with greater divergence in form than this. The affinity between *rahniaunian*, which means "his son's wife" or "his daughter's husband," and the word for "skirt," *niaua*, has led to the hypothesis put forward by some that there is in this term the implication of a former existence of a dual organization of society with matrilineal descent. It is perfectly true that the person spoken of as a *rahniaunian* of a man would always be of the same moiety as himself in a dual organization of society with descent through the mother, but the possibilities of establishing a clue to an ancient order of society on such a hypothesis must not be pressed too far. If this were true of Waisisi and Lenakel it would not be true of the *kunkwanien* and *rous* of Kwamera, where the descent must have been purely patrilineal.

There are four case forms in the Waisisi dialect as applied to pronouns. They are as follows.

---

[1] This agrees with Ray (1894, p. 227) quoting Gray.

First person—exclusive or inclusive of person or persons addressed—different forms for each.

> Singular: I.   Trial: we three.
> Dual: we two.   Plural: we four, or more.

Second person—one form only for inclusive and exclusive[1].

> Singular: you.   Trial: you three.
> Dual: you two.   Plural: you four, or more.

Third person—one form only as in second person.

> Singular: he or she.   Trial: they three.
> Dual: they two.   Plural: they four, or more.

For example, when a man asks for medicine for his wife only, when she has no child, he asks for it "for her." If she has a child, recently born, he asks for it "for the two of them," even if the medicine is desired for the wife only.

Some of the names for weapons used in the olden time may be added. The killing stones are called *kawa*, the bow *numan* (*faga*), the blunt arrow is called *noanpara*. Also the sharp arrow, *nefaga*, combines the ancient and the present-day name in the one word. The names of the sling, *kuteliu*, of the spear, *niro*, and the club, *nium*, were all given to these arms in the fighting days, and they are still used today when these weapons are mentioned. The word for bow has great variety in different islands of this part of the Pacific. In Tanna it is *faga*, or *numan faga*, in Anaiteum it is *fana*, in Efate it is *asu*, in Epi *viu*, in Paama *hisu*, in Nengone and Mare in the Loyalties, *pehna*, while in islands as remote from Tanna as Florida and Savo in the Solomons, it is *bage*, which is more like the Tannese word than that of an island no farther away than Efate. This example will prove, if proof is still necessary, what an involved question that of the Oceanic language is.

Forster (p. 267) found words in Tannese corresponding to those of Tonga and the Friendly Islands, and resemblances between Tanna and Tongatabou were noted by Cook.

---

[1] The pronoun, second person singular, *ik* in Tanna, becomes *kik* in Eromanga and *aiek* in Anaiteum. See McDonald, Rev. D., *Trans. and Proc. Roy. Soc. Victoria*, XXIII. O.S. pp. 8–9.

At Waisisi the names for the regular feasts throughout the year are as follows: *Nabok, Taka, Kaielaoulaou, Kasasiwa, Nalera, Nao nasil, Noaneriou, Iale, Bulugi,* but the meanings of these words have disappeared entirely. There are not many words for colours and not many colours have names. One chief called red and brown by the same name. The principal names, with the addition of light brown or pig colour which has a special name, *kamra,* are: yellow, *taburhel*; red, *taravarev* (green and blue share the native name of *tamenta*); black, or dark, *taben*; white or light, *taruan.*

CHAPTER II

ANAITEUM[1]

THE tribal groups in Anaiteum seem to be somewhat akin
to those of Tanna. A group of villages forms a tribe, but it
is not known if the dialectal differences that form the
basis of the tribal unit in Tanna exist in Anaiteum. There are
six coastal tribal groups and two interior tribes more or less
subject to the former. These coastal tribes are separated, as
far as their sea boundaries are concerned, by the more important headlands (Lawrie, p. 709). In Anaiteum each tribe has
a chief (Inglis, p. 24). Each village group in the tribe also has
its head man or chief, who seems to be somewhat subservient
to the tribal chief, more so at least than in Tanna. The six
coastal tribal groups are of very unequal size territorially, the
boundaries between the different tribes being formed by natural
barriers. There are four large and several smaller valleys running
from the sea into the mountain range that rises to some 3000 feet
in the centre of the island. The slopes of the mountains are
steep and the valleys deep and narrow. One result of this inequality in the size of the tribal districts seems to be that certain
tribal chiefs were more powerful than others in the old days
(Inglis, p. 24). Three chiefs of more authority than their neighbours are reported by Brenchley (p. 198). The chief of each
village group is a member of the tribal council, but the meetings
of this body are never held without the tribal chief at hand
(Lawrie, p. 710). At these meetings all infractions of tribal law
are discussed, judgements pronounced and punishments ordered.
It is not possible to learn if unanimity of agreement is necessary
in order to convict a delinquent or whether a tribal chief has
any special prerogatives, such as a deciding vote or the power
of a veto. Punishment takes various forms, but a common
method is to order the culprit to be bound with his arms behind
him in the public place, or general meeting place and dancing

[1] According to Inglis (p. 19) the island is called *Anattom* by the Tannese.
It was so spelled by Capt. Cook. It is called *Ekiano* by the Futunese.

ground of the village. For lesser offences the culprit may be ordered to seek for food for the chief and the old men of the village.

Chieftainship is hereditary, the descent going from father to son or, if there be no son, to the son of a brother or sister of the deceased, but no authority notes whether, in this case, any preference is given the brother's son or the sister's son. There have been female chiefs in the island, but all detail as to this is lacking (Lawrie, p. 710). The tribal chiefs seem to have a more priestly than secular power and this power is in no sense absolute. In fact, it is stated by Inglis (p. 24) that the men who hold the true power in the community are the warriors and the magicians.

With regard to clan organization or the existence of clan symbolism, nothing is known, and no indications have been noted by the few who have written of the island. Nor is it stated whether the descent is through the mother or the father or through both, one after the other. Of adoption there is no recorded evidence; of kinship terms the evidence is scanty and what few are given suggest an affinity with those of Tanna only in the suffixed pronouns to indicate the person intended. Thus "my father," *etmak*, becomes *etmam* in the second person singular, and *etman* in the third person; "my mother," *risek*, "thy mother," *risem*, "his" or "her mother," *risen*. The same suffixes apply to other words, as *etoak wak*, "my brother," and *natahaigirak*, "my sister" (Lawrie, p. 716).

I cannot find any records of physical characteristics and measurements of the Anaiteumese. Brenchley (pp. 196–7) speaks of them quaintly as a moral people, whatever that may mean.

The domestic conditions seem to bear some resemblance to those of Tanna. The corded hair and ear ornaments of the Anaiteumese have a strong resemblance to those worn by the Tannese, the women, in the old days at least, wore the pandanus skirt as in the northern island, and the houses were like the old-time Tanna houses (Lawrie, p. 710). Every village has its "sacred ground," where feasts and other ceremonies were formerly held (Inglis, pp. 29–30).

Marriages are arranged generally by the chiefs; whether of

the tribe or the village group, is not stated. The marriage is often planned soon after the birth of a female child, but the girl does not go to live with her affianced husband until she has reached puberty, which occurs in females at about fourteen, in males from sixteen to eighteen years. When the formal union takes place and the husband begins to cohabit regularly with his wife a feast is given. The only restriction to marriage is with a near blood-relation, and marriage seems to take place within the tribe in most instances. Cross-cousin marriage is allowed, but not that with the daughter of the father's brother or of the mother's sister. Polygyny was once common and widows were sometimes strangled at their own request by a son or a near relative, for it was considered a disgrace to live in widowhood. There was a feeling that the wife should be near her husband in their future home, for wives are little more than slaves of their husbands. In a community where polygyny was common disputes about women were continuous, and these and disagreements about land were the usual causes of war, as in Tanna. Of adultery, prostitution, avoidance and perversions, no record exists (Lawrie, pp. 709–10).

Boys are welcomed at birth but girls are received in silence, infanticide, in the case of female children, being common in the old days, when it was accomplished by leaving the unfortunate infant to perish in the bush. The nearest female relative names the girls, and the nearest male relative performs the same office for the boys, but, unfortunately, the exact relationship of these persons to the parents is not stated. Children are often suckled for two years even today and, formerly, a feast was made by the father of the boy when he was weaned (Lawrie, pp. 708–9). Deformed or sickly children were not killed but were neglected and allowed to grow up as best they might. Children are still carried in the old manner, sitting astride on the mother's hip. The children do not seem to be well disciplined. Lawrie (p. 710) says that both male and female children inherit equally from the parents.

Of childhood, children's games and pastimes, nothing has been recorded; of native emotions none has been noted by the few visitors who have been in the island. Neither can anything be gleaned from the brief accounts of the island in regard to respect for law, the enforcement of rules and the force of public opinion.

Of warfare very little is recorded. Lawrie (p. 709) states that certain tribes stood together in war, but whether the tribes of the island were generally divided into two groups when war was in progress, or whether he refers to the distinction between the stronger coastal people and the weaker interior tribes, it is impossible to learn. Fighting was much less common on Anaiteum than on Tanna (Turner, p. 326), but cannibalism was common after warfare[1], for it is stated that the men killed in combat were invariably cooked and eaten by the tribe of the men who obtained possession of their bodies (Lawrie, p. 712).

The island is small[2] and rather poor for a tropical island (Inglis, p. 22). The fertile portions are limited, practically, to the level bottoms of the larger valleys, and to a narrow fringe along the shore, which is protected by reefs over a large part of the circumference. In these regions grow coconut, bread-fruit, taro, sugar, banana and yam, but the latter is not a food staple as it is in Tanna. A source of revenue to the white man since his advent has been found in the rich forests of the higher parts of the island, where the soil is very rich and well watered. These forests are composed largely of a kind of pine, the *Dammara australis* (Turner, p. 325), which has been shipped away to various parts of the world for many years. The indigenous foods are the bread-fruit, banana, coconut, "horse chestnut," sago, sugar, taro, yam, sweet potato and arrowroot. The introduced fruits are the lime, lemon, citron, pineapple, custard-apple and pawpaw (Brenchley, p. 199).

The land is cultivated by the family, but waste land belongs to the tribe. The statements made (Inglis, p. 24) in regard to land ownership are too uncertain to be accepted without reservations. Digging sticks were used for preparing gardens in the old days but are superseded now by agricultural implements of the white man. In the swampy parts of the island the taro is plentiful, yams being less common than in many islands of

---

[1] According to Brenchley (p. 197) the last case was in 1852.

[2] Brenchley (p. 195) says it is fourteen miles by eight.

the New Hebrides, as noted above, and food is cooked in earth ovens by means of heated stones, without steam, as in Tanna (Lawrie, p. 710).

Fishing is not a very common method of procuring food. Pigs and fowls constitute almost the only fauna.

Handicraft is of a very inferior quality as Inglis notes (p. 25), "Houses, canoes, ornaments and weapons show the least possible skill in their form and workmanship."

Concerning magico-religious ideas and practices little is recorded. No distinction between the idea of spirits and ghosts could be made by anyone who has visited the island. The *natmas*, or, great spirit, was feared and propitiated in the old days and the common people dared not pronounce his name aloud (Lawrie, p. 712). The ghost of the dead left the body, went to the west end of the island, plunged into the sea and swam to the abode of the departed (Turner, p. 326). The word for "ghosts" in the Banks' Islands is much like the Anaiteumese word (Codrington, 1891, p. 123), and it seems as if a connection between the two may be possible.

Of magic in general we have no more information than we have in the case of spirits and ghosts. Certain persons have magical powers which are said to have descended from father to son; these men are held in great veneration by the people of the island and are believed to have much power for good or evil. Some persons, possibly not the same as the above, have power to prepare earth from a certain part of the island into love charms. Another way of preparing magical potions is to mix a bit of charcoal with some wood and a banana leaf and parts of the anatomy of a lizard, all of which are placed in a section of bamboo, which resembles the Tanna method with the exception of the lizard (Lawrie, p. 711). The *natmasses* or magical stones have a resemblance to the *natuk* of Tanna, but Inglis insists that they are evidences of "secret idolatry" in Anaiteum (Inglis, pp. 31–2). A sacred staff, said to be used in illness, was seen by Turner (pp. 327–8).

Circumcision is performed on lads usually between the ages of seven and ten by certain men who do the operation as an hereditary right, a knife being used, as in Tanna.

The natives think that the performance of this rite increases the stature and improves the physical condition of the youth. As circumcision is general it is difficult to prove that this is not the case. The food prepared for the boys during seclusion is cooked at a special oven and the boys are carefully watched and tended as in Tanna and, on recovery, a special fowl or fish is cooked and given to the lad. It is not stated if this refers to the food partaken of at the feast at the end of the seclusion, or if it is a separate case of special feeding. The seclusion seems to last from one to three months. The adoption of the belt and penis case is, as in Tanna, the culminating act whereby the lad passes to man's estate (Lawrie, p. 709). Turner's account of the ceremony in Anaiteum agrees substantially with this, though he says (p. 326) that it is usually performed at the age of five.

The death of a chief is attributed always to black magic; something belonging to the deceased has come into the power of a magician and has been imbued with power for evil by the latter. It may be nothing more than a banana skin which the deceased has tossed away carelessly or some chewings of sugar cane which he has expectorated. For this reason great care is taken to dispose of such things, so that they may not be found by an enemy or, if found, identified (Lawrie, p. 711).

As to disposal of the dead, the body of a chief is bound with strips of native cloth tied around the arms and legs, while stones are attached to the feet and the face is painted with red clay. Whether the legs are flexed or not is not stated. When all these preparations are made the body is carried to the edge of a cliff and dropped into the sea. Some great chiefs used to be buried in the ground, in an erect position, with the head exposed, female mourners watching the body until decomposition began. When all the flesh disappeared, the skull was placed in a cave or sacred enclosure, all this being very different from the disposal practised by the Tannese. Food was placed in a basket and hung in a tree near the grave. Sea burial was accompanied by a fire on the beach, at which the ghost of the deceased was thought to warm itself, and widows were strangled after the death of a chief (Inglis, p. 31; Turner, p. 326). In sea burial men were nude except for the cloth bindings referred to above, and women were wrapped in the grass skirt worn commonly by their sex. The future home of the deceased is divided into two parts. The word for this place is *uma atmas*, and one part is for the good and the other for the bad, although ideas of reward and punishment seem to be rudimentary. Perhaps the greatest sin is stinginess. The entrance to this abode of the dead, according to some ideas at least, is through the vent of an extinct volcano at the west extremity of the island (Lawrie, p. 712), possibly the same spot from which the ghost of the departed began its swim to its future home, as noted above, but whether the two ideas are connected does not appear. The home of the dead who lived good lives, according to native ideas, is a place of sensual delights, particularly those involved in feasting. The abode of the bad is furnished with food of a loathsome description, and those who have been niggardly in their gifts of food for feasts on earth are obliged to eat this as punishment. Ancestors were worshipped, prayers and offerings being made to one when taro was planted, to another when a canoe was made, to another when war was undertaken, etc. This seems to resemble propitiation rather than worship of ancestors, but the material at hand is too scant to hazard an opinion.

The folk lore of the Anaiteumese resembles that of the Tannese, in the few evidences that have been recorded. MATIKTIK of the Tannese becomes MAUITIKITIKI in Aniateum as he does in Efate and Nguna (Ray, 1901, p. 147). There is an interesting tale of the creation of the island:

INHUGARAIG, or the great NATMAS, went out to sea to fish on the leaf of a native tree with no midrib, called *nesiaig*. As he fished he finally caught something on his line, which he pulled and pulled and drew a mountain peak from the sea. On this he sat and then pulled up land which he set alongside the mountain. Thus the island was formed and on this, eventually, he set man and woman.

INPOTHETH is a mischievous spirit feared especially on moonlight nights when shadows are cast by the trees, but whether he is a spirit which was never human or the ghost of some departed chief is uncertain.

Counting is not clearly defined, and it is not easy to determine if it is done by fives in the Melanesian manner or by tens in the Polynesian[1], though the former method seems to be more likely. The word for five means "one hand," that for six "one hand plus one finger." Eleven is "two hands and one toe," the word for twenty means "all fingers and toes" or "hands and feet" (Lawrie, p. 713).

Dialectal differences between tribes are negligible in this island. Nouns begin generally with *n* or *in*, and the plural is often expressed by dropping these prefixes. The personal pronouns have four persons: singular, dual, trial and plural. The first person of the three latter has inclusive and exclusive forms, the inclusive referring to the speaker and the person or persons spoken of. The verb has three tenses, present, past and future. The grammar of the island is the one thing that has been treated fully and well by an authority on such matters.

The songs of the Anaiteumese have no relation to poetry, except that they have a certain rhythm of their own; they are always short and are not products of ancient times[2].

Some rock drawings found in the island are given by Speiser (1923, Table 107).

[1] See Inglis, J., *Dictionary of Aneityumese*, London, 1882, p. x.
[2] Inglis, *loc. cit.* pp. xxv–xxvii.

CHAPTER III

FUTUNA[1]

THE FUTUNESE seem to be of a mixed type with distinct Polynesian affinities. There is no definite evidence, in the little that has been written about the island, of the status of the tribe, the village community or the clan. Chieftainship exists certainly and an energetic chief sometimes used to get control of a chief superior to himself, as well as of the men endowed with magical powers (p. 201). This would suggest a chief or chiefs in the island with powers over the lesser village chiefs, as in Anaiteum and west Tanna, but distinct from the chieftainship found in the Waisisi region of Tanna. Trees are owned by the individual, or at least by the family, in Futuna, and the land belongs to the tribe or group (p. 202). There is no evidence of totemism (p. 207), but the descent was through the mother before the conversion of the entire population to Christianity changed the social organization of the Futunese. The sons always belonged to the mother's group, and the chiefly office descended to the late chief's sister's son, or to his sister's daughter's son (p. 205). Indeed, the system of relationship was of the simple classificatory kind, a man having rights to all the sisters of his wife as potential wives (pp. 205–6), which seems odd in a community that was distinctly Polynesian in many of its customs.

In personal appearance and physical characteristics the Futunese is not so much Polynesian as would be expected when one considers the preponderance of Polynesian over Melanesian culture in the island. The hair of the men is dressed as in Tanna but is allowed to grow longer, and it is said that this manner of dressing the hair was once common among the women as well as among the men (p. 193), yet Cook (II. p. 78, 2nd ed.) mentions hair like that of Europeans on the Futunese he saw in Tanna in the eighteenth century. It is

[1] Except where otherwise stated, all the references are to the Rev. W. Gunn's *The Gospel in Futuna*.

difficult to reconcile the two statements. The septum of the nose is pierced as well as the lobe of the ear, and an interesting legend of ear-boring is recorded (p. 194). Pendants of pearl shell or disks of green stone are worn (p. 192). It seems that the Futunese in the old days suited his dress and adornment to the dictates of the combined Melanesian-Polynesian influence in which he lived.

Of sex matters and the regulation of marriage very little is recorded. Wives were purchased, though it is possible that the description of the manner of obtaining wives has more reference to bride price than to marriage by purchase (p. 202). Unfaithfulness to their marriage vows among men is condoned, but this is not the case with women, where the strictest circumspection is demanded. Polygyny was very common in the days before Christian influence, especially among the chiefly class, and all who were able to afford it had two or three wives, and some are said to have had as many as ten, or even more (p. 203). Most of the quarrelling in the island was about women. Prostitution is regulated as in Tanna and Anaiteum[1]. No information as to avoidance, adultery or sexual perversions has been collected. The birth of a boy is the occasion for rejoicing, and the women who attend the mother give a cry when the infant is found to be a male, while the men celebrate the event by a sham fight with clubs. Girls are not welcome, and female infanticide was common in the old days, when the infant was thrown into the bush. Sometimes she was rescued and adopted (p. 204), this seeming to be the only evidence of this practice, but it would not come under the caption of adoption in the ethnological sense. A name is given to the child soon after birth by the father or the mother, but if the child cries a great deal, the name may be changed. Of childhood games and native emotions no records have been made.

The weapons used in war were more elaborately carved and worked than those used in Tanna. Clubs were diamond-shaped, bows were five or six feet long, killing stones were cut from the coralline rock which is so common in the island (p. 196). No dependable account of warfare in the old days has come to the

---

[1] This is on the evidence of KUOKAREI, chief of Whitesands, Tanna.

notice of the writer. It is stated that the Futunese are a cruel people (p. 253), but whether this refers to actions in warfare and treatment of captives or to their general attitude toward children and animals is not clear.

Food is said to be planted by one group but is never eaten by that group, a feast being made and the food exchanged for some raised by the invited group or groups (p. 209). Ovens are dug in the ground as in Tanna and the method of cooking seems to be the same as in that island, and no evidence appears as to the use of steam (p. 210).

Fishing is an important activity, being either with hook and line, with net and basket, with spear or with bow and arrow (p. 197); women sometimes fish with rod and line (p. 198). The native-made fishing line is so strong that it will outlast the European article (p. 199). Torchlight fishing is common (p. 198), and in general fishing as a means of obtaining food seems to be much more commonly practised and more profitable than in Tanna.

Basket making of a fine kind of plait was common in Futuna in the old days (p. 200), and baskets may sometimes be found in other islands that were made in Futuna. Canoes have a recess hollowed out of the bow or stern for holding fish baskets, and an ornament in the stern resembling the tail of a fowl. The sides are raised by rows of planks attached to the main body of the dugout by cords of sennet, the holes through which the sennet is passed being plugged with coconut fibre. The larger canoes are built by joining two hollowed-out tree trunks so skilfully that no water ever enters at the point of jointure, these larger craft being used in catching flying fish and, formerly, for voyages to other islands. A baling implement, in the form of a wooden scoop with a handle (pp. 198–9), is always carried, but what wood is used for this or for canoe making is not clear. All handicraft has degenerated with the diminution of the population.

Of belief in spirits, ghosts, or a superior being or beings, no accounts have been given; of magic almost nothing has been written, although magical stones in the shape of bread-fruit are mentioned (p. 221). There are references to altars with posts, of

which the two tallest were dedicated to the sun and moon
(p. 218), and a "temple" is also referred to, with high walls
and gable ends, which was rebuilt for the last time in 1859
(p. 219), but there is no reliable account of anything of this
nature to be obtained now. Gunn mentions certain magical
rites, notably one performed over a boy who fell from a coconut
tree in the act of gathering nuts (pp. 223-4), and of a special
test for discovering a thief (p. 214).

An important supernatural being is given the name of
AMOSHISHIKI (p. 217), but whether he is a spirit which has never
had human shape or the ghost of some departed ancestor of
the Futunese is not stated, although the name suggests a connection with the MATIKTIK of Tanna (Ray, 1901, p. 147).

Circumcision is mentioned as a Futunese custom, but no
description of the rite has been found (p. 207).

When a feast is made the food is piled in the centre of the
dancing ground or village square, word being sent to the group
for which the feast is being given that all is ready (p. 209). Men
wear a bright coloured dracaena when a pig is brought to the
feast (p. 193). Except during feasts, men and women live together in their houses and work together in their gardens, but
the men always eat in a group by themselves at evening in the
public square (p. 203), the women doing the same. Promiscuity
was permitted at the end of certain feasts in the old days, if not
after all gatherings of this kind (p. 210). There is no account of
special feasts at certain seasons, with one exception, when a
special feast is held during the annual visit of the flying fish
(p. 211).

The scant account of the preparation of kava leaves much
doubt whether the rite is performed in the Polynesian or the
Melanesian manner. Beyond the fact that it is prepared by
boys, that no women are allowed to be present, that the men
spit out the first mouthful calling on some supernatural being
or ghost and then finish the draught, sinking afterwards into a
deep sleep (p. 203), nothing is recorded. It would seem as if
the manner of preparation had more Polynesian than Melanesian
affinity since all male members of the village group partake of
the drink at the same time (Rivers, 1914, II. p. 245).

Disposal of the dead occurs in more than one manner, although the most common form seems to be sea burial. In this case the bodies are weighted with stones. Sporadic cases of grave burial occur, the body being left half buried formerly until the person who caused the death of the corpse had been killed in revenge (p. 214). Fruit trees are cut down after the death of the owner, as in Tanna (p. 215).

Of myths and traditions very little is recorded. The resemblance between those of Futuna and Tanna is apparent in the few cases extant. AMOSHISHIKI, the Futunese superhuman being corresponding to the MATIKTIK of Tanna, is credited with forbidding the introduction of sorcery into the island, which is a distinct variant of the Tannese version. A partially submerged rock some distance from the Futunese coast is pointed out as the canoe that was bringing this curse to the island[1]. A story of AMOSHISHIKI, or MOSHI as he is called at times, is related, that agrees in all essential features with that told of MATIKTIK on Tanna. There are differences of detail but they are unimportant. Another tale is about the origin of man and woman. Two yams were lying together on the ground. The next morning one had turned into a man, the other into a woman (p. 216). A legend of a man swallowed by a big fish, something like the story of Jonah, is told. One, YAWIA, is swallowed in this manner and escapes alive (p. 218). A story of creation, temptation and consequent loss of divinity is related by Suas (p. 906). Folk lore is not the specialty of any one island (p. 241), and it is exceedingly difficult to determine where stories are original and where they are derivations.

No account of general knowledge of the Futunese has been given us. It is said that the names for certain constellations such as the Pleiades, the Great Bear, the Milky Way and Orion are known (p. 251), but the evidence is not convincing. Counting is by multiples of ten, and there is a special word for each number from one to ten (p. 233).

The similarity between the languages of Futuna and Tonga is noted by Forster (II. p. 294), and Ray (*J.A.I.* 1901, p. 147) remarks that the language of Futuna is closely akin to that of

---

[1] Ray, *J.A.I.* 1901, p. 147.

Eastern Polynesia. Words for anger are said to be more numerous in Futunese than in English; there are only one or two words for "love," "like" and so forth, and there is only one word for "good," "excellent," "beautiful" (p. 231). Altogether, the language is Polynesian with Melanesian mixture, rather than Melanesian with Polynesian affinities, as in Tanna. There is a nice distinction between poetry and prose; the former must be sung while the latter must be spoken (p. 239).

CHAPTER IV

ANIWA

So little has been given to the world about this small island that the few facts set forth here can do little more than suggest a few contrasts between the cultures of Aniwa and Tanna.

The island represents an excellent example of a Melanesian-Polynesian culture complex (Gunn, p. 108), but no evidence of tribal, village or clan organization is at hand as far as can be learned. The kinship terms have strong Polynesian affinities and are quite unlike those of either language division of the island of Tanna. The one measurement taken of an Aniwan on the island of Tanna has no anthropological value, and it is a matter of regret that more measurements of visiting Aniwans were not recorded during my stay on that island. The cephalic index of this one case is high—84·2—but this may be a sporadic case of brachycephaly. Paton (p. 369) calls all Aniwans Malays, but the loose use of this term in the early days of anthropological research leaves one in doubt as to what is really meant.

No record as to the status of chiefs has been recorded of Aniwa. As all the inhabitants of the island were converted to Christianity many years ago, the recollection of customs of the heathen days is very vague. Even when some are recalled it is very difficult to get at the exact facts. The Christianized native is very prone to think that the white man will not approve of his heathen customs and he will not talk frankly about them until his confidence has been completely won.

The septum of the nose used to be pierced (Gunn, p. 193) and ear-boring is still common, together with the wearing of shell ear-ornaments as among the Tannese. It is said (Paton, p. 337) that the latter are given to a man by a woman as a sign of love. Nothing of marriage regulations or of sex matters has come to us. A report that a woman may beat her husband can hardly be accepted without some reservations (Paton, pp. 368–9).

It seems that the young women must have been monopolized
by the old men in the old days, since there is a record of thirty
young men in an Aniwan village wanting wives, who could not
procure them (Paton, p. 338). Infanticide was practised and
three cases are mentioned by Paton (p. 334), but whether it
was a regular custom and whether it was limited to female
infants is not known. Prostitution is practised exactly as in
Tanna.

Of warfare there is no record as far as can be discovered. On
an island that never had a large population and which has no
safe anchorage or harbour, it is difficult to see how warfare
could have played much part in the social life of the people.

Horticulture and hunting must have been restricted because
of the coralline nature of the island and the scarcity of wooded
regions. Fishing was always an important occupation and is still
carried on, often by torchlight (Gunn, pp. 197–8).

In marked contrast to Tanna, baskets are still made here with
real artistry of design and workmanship.

Of spirits, ghosts and magic in general nothing is recorded.
Neither is there any evidence of the use of kava or of feasts and
other expressions of the people in ceremonial life. Dancing is
performed as in Tanna (Paton, p. 336). Serpent worship was
practised in Aniwa, according to KUOKAREI, and the sea snake
is the totem of some of the people there.

Paton records one or two legends. MOSHIKISHIKI, or MAT-
SHIKTSHIKI, evidently the MATIKTIK of Tanna, placed men and
women in the island, and there is a tale resembling the flood
story of other peoples. According to this account the volcano
on Tanna was a part of the island of Aniwa at one time. Rain
fell day after day and the sea rose and began to cover every-
thing. All the people, except the few who climbed the cone
of the volcano, were drowned. MATSHIKTSHIKI, fearing the
fires of the volcano would be extinguished by the flood, split it
off from the submerged part of the island and floated it across
to Tanna, where it still is. When the sea subsided Aniwa was
left without a volcano, but nothing is recorded of the fate of
the few people who sought refuge on the summit.

The origin of coconuts is told almost as in Tanna (Ray, 1901, pp. 150–1). The end of the tale, with the throwing away of the *tanojiro*, or central leaf of the coconut palm, is added in the Aniwan version. Ray (1901, p. 147) notes that the language of Aniwa is related closely to that of Eastern Polynesia, rather than to Melanesian.

Relationship Terms

ANIWA.

	Term	Reciprocal	
Father	TAMANA	NOTARIKI TENTAMA	Son
Mother	NANA	NOFINE TENTAMA	Daughter
Elder Brother	NOSOATASORI	NOSOATASISI	Younger Brother
Elder Sister	NOKAVE	NOKAVE	*Younger Brother*
Younger Sister	NOKAVE	NOKAVE	*Elder Brother*
Elder Sister	NOSOATASISI	NOSOATASISI	*Younger Sister*
Father's Sister	NANFANGAVAI	NOSOATASORE	*Brother's Son*
" "	NANFANGAVAI	NOSOATASORE	*Brother's Daughter*
Father's Sister's Husband	—	—	Wife's Brother's Son
" "			Wife's Brother's Daughter
Father's Sister's Son	—	—	Mother's Brother's Son
" "			Mother's Brother's Daughter
Father's Sister's Daughter	—	—	*Mother's Brother's Son*
" "			*Mother's Brother's Daughter*
Mother's Brother "	TOMANA	—	Sister's Son
" "	TOMANA	—	Sister's Daughter
Mother's Brother's Wife	—	—	*Husband's Sister's Son*
" " "			*Husband's Sister's Daughter*
Father's Father	TUPUNA	TAMPUPUNA	Son's Son
" "	TUPUNA	TAMPUPUNA	Son's Daughter
Father's Mother	TUPUNA	TAMPUPUNA	*Son's Son*
" "	TUPUNA	TAMPUPUNA	*Son's Daughter*
Mother's Father	TUPUNA	TAMPUPUNA	Daughter's Son
" "	TUPUNA	TAMPUPUNA	Daughter's Daughter
Mother's Mother	TUPUNA	TAMPUPUNA	*Daughter's Son*
" "	TUPUNA	TAMPUPUNA	*Daughter's Daughter*
Wife's Father	—	—	Daughter's Husband
Wife's Mother	—	—	
Husband's Father	—	—	Son's Wife "
Husband's Mother	—	—	" "
Wife	TAFOINA FUNE	NENUANE	*Husband*
Wife's Sister	NANUFUNE	—	*Sister's Husband*
Brother's Wife	—	—	*Husband's Brother*
Wife's Brother	NOSAFE	—	Sister's Husband
Brother's Wife	—	RUFEIMA	*Husband's Sister*

Collected from *Internationales Archiv für Ethnographie*, Band VII, p. 238.

CHAPTER V

EROMANGA

PHYSICAL CHARACTERISTICS
AND MEASUREMENTS

THE EROMANGAN is of a less fine type than the Tannese. This may be due to the decimation of the population, for the warlike character of the native of this island in the old days leads one to believe that a much more vigorous type prevailed when Cook had his trouble with the natives in Polinia Bay.

The fifty-nine measurements of adult males recorded represent about half the number in the island, for the preponderance of women in the known villages leads one to presume that this inequality in the sexes is constant throughout. While the measurements recorded represent groups from certain sections of the island, no one group is of sufficient size to establish an average for a particular locality. The largest single group, from Unupunkor near Dillon's Bay on the west coast, numbers only twenty-two adult males and, in this case, every one is recorded, while from the south—Unapang and its vicinity—there are twenty-six adult males recorded, almost the entire male suffrage of that part of the island. In the latter case, however, some of the men, while coming from the district around Unapang, actually live at some distance from it and the value of the average for that part of the island is manifestly weakened thereby. For the north and north-west we have only seven and four recorded measurements, so the averages must be given for the island as a whole and not for any particular part, although all the measurements record persons who live to the west of a line dividing the island from north to south and intersecting a point midway between Dillon's Bay on the west and Traitor's Head, the extreme easterly point. The upland grassy tableland is very sparsely populated and the villages are usually on or near the coast.

The average height of 48 adult males—for 11 men from the south were measured at one time on uneven ground, where height measurements were quite impossible—is 1656·4 millimetres with a maximum of 1790 and a minimum of 1496; 8·3 per cent. are short, 50 per cent. medium, 29·2 per cent. tall and 12·5 per cent. of very tall stature.

The hair is woolly but does not grow to the length worn by the Tannese, and there is no elaborate manner of dressing it as in Tanna, but it is impossible to state if the present manner of wearing it is the result of Christian influence or not. The only certainty is that it was never dressed in the Tannese fashion. The normal colour is dark brown, never absolutely black, and there are varying lighter and darker shades; but it is not possible to agree with Robertson (p. 362) in saying that it is darker in colour than the hair of the Tannese.

The eyes of the 59 males measured are dark and in four cases the term very dark may be used in describing them, the rest showing astonishing uniformity.

The skin colour is very regular and the number of men who may be described as having a brown skin include practically all those recorded. In two or three cases the definition of dark brown may be used but there is no one case that may be called light. Here again Robertson's statement, that while a native with black skin is rare, he does exist, is not in agreement with the writer's experience[1].

The average cephalic index of the 59 adult males is 74·9, with a maximum of 84·6, and a minimum of 68·1. This is a most astonishing contrast to the conditions prevailing on Tanna, and reference to the measurements taken on both the east and west coasts of that island will show how little the brachycephalic influence there has had any appreciable effect in Eromanga.

Taking 77–82 as the range for mesocephaly the percentages of cephalic index are as follows:

Dolichocephals	67·7
Mesocephals	28·5
Brachycephals	3·8
	100

[1] Robertson, p. 362; see also Cook, II. p. 49.

Eromanga Measurements. All males over 18

Name	Height	Head		Facial Height	Bi-zy. Breadth	Nasal		Indices		
		Length	Breadth			Height	Breadth	Cephalic	Facial	Nasal
From the North-west										
1. Naling ...	1690·4	190	147·7	123·5	141·5	43·2	38·5	77·7	87·2	89·1
2. Aliaui ...	1668	190·5	143·1	128·2	148·5	41·5	37·5	75·1	86·3	90·3
3. Villivill ...	1635·6	195·5	147·5	128	139·5	58·1	42·5	75	91·7	73·1
4. Narai ...	1584·2	175·5	138·2	102·3	130·6	44·1	41·6	78·7	78·3	94·3
From the South. No height measurements taken										
5. Ialiniau ...	—	195	149·1	116·5	142·3	52	44·2	76·4	81·8	85
6. Natun... ...	—	191·5	142·5	112·2	140·1	42·2	41·1	74·4	80	98·3
7. Unpoke ...	—	205	144·2	121	143·7	43	42	70·3	84·2	97·6
8. Natun (2) ...	—	191·2	150	112	147·7	41·5	44·2	78·4	75·8	106·5
9. Ialimiau ...	—	193·2	150·2	125·2	139	47·8	34·7	77·7	90	72
10. Netawune ...	—	190	147·2	123·5	149·3	48·5	34·7	77·4	82·7	71·5
11. Atnelo ...	—	202·8	145·6	133·9	150	45·2	41·6	71·7	89·2	92
12. Alial	—	198·6	149·9	126·2	150·1	48·6	43	75·4	84	88·4
13. Atnelo (2) ...	—	186	157·4	124·6	144	49·1	43·2	84·6	86·5	87·9
14. Nilselu ...	—	185·8	146·4	122·5	145·5	51·2	39·6	78·8	84·1	77·3
15. Uma	—	191·1	143·2	135·5	150·1	51·2	44·2	74·9	90·2	86·3
From Unupunkor. West Coast										
16. Waris	1567	191·2	139	133·2	136·7	51·2	43	72·6	96·7	87·9
17. Mana	1664	193·2	147·5	121	144	49·5	43·5	76·3	84	87·8
18. Noia	1654	175·7	139·8	118·8	132	52·2	40	79·5	90	76·6
19. Waris Buro ...	1667	195	136·8	137	141·4	53	45·5	70·1	96·8	85·8

Eromanga Measurements. All males over 18 (continued)

Name	Height	Head		Facial Height	Bi-zy. Breadth	Nasal		Indices		
		Length	Breadth			Height	Breadth	Cephalic	Facial	Nasal
From Unupunkor. West Coast. (Continued)										
20. NONPURON	1667	197	154	117·5	140·6	45	45	78·1	83·5	100
21. PORKE	1590	190·5	138	114·8	135·4	50	44·8	72·4	84·7	89·6
22. UMETE	1615	197	147·5	134	142	63	42·2	74·8	94·3	66·9
23. TAINOO	1730	197·2	140·2	136·5	141	57·5	41·2	71	96·8	71·6
24. NATUNGA	1693	195·5	142	122·6	145·7	57·2	40·5	72·6	84·1	70·8
25. IAUIIAUI	1635	195·2	145·4	133	138·6	57·2	40·4	74·4	95·9	70·6
26. WARU	1635	195·6	143·1	128·1	139·2	66·7	42·2	73·1	92	63·2
27. NETAVURAK	1634	201	137	130	135·3	64	42·5	68·1	96	66·4
28. WARIS NOLL	1662·2	189·1	146	132·7	137	60·5	45	77·2	96·8	74·3
29. LIFU	1610	200·5	146	129·5	147·2	60	44·5	72·8	87·9	74·1
30. TAREVI	1728	199·5	146·4	130·4	148·6	69·2	41	73·3	87·7	59·2
31. NEPMINUM	1630	190·5	140·5	137·2	138	56·8	44·5	73·7	99·4	78·3
32. NOKILIEN	1768	201	144·5	144	153·7	72·8	42	71·8	93·6	57·6
33. IAMTAO	1671	202·5	148	126	140·6	55·5	46	73	89·6	82·8
34. NESOK	1680	192·4	152·2	116·8	133·5	58	27·6	79·1	87·4	64·8
35. WARIS-NIMATANI	1596·5	198	151	131·5	145·6	63	43·7	76·2	90·3	69·3
36. NUMPUAT	1669·5	200·1	138	133·8	140·8	58·5	48·6	68·9	95	83
37. NARAI	1669·5	195·6	135·2	130·5	135·2	56·5	44	69·1	96·5	77·8

From Etefate. Northern point of island

38. NAIWAN	1612	184	140·1	117·5	143·2	55	39·5	76·1	82·2	71·8
39. NAPENU	1544	190·5	138·5	123·2	136·2	59·3	41	72·2	90·4	69·1
40. UMO	1698	192·3	141	113	135·6	56	37·5	73·3	83·3	66·9
41. NAVIAN	1695	191	139·5	123·1	137·6	62	44·2	73	89·4	71·2
42. MATTHEW	1643·5	185	149	123·5	135·5	58	40·5	80·5	91·1	69·1
43. NARE	1661	184·8	131·2	118	119·6	55·8	37·5	70·9	98·6	67·2
44. NARIVAS	1641	189	138·6	118·4	143·5	49	41	73·3	82·5	83·6

From Unapang. In the South

45. NOMORKINA	1636·5	194	138·2	121·5	132	60·5	41·2	71·2	92	68
46. NALUA	1636	195·5	146·5	126	140·8	62	42·5	74·9	88·4	68·5
47. LOVA	1731	183·2	148	133	139·6	61·5	40	80·7	95·2	65
48. NATUNG	1698	197·5	142·2	113·5	137	60·5	45·5	72	82·8	75·1
49. MOLO	1690	196·5	151·5	139·5	147·4	59·8	44	77	94·6	73·5
50. KIRI	1575	183	145	121	137	61	46·5	79·2	88·3	76·2
51. UVEN	1650	207·5	145	132	135	59	48	69·8	97·7	81·3
52. NARIOVE	1673	190	152	126·5	146	53	47	80	86·6	88·4
53. NALING	1496	189	144	128·5	142·4	61·4	36	76·1	90·2	58·6
54. TOM	1671	184	153·5	126·4	145·5	65	44	83·4	86·8	67·6
55. ELIMIAU	1765	191	144·5	121	135	55	45	75·6	89·6	81·8
56. NOWAU	1690	195·5	139	121	138	60	45	71·9	87·6	75
57. NALAU	1790	189	148·5	122	150	45·5	45	78·5	81·3	98·9
58. RUMTAU	1664	190	142	122·5	140·5	59	32·5	74·4	87·1	55
59. UMAS	1635	184	136·5	123·5	145·5	63·5	45·5	74·1	84·8	71·6

The average facial index for the 59 persons measured is 88·6 with a maximum of 99·4 and a minimum of 75·8.

Taking 79–84 as the range for euryprosophy, 84–88 for mesoprosophy and 88–93 for leptoprosophy, the percentages of facial index are:

Hypereuryprosops (– 79)	4·2
Euryprosops	12·8
Mesoprosops	27·9
Leptoprosops	27·5
Hyperleptoprosops (93 +)	27·6
	100

For the nasal index the average is 77·4 for the 59 individuals, with a maximum of 106·5 and one other of 100 and a minimum of 55, the extreme maximum being possibly a sporadic case of nose deformity.

Taking 70–85 as the range for mesorrhiny the percentages of nasal index are:

Leptorrhines	24·1
Mesorrhines	41·6
Chamaerrhines	34·3
	100

SOCIAL MORPHOLOGY

THE TRIBE. Years ago, when the population of Eromanga was much more numerous than it is today, tribal organization was an important part of the culture of the island, each tribe consisting of several villages, sometimes of two or three only, sometimes of a score, in which case they may be called, more properly, tribal districts. The tribal limits were not geographical, as in Anaiteum, and it is impossible to assign them to the dialectal divisions, which, as we shall see later, divide the island into groups. The terrible decline of the population, which shows no sign of abatement today, makes an attempt to locate the old tribal limits futile. The island, thirty-five miles in length at its longest part, with a coast line of 100 miles (Robertson, p. 8), has today about 420 natives, some villages being reduced to seven individuals. The result is that the two or three survivors in these cases go to live, finally, in some other village and their old home soon disappears entirely in the tangled vegetation of the bush. All this has helped to obliterate the memory of many things in connection with tribal organization.

Yet there is one outstanding fact with regard to the tribal
life of the island in which all the old chiefs agree. The tribe was
responsible for the deeds of every one of its members and all
the people banded together were so well instructed in the unwritten law of the community that disobedience to the will of
the chief was unknown. Unwritten law is always stronger than
that which is written. There is plenty of evidence today of the
arbitrary power of the district chief, who, as we shall see later,
presides over a large territory.

THE CLAN. In spite of diligent search, no evidence of a
division of the people into clans of any sort, exogamous or endo-
gamous, appears, nor is there the least sign of anything suggesting clan symbolism.

FAMILY AND KINSHIP

As the entire population of Eromanga has been Christianized
for a period of something over fifty years, it has completely forgotten the days when polygyny prevailed. If this is not strictly
true there is at least an insuperable fear in the native mind in
talking about such things which no amount of confidence established with the older chiefs succeeded in banishing. We shall
see later, in several instances, how depressing an influence the
decrease in the population of the island has had on the native
mind. Is it not possible that this despondency affects the native
in more ways than one? However this may be, the Eromangan
today will tell you that the family consists of the father, mother
and children and nothing more can be wrung from him. The
following facts in connection with the family are all that may
be relied on as true in the mass collected on the island.

The descent is purely patrilineal, nor does anyone recall a
time when matrilineal descent, or anything like it, prevailed.

There is one name which stands out in the kinship terms,
which otherwise are quite regular, and bear more resemblance
to those of Tanna than one would expect. A woman directly
she marries is called *retepun* by all when speaking of her as the
wife of such and such a man, but after she has borne her first

child she becomes his *netnime*. Unfortunately the exact meaning of this term is not clear. A man may beat his wife if she does not bear him children in a reasonable time, and if the woman proves to be barren he may put her away and take another wife, the discarded woman remaining in his house, often in a menial position, subject to the taunts of her successor. In this case she does not occupy the position of a concubine and the custom has no connection with polygyny, although it may have had in former times.

In the kinship terms there is a special term, *detuun*, for the father's sister of a man or of a woman; the father's sister's husband, the mother's brother and the mother's brother's wife, be it of a man or a woman, being called uniformly *metan*. This suggests a special prerogative for this person in connection with her brother's children, but diligent search fails to reveal any such thing today or any recollection of it in the past. The other relatives in this category—the brother's son or daughter, the sister's son or daughter, the father's sister's son or daughter or the mother's brother's son or daughter are all called the *aluwan*, be it of a man or woman that one speaks. There is no counterpart of the *rahniaunian* of Tanna, the designation used for a man's daughter's husband or son's wife; the term used for this relationship in Eromanga, *etemarsi*, is applied to the father and mother of the husband or wife of any individual indiscriminately, and is extended to a man's wife's brother and sister's husband as well as to a woman's husband's sister.

Cross-cousin marriage does not prevail in the island, and there is a strong aversion to marrying a first cousin, in the European sense, whether that individual be the child of the father's sister or brother, or of the mother's brother or sister, and in spite of extended inquiry not one case of such a marriage was discovered. It is difficult to believe that a system of marriage regulation that has made such an impress in many islands of the New Hebrides has never existed in Eromanga, but the fact remains that there is no evidence today of any such alliance. The children of two sisters married to men who are not brothers are spoken of as *niten*, as are the children of two brothers married to two women who are not sisters, but the term is not used if the children spoken of are the result of a union between two sisters married to two brothers. This relationship does not exist, and no native has the intrepidity to declare what the kinship term in this case will be, for, if the case does not exist, why have a word by which to express it?

Illegitimate children are given the name of *unalau untapalo*, or "born in the bush."

Relationship Terms

EROMANGA.

	Term	Reciprocal	
Father	ETAMIN	NITEN	Son
Mother	DINIME	NITEN	Daughter
Elder Brother	AVENSAI	AVENSAI	Younger Brother
Elder Sister	VEVEN	MAN	*Younger Brother*
Younger Sister	VEVEN	MAN	*Elder Brother*
Elder Sister	AVENSAI	AVENSAI	*Younger Sister*
Father's Sister	DETUUN	ALUWAN	*Brother's Son*
,, ,,	DETUUN	ALUWAN	*Brother's Daughter*
Father's Sister's Husband	METAN	NITEN	Wife's Brother's Son
,, ,, ,,	METAN	NITEN	Wife's Brother's Daughter
Father's Sister's Son	ALUWAN	ALUWAN	Mother's Brother's Son
,, ,, ,,	ALUWAN	ALUWAN	Mother's Brother's Daughter
Father's Sister's Daughter	ALUWAN	ALUWAN	*Mother's Brother's Son*
,, ,, ,,	ALUWAN	ALUWAN	*Mother's Brother's Daughter*
Mother's Brother ,,	METAN	ALUWAN	*Sister's Son*
,, ,,	METAN	ALUWAN	Sister's Daughter
Mother's Brother's Wife	METAN	NITEN	*Husband's Sister's Son*
,, ,, ,,	METAN	NITEN	*Husband's Sister's Daughter*
Father's Father	ITUN	MORPUN	Son's Son
,, ,,	ITUN	MORPUN	Son's Daughter
Father's Mother	NOVUN	MORPUN	*Son's Son*
,, ,,	NOVUN	MORPUN	*Son's Daughter*
Mother's Father	ITUN	MORPUN	Daughter's Son
,, ,,	ITUN	MORPUN	Daughter's Daughter
Mother's Mother	NOVUN	MORPUN	*Daughter's Son*
,, ,,	NOVUN	MORPUN	*Daughter's Daughter*
Wife's Father	ETEMARSI	ETEMARSI	Daughter's Husband
Wife's Mother	ETEMARSI	ETEMARSI	,, ,,
Husband's Father	ETEMARSI	ETEMARSI	Son's Wife
Husband's Mother	ETEMARSI	ETEMARSI	,, ,,
Wife	RETEPUN	ASUN	*Husband*
Wife's Sister	RETEPUN	ASUN	*Sister's Husband*
Brother's Wife	ROVUNUN	ETEMARSI	*Husband's Brother*
Wife's Brother	ETEMARSI	ETEMARSI	Sister's Husband
Brother's Wife	ROVUNUN	ETEMARSI	*Husband's Sister*

In Eromanga the aversion to mentioning the name of certain relatives is very strong, much stronger than in Tanna. No man will speak his wife's name aloud and, if he is asked her name by a stranger, he invariably asks one of his neighbours to speak for him but, in the case of the wife at least, this friendly act must be performed by a member of his group of villages and cannot be done by an outsider, for no such person may mention her name aloud. In some parts of the island this restriction allows the name to be spoken by a near relative of the woman, that is, by one of her brothers or the brothers of her father. In addition to this, no man will speak his own name aloud willingly. Two men addressing each other use invariably the second person *kik*, and the name itself is never mentioned. If a man not present is mentioned, he is never referred to by name but is usually mentioned as "the son of the son of so-and-so," doubling the paternity having a particular virtue which the native cannot explain but which seems to have some significance beyond a clear definition. Relatives by marriage are in the same category with the man's own family as far as speaking aloud the name of the individual is concerned, but they are certainly not treated to a special taboo as they are in the Banks' Islands[1].

Adoption is perfectly free and there is no particular cere-monial attached to the custom. In the case of a chief adopting a son the boy must belong to the chiefly class, but whether he belongs to the chief's own group or to another group in a different part of the island is immaterial.

CHIEFTAINSHIP. When chieftainship flourished in the island there were several districts, each with its high chief, *Fanlo*, who had jurisdiction over all the villages in his territory, while each village had its own *Fanlo* as well, who had local authority, chiefs with varying rank having a wide distribution in the Pacific (Rivers, 1914, p. 380). At the present time there is but one high chief living, WARIS, whose territory consists of several villages but, owing to the decrease in the population of the island, only three village chiefs are left in his district. The word *Fanlo* seems to mean a man of the chiefly class and is not the special title of the high chief. Women of the chiefly class are called *Nasimnalan*, and all commoners, men and women, enjoy the name of *Taui natimono*, or sometimes *Nefore* or *Nevsen*. Formerly, of course, no village would be allowed to languish

[1] See Frazer, 1923, p. 251.

without a chief, but this neglect is only another of the evidences of the apathy of the present-day Eromangan and his general idea that nothing matters.

The authority of the high chief was absolute in the old days. He held councils and asked the advice of the old men of his district, though only those of the *Fanlo* were invited to air their views, and frank opinions were expressed and extreme divergences of opinion thrashed out. The final decision was with the high chief, and even today old WARIS decides matters for his district more or less in the old way. Fear was the controlling motive for this custom according to WARIS. The councils often lasted for several days and, as everyone present talked volubly and at length, the mass of opinion must have been enormous. One thing is certain. When the high chief announced his final judgement in the matter this opinion was never questioned, and the meeting broke up. Judgement and punishment were meted out to the offenders if the matter required it; and if it was a question of warfare the decision for or against rested in the hands of the high chief.

If lesser offences were committed by a man of one district against a person or persons of another, the high chief and all his advisers of the district of the injured person or persons discussed the matter freely; but, if it was not considered of sufficient importance to fight about, nothing was done at the moment, though if a more serious disagreement took place at a later time, the old grudge was recalled and had a decided influence in determining the course of action. Petty quarrels between men of different districts might be discussed by the high chief and his advisers but the matter was left, usually, to the injured men to settle in their own way. There was always the chance, however, if the injured man took matters into his own hands and killed his foe from ambush, that the quarrel would become general and lead to warfare.

Succession went usually to a son of the late chief, or to one of his brothers, if he had no son, the only qualification being that the youth must be born of a woman of the *Nasimnalan*. With the facility accorded by the practice ·of adoption a successor was usually provided by the *Fanlo*, but he must be *persona grata* to the community or he would not be allowed to assume power at all.

Under Christian influence the control is largely in the hands of the elders of the church, who usually belong to the *Fanlo* and continue the prerogatives of that class, subject to the infrequent visits of the Government Agent whose headquarters are in Tanna. The old order of chieftainship and its prerogatives is practically extinct.

TRIBAL LIFE

DOMESTIC CONDITIONS. The clothing worn by the male Eromangan, when he discards the ubiquitous *lavalava* of the Pacific, is, like that of the Tannese, extremely simple. In addition to a belt of tapa very like the one worn in Tanna and the penis case he wears nothing at all except one or more ornaments. The penis case is made very simply of any convenient leaves much longer than the organ, so that the covering hangs down sometimes below the knees, for the case is not inserted in the belt as in Tanna. It is held in place by a twist of native fibre or by European twine. The name of this covering is *yelau* and, in the case of a high chief of the *Fanlo* in the old days, the *yelau* was worn longer than that of any other man, often reaching nearly to the ankles and was one of the symbols of chieftainship.

Concealment of the penis is a *sine qua non* of Eromangan life, and it is considered indelicate for the men to appear entirely nude in the presence of their own sex and, of course, it is taboo to do so in the sight of a woman. Great circumspection is observed, but it is true that this custom shows signs of breaking down in Eromanga at the present time, as far as the men alone are concerned, and in bathing the Eromangan is not nearly so particular as is his neighbouring islander, the Tannese. In the old days, the *yelau* might be spoken of even in the presence of women, but to exhibit the uncovered penis to a woman was an insult that might be avenged by death. Cook (1st ed. p. 49) reports the *yelau* of the Eromangan to be worn like that of the Great Nambas people of Malekula, and the engraving in the first edition of his immortal work (1st ed. p. 46) represents this article of dress in that fashion. One can only suppose that, in his haste, his usual accuracy in observation deserted him and that his recollection became mixed with that of Malekula, for the *yelau* of Eromanga has never been worn inserted in the belt. There is a rooted aversion to wetting the end of the *yelau*, however, which may account for his mistake, for, in crossing a river or wading in any water the Eromangan is very particular to hold the *yelau* up in one hand to prevent it from getting wet and this may have deceived Cook as it did the earlier missionaries in the island. The Eromangan is not so cleanly in his habits as the Tannese, and the absence of people in the water at all times at the coastal villages contrasts strangely with the joy that the Tannese takes in entering the water at least once a day.

The hair of the adult male in the old days was allowed to grow long, and, being woolly, had an appearance more like the hair of some of the Solomon Islanders. Even today an occasional head of hair is seen that is thick and bushy, but the usual mode is to clip it fairly short. The old custom of wearing a comb in front, over the right eye, is still observed, and all young men appear in this manner on all festive occasions, when the hair is rubbed well with coconut oil and sometimes a flower is worn inserted under the comb.

The comb is neatly made of wood with a varying number of teeth and the design is extremely simple but shows a rudimentary idea of decorative effect. A drawing is given on page 136.

Perforation of the ear lobe is still practised extensively and is done in the usual way, by the insertion of a round, sharp-pointed stick of hard wood—this is put through the hole several times a day—and the stick turned frequently to increase the size of the hole. The substitution of a larger stick does not follow in this island and the constant turning of the one stick used is depended on to make the hole of the desired size. It is common to see a man carrying his pipe, or sometimes a flower, in the perforation. Smoking is universal now and has been for a number of years, although it was introduced in the beginning by the white man as in the other islands of Melanesia.

A simple form of tattooing is practised by the men, the more elaborate forms being left to the women, though they are gradually giving up this mode of adornment (Robertson, p. 367). In the case of the men, the usual form is to make lateral blue or green lines across the face, as indicated by the rude drawing below, any variation from this form being extremely rare.

The men often sling a native basket over the shoulder for carrying a few necessities such as pipe and tobacco, but this is said to be an innovation since the advent of the white man. Arm bands of coconut shell, highly polished and sometimes carved with a design not unlike that of the combs, are very

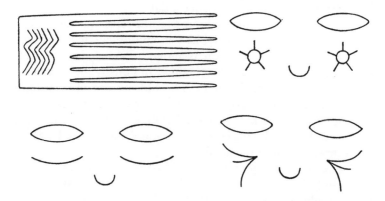

common; anklets of small shells are worn just below the knee of one leg[1], and both men and women wear necklaces of plaited pandanus, sometimes with small sea shells attached. The men wear gold rings in their ears, sometimes with a small shell pendant attached, but this seems to be a modern custom, perhaps replacing that of wearing two or three prongs of turtle shell in the ear lobe, which was common in the old days, but has now entirely disappeared. The women have never resorted to ear adornment.

The *numplat* or skirts made and worn by the women are the most noteworthy articles of women's attire, for the Eromangan female wears very little else. Her hair is not allowed to grow

---

[1] This agrees with Robertson, p. 367.

long, nor is it dressed in any way; she wears few ornaments, even on festive occasions, but in the length and number of her *numplat* and the decoration of her face by tattooing she leaves her lord and master far behind. The *numplat* is made of the leaves of pandanus, banana, coconut, hibiscus, native cabbage or other green plants[1]. It is such an important part of Eromangan culture that it will be described in full in treating of handicraft in a later chapter.

The decoration of the face employed by the women is the survival of an elaborate form of tattooing which was practised in the old days. In some cases the design is exactly like that of the men, as shown in the drawing already referred to. In addition to this, a favourite design is done in blue looking like an object that may very well be intended to represent the sun, an octopus or a crab. This form is very common and is sometimes done in green, although blue is in greater favour.

Tattooing, which, as we have seen, is performed in the majority of cases on women, is always done by them. The pattern is made on the skin by a sharp piece of bamboo. A cutting from the wood of the *nangai* tree—a kind of nut—is placed in the fire till the sap oozes out, which, when collected and mixed with water, forms a paste-like substance, which is smeared over the body where the pattern has been traced and left in this position for a month or so. When it is finally washed off, a well-defined design remains, which seems to resist all the bathing indulged in by the Eromangan female. Although the process is very painful during the first part of the operation when the design is being traced, no woman ever objects to the treatment and it is *infra dig.* to show the least sign of suffering.

The pattern is usually traced in lines, straight or curved, and figures are often made, as we have seen. One of the old men, VILLIVILL by name, insisted that no aquatic animals are ever used in native designs in this island, nor is there evidence of the use of the sun, moon or stars in this connection. If this is true, the objects ornamenting the cheeks of the women noted above must be a flower, which this man admits are common,

[1] Cf. Robertson, p. 365.

and not an octopus or the sun. The same man insisted that no woman selects the design herself but that the choice lies in the momentary whim of the old woman who does the work. Certain women have a reputation for being experts in this art, but the right to perform it is not hereditary and there is no apprenticing of young girls, no woman undertaking the work until she is married.

The house—domiciliary, kava, or *siman lo*, where the unmarried men live—will be described in connection with handicraft on p. 155. Suffice it to say here that there is no attempt at symmetry in arrangement, and the houses of a village are put wherever convenience and other reasons dictate, there being no open dancing ground with its banyan tree, as in Tanna, although the banyan tree may exist in or near the village. Light reed fences are built around the gardens and strongly built wooden fences of logs are built around the village, at considerable distance from the latter and including the gardens, to exclude the wild pigs. These are rough affairs and contrast unfavourably with the excellent work in this particular done in Tanna, which is odd, since the handicraft of Eromanga, in other respects is, on the whole, superior to that of the southern island. While these fences are quite efficacious in performing their appointed function, they have no design in particular and often consist of a number of stout trunks piled upon each other, stoutly bound together to resist the impetus of the largest wild pig. This creature in Eromanga reaches a size and ferocity unknown on the neighbouring island of Tanna, and hunting expeditions are often organized. Curiously enough, these expeditions are now organized invariably by the Tannese in the island employed by the owner of the sheep station, and have the rather faint-hearted support of two or three of the less languid Eromangans.

The preparation of food is as follows: a large round hole in the ground, perhaps six feet across and two feet deep, is found in every village, and in this a layer of red-hot stones from a neighbouring fire is placed. A native pudding or whatever the native may desire to cook is wrapped in banana leaves, and laid on the stones; another layer of hot stones is placed on top and the whole covered in with leaves. It is left for varying lengths of time, according to the contents, pigs, for example, taking about one hour to come to a perfect state of delicacy. Then the oven is opened, the upper layer of stones removed, and the wrappings are taken off the puddings, which are cut in slices and eaten at once. No use of steam is made in this process and water is not poured in at any stage of the cooking.

Many varieties of fruit and vegetables are used in the preparation of puddings and all sorts of combinations are common, yams, *nuup*, taro, *ptala*, coconut, *noki* (young and tender coconut, *neseruk*, dried coconut, *numkai*), native cabbage, *tampele*, sugar cane, *polie*, tapioca, *manieka*, sweet potato, *ufulei*, and, last but not least, the banana, *novos*, all having a place in the housewife's resources. With the changes in the seasons and the recurrence in crops, there is always a supply of material for food preparation. Another dish of yam, *nuup*, cooked with fowl and called *tampunpie*, is mentioned by Robertson (p. 380), but it is doubtful if dishes in which fowl appears as an ingredient were common in the old days before the advent of the white man.

The preparation of the pudding ingredients is as follows. Taro or yam, the constant ingredients in most puddings, are grated on the stalk of the tree fern, and slightly mixed with water until a dough-like substance is formed. The other ingredients are then grated and laid with the moist pulpy formation of yam or taro, but not mixed with it at the moment. Prawns are often added as a special delicacy and the whole is then kneaded into a compact mass. A banana leaf is set on the smoking fire for a moment after the mid-rib has been removed, and the mass is wrapped in this so that every part is securely covered, the mid-rib being used to tie the whole so that it shall not come undone before the cooking process has begun. The *noeki* is a special favourite, made of yam, coconut and prawns and must cook for two hours; the *opiopi*, in which shredded cabbage replaces the coconut, is also popular.

Fish, which is cooked commonly also, is wrapped in a banana leaf without being cleaned, the entrails being thrown away by the person who consumes the titbit. Turtle is laid on its back, wrapped in banana leaves, on the lower layer of stones, the shell having been removed, and the process is continued as in the case of the puddings. Pig is prepared in exactly the same way. Large pigs are cut up first, singed and scraped with a bamboo knife (except in the case of a very big feast), but little pigs are often cooked whole and come out done to a turn. Young sharks are eaten, the preparation being the same as with all fish and, in the old days, large pieces of shark were cut off and cooked separately. This custom has never been practised since the Eromangan went first to Queensland to work on the plantations, though the reason does not appear.

The evening meal is the chief repast of the day, the native picking up odd things during the day, fruit as he passes the trees of one of whose fruit he may partake, but, until the evening, eating is not a serious matter. Even then it is common to see several men eating noisily and earnestly and others sitting about not having begun, although the food is there to their hand. In Eromanga men sometimes take part in the preparation of the food, busying themselves about the oven but rarely doing the entire preparation of the native pudding. The men sit together in groups, as do the women and children, at the usual evening meal as well as at any feast, large or small.

Fire-making is done by the friction method, the native squatting with a foot on either side of a grooved stick, lying on the ground groove upwards and held in place by one hand, always the left, as far as observed. This stick is of soft wood and a pointed stick of hard wood is taken by the native in his right hand, firmly held by the thumb underneath, the four fingers lying unflexed across the stick and above it, the friction being brought to bear away from the operator. A pointed stick of fairly soft wood is seen occasionally. The grooved stick of soft wood is kept carefully and used many times in fire-making, but more important than this is the fire stick, of very soft wood, which remains kindled for hours, so that the arduous work of making fire by friction has to be performed rarely, as when the native is on the track in the bush. The fire stick in the village is used so often to light a pipe or a small fire that it is practically never extinguished.

Water is carried in bamboo stalks, some being of enormous size. In this case the carriers come from Tanna, where, in turn, one is told that they come from Norfolk Island. However this may be, it is certain that no bamboo of such size is found on Eromanga. A native carrying a bamboo stalk filled with water, six feet long and at least six inches in diameter, is a common sight.

SEX AND MARRIAGE. District exogamy prevailed extensively in the old days, and there was allied with it a system of return marriages between the two districts involved, and even today the wife for a man is usually chosen from another district, although marriage between two villages of a district occurs occasionally. Dislike to marriage within the tribe is strongly marked and it is stoutly maintained that not only is marriage between the children of two sisters or of two brothers prohibited, but the cross-cousin marriage itself, between the children of a brother and a sister, is likewise condemned and, until very lately, had never occurred. This prohibition does not now apply to the children of these cross-cousins, for they may marry each other, but it is likely that this concession has been granted on account of the rapid decline in the population of the island and is of recent adoption. The kinship terms suggest that at one time, perhaps in the dim past, a system of cross-cousin marriage was introduced but it found less favour here, apparently, than in most of the other islands of the New Hebrides, and was never an important part of Eromangan marriage regulation. When asked why a man may not marry a woman of his own village the answer is, invariably, that such a woman is his *veven* (sister) and of course it cannot be, but he does not know any reason why a man may not marry a woman from other villages of his district except that it is not usually done.

As in other islands, a woman is frequently set apart for a certain marriage when she is very young but the marriage is not consummated until she has reached puberty, and the payment of the bride price has been faithfully performed. But in

Eromanga, in this case, a young woman of the district of the bridegroom-to-be must be set aside for a man of similar rank in the other district, a simple form of return marriage. The chief of the district, in the old days, approved the young woman as a suitable wife for his man, and the same approval was necessary on the part of his neighbouring district chief before the two parties to the return agreement could be considered as pledged to each other.

With the division of the people into two classes of society, a very important marriage restriction is that no woman of the *Fanlo* class may marry a man of the *Taui natimono* under any circumstances, but that a man of the *Fanlo* may, under certain conditions, marry a woman of the *Taui natimono*. As the distinction, in the case of a *Fanlo* man, in choosing a wife from one class or the other, seems to be that he pays for a woman from the *Fanlo* class while, for one from the *Taui natimono*, he pays nothing at all, the union in the case of the latter seems at first to be more like a form of concubinage than a proper marriage. This is however not the case, as the children of the *Taui natimono* woman had the same rights as those by any *Fanlo* wife he may have possessed in the old days when polygyny was common, and a son by the common woman might, if he had other qualifications, succeed his father as chief, to the exclusion of any sons by the *Fanlo* wife or wives. In this case the son became of the chiefly class through his father, at birth, but the mother had no special rank or honours for being the mother of her husband's successor. Three wives to a chief were the average in the days of polygyny, although more were not uncommon, and the father of WARIS, YALIMIAU, had eleven wives to his credit. The new wife in each case seems to have been the favourite, at least for a season, and the lives of her predecessors were made miserable and they were treated as little better than slaves, whether they were *Fanlo* or *Taui natimono* women.

When a man has seen a woman of another district who takes his fancy, he goes to his chief with the request that he may marry the woman, but the chief has no scruples in denying his suit, if he has other plans for the man, or the woman is known to be set apart for someone else. More commonly than would be supposed, however, the man has his way and, if there is no other objection on the ground of consanguinity or unfitness of any kind, the necessary consent of the district chief is granted. Thereupon, the man asks a friend in a third district, not the district of the favoured woman, to act for him as a go-between. No special person has any prerogative for this friendly act and the native name for this personage, *tantavinidme*, seems to mean, as nearly as it can be translated, "avoidance," and may be given because the suitor is not permitted to speak with or have any association with the men of the young woman's district during the proceedings.

The bride price is divided into two part-payments, for a present of sharks' teeth is given at once in earnest of the feast, or *nerom*, that must inevitably follow before the young woman will be permitted to become the wife of the suitor. In the case of a return marriage arrangement later on, these teeth may be used as the preliminary gift in the return bride price, but today, when the custom of return marriage arrangements shows signs of breaking down, the teeth are often kept by the father of the young woman, and the present itself shows signs of being discontinued altogether. The young man, in the old days, had the right to sleep once with his bride before the feast was given and, in the cases where the poor fellow could not accumulate the necessaries for the *nerom* without considerable delay, there was sometimes a long period between this occasion and the final union of the couple. Cases occurred, though rarely it seems, when there was no woman available in the suitor's district for the return marriage, in which case he, or his neighbours, it is not certain which, must make presents of other things than sharks' teeth to the district of the young woman, in recompense. Sometimes the young fellow takes special presents of shell, the *navela nunpuri*, to the father of the young woman, but they are always in addition to the sharks' teeth, and if the young man carries them to the village of his sweetheart himself, he must speak to no one, not even to her father. Sometimes, indeed, a boy begins to take presents to the young woman whom he knows has been set apart for him, before puberty, but this does not seem to be a common custom.

After all the necessary presents have been made and the *nerom* is over, the bridegroom-elect lets it be known that he will be coming for his bride on a certain night. Thereupon, her mother and sisters tell her to go out to gather firewood, which is collected before the house and an axe is placed on the top of it. Of course the young woman knows the meaning of all this but it is not seemly for her to appear to do so. Her mother, or some older woman, lies down by the girl, the other sisters taking themselves off for the night. When the bridegroom and his friends come stealing into the village, they see the axe lying on the pile of brush and know that they are expected. He, or sometimes they, then enters the house and he places a star club beside the girl, who is pretending to be asleep, even if she is not. Her mother, who has not slept all the while, now arises, bids the young man welcome and awakens her daughter, who is dressed for the first time in the trailing *namplat* of a married woman, and goes away with her husband and his friends without seeing any of her own people again. There is no further ceremony and the young man takes her to the house he has built in his village, or, in case that is not yet ready, to his father's house. If he has cohabited with the young woman on one previous occasion this has taken place in the bush and not in the house of the young woman's father. After leaving the sleeping village the bridal party begin to call out *nem brolak*, "we are going to be married," or more properly, "we are going to consummate the marriage," as they pass along.

Adultery. In spite of Brenchley's statement (p. 319) that adultery was punished by death in the old days, the death penalty seems to have been rare, and with one or two exceptions never to have been administered to the woman, although the man was often ambushed and killed by the injured husband, when he belonged to another district. Warfare was a very common result of this offence when a man eloped with a woman, the chief of the district of the injured husband usually summoning a council and deliberating the matter, as we have seen was the custom in all emergencies. If the woman belonged to the *Fanlo* class the measures taken for revenge seem to have been more stringent than if she were one of the *Taui natimono*. If the woman succeeded in reaching the district of her paramour she was allowed to remain there, even if war resulted, and she never returned to her people; if she was taken in flight by her people nothing more than a scolding resulted, though if she continued her efforts to escape she was perhaps given a beating.

Prostitution. All the chiefs deny resolutely that anything like the *iowhanan* of Tanna ever existed in this island, and all men are presumed to remain virgin after the incision ceremony until they marry. Patient inquiry elicits the information that promiscuity exists among the young people but that it is condoned and does not lead to marriage. If the young people are caught by the father of the girl there is sometimes some public reprimand administered to the lad, but it is of a perfunctory sort and the offence is tacitly admitted and approved of, a practice common enough in the other parts of Melanesia (Codrington, 1891, p. 235). Many youths, so several of the old chiefs assert, remain pure until they marry, this taking place usually not long after puberty.

Perversions. These seem to be practically unknown and, when occurring, are the result of habits acquired during the Queensland days, or by contact with natives from other islands.

Avoidance. No brother-sister avoidance before puberty occurs and even afterwards, today, brother and sister may stop and talk if they meet in the bush, though this is undoubtedly a development of Christian influence. In the old days, no woman spoke to a man if she met him walking beyond her village and, today, no woman will speak to any man who is not a member of her own village group, nor to any boy who has been through the incision ceremony. She invariably leaves the track and makes a detour around the man who, in turn, pays not the slightest attention to her. Natives walking through the woodland tracks with their women always precede them, armed with bow and arrow; these serve if birds are seen and not for any other use. The women follow carrying all the goods and chattels of the family as well as those children who are too little to walk alone. Men seem extremely fond of their children and can be seen at almost any time carrying them about the villages.

Nothing resembling polyandry is found in this island, a fact that we accept with equanimity considering Codrington's contention (1891, p. 245). Infanticide, except when the mother dies in childbirth and the child is buried alive with her, seems to be unknown[1]. Couvade, deformation of the skull, and skull trepanning, are all unknown, as is the use of the bull-roarer or the boomerang. It is perhaps needless to remark that this island is far beyond the easterly limits of the use of betel and that the betel nut is unknown.

GAMES AND ENTERTAINMENTS. One game only is common to the childhood of the island, and one wonders if the scarcity of children and the general apathy may not be responsible for the poverty of this important cultural unit. The game referred to is played as follows. A child is selected and covers his eyes with his hands and counts a certain number in multiples of five, while the other children stow themselves in convenient shelters hard by. He then hunts for the children, who usually call out to him jeeringly until he comes near to them, when they are perfectly silent. The first person found then takes his turn at seeking the others, and so on as long as the children wish to play. It is our game of hide-and-seek with variations and the children never tire of it, usually playing it at dusk or on moonlight nights.

Three forms of Cat's Cradle are found, the native names of which are *denun*, meaning unknown, which is very elaborate and involves the use of the mouth, *netuo*, meaning a "fowl," and *morulu*, a kind of yam. It is to be regretted that actual description of them was one of the things undone when the time came for me to sail away.

NATIVE EMOTIONS. In spite of what has been said about primitive people not feeling keenly about intimate matters and not suffering greatly from pain (Williams, I. pp. 134–5), several months' residence among the New Hebrideans of the southerly islands of the group convinces the writer that the native is much more like ourselves than is usually believed. While the Ero-

---

[1] See Brenchley, p. 319.

mangan is not so expressive of his emotions as the Tannese, a few remarks on this subject may be interesting.

The Eromangans had the reputation of being the most cruel people in the southern part of the group in the early days, but this is due, probably, more to the treatment of John Williams and the two Gordons and to the reception which Cook had at their hands at Polinia Bay. Still, it is true that the Eromangan impresses the visitor as more taciturn than the Tannese, and an excellent opportunity to study the two peoples together was afforded by the presence on the island of twenty or more Tannese, employed, as has been said already, at the sheep station. The Tannese are a jolly, vivacious lot as compared with the Eromangans, their laughter is more hearty and they are better developed physically. Whenever the two peoples came together for a merrymaking at the station, as they did at Christmas and New Year, they never mixed but kept in two groups. No animosity was shown, but there was no tendency to fraternize, at least at a general gathering. At other times one Eromangan and two or three Tannese might go together to shoot birds or wild pigs and there seemed to be no strained relations whatever. At the festivals referred to above the Tannese were always ready to dance for the entertainment of the white man and his guests, and they performed this with much gusto in precisely the same manner as their fellow islanders when at their native feasts in the bush, as recorded above.

Like all primitive peoples, the native is very prone to suggestion, and cases of death due entirely to discouragement and the rooted idea of an incurable malady are known to have happened when no bodily ill made its appearance, although, in these cases, the failure to perform an autopsy makes it impossible to state that something organically wrong had no controlling force. Men say, sometimes, that they will be dead at a certain hour on a certain day and they are, the end coming at the precise time stated. However we may try to explain this phenomenon we cannot deny the fact of its existence.

Children are disciplined very badly by Eromangan mothers, and they cry much more often than their Tannese neighbours, although, here again, we must be cautious in judging such differences, which may have a root in the decline of the population and its consequent discouragement. It is true that the boys of six or seven begin to order their mothers about in most arbitrary fashion, and the woman accepts this treatment meekly and makes no protest whatever. No Eromangan will speak if a nod or movement of the facial muscles will answer instead, and the variety of expressions and shades of meaning in two gestures almost alike is remarkable. Assent is by lifting the eyebrows, as in Tanna, and Guppy (1887, p. 126) has shown us how common this form is in the Solomons and elsewhere. The exception to this resource to facial movement and gesture in the place of speech is the word for "no," *ei*, which is said without the twitch of a single facial muscle. Occasionally a variant for assent is the word *aa*, spoken with considerable emphasis, while uncertainty is expressed by a variety of telling gestures and shrugs and, occasionally, by the sound *kai*. There has been only one dumb man in the island in the memory of the oldest chiefs, and he was so remarkable that he was commented on constantly during his life and has never been forgotten, though he died many years ago. An albino on the east coast, on the other hand, seems to be accepted by all and is not regarded curiously by anybody.

WARFARE. Fighting, which has been entirely discontinued in Eromanga since the establishment of the Condominium Government of Britain and France in 1906, was due, usually, to quarrels about women, land or distribution of the *navela* stones. In any case the procedure was as follows. A council was held to decide for or against war, the final vote, perhaps after almost interminable discussion, being given by the district *Fanlo*, as noted above. If the decision was in favour of hostilities, the matter was pressed with all speed, but there is no evidence that invitations to join were sent to neighbouring districts as in Tanna. Surprise attack by the enemy was sporadic and rare, a direct challenge being the usual means of beginning hostilities, these taking the form of burning a house in one of the enemy's villages, cutting down banana trees belonging to some of his people or, though this last means is not too well authenticated, shooting an arrow into one of his villages. The district to be attacked built stockades about the village as rapidly as possible, a custom not common in all parts of Melanesia. Fighting was intermittent and more or less perfunctory (Erskine, p. 304), and if no one happened to be killed in the first encounter, the chiefs of the defensive district met in council, after an interim during which the wounds of the warriors had healed, to discuss whether the hostilities should be continued. It was common to offer a feast to the aggressors and to make peace, *navela* stones being sent as a sign of amity and pigs furnished for the feast. If the warfare had been begun on account of a dispute about women, the owners of these women in the injured district received *navela* and sometimes tusks of pig and cowrie shells strung on sennet.

If a man was killed on one side in the first encounter, the result was quite different, and one must be killed on the opposite side before peace, or even a temporary suspension of hostilities, could be considered. At any time, however, a truce might be declared by either side for the purpose of garden cultivation, which was never allowed to languish, or an important feast that must be held in a certain month. When a chief was killed on either side a temporary truce was agreed upon, although a chief must be killed on the other side in return before a permanent peace could be made, which is a common form of warfare in Melanesia, observed by Codrington (1891, p. 305), and already referred to in the case of the Tannese.

If other district chiefs took sides in the quarrel they sometimes went in on one side or the other, and the entire island was frequently involved in general conflict and, as usual in these cases, fighting between districts in which two or more were involved was practically continuous, as it was in the neighbouring island, as mentioned by Turner (p. 312). In addition to general participation of other districts in the fighting, offers to act as intermediary to seek for a cessation of hostilities might come from a neutral district, and there is a well authenticated report of one case where a district *Fanlo* of a neutral group went to the battlefield and commanded the belligerents to cease fighting. Brenchley (p. 298) found two district groups at war with each other in his time, but it is doubtful if he saw enough of the island to be certain that no other groups were involved.

When the chief of the injured district had had enough to satisfy his revenge, a woman was sent to arrange for a peace, but no evidence is given whether she was provided with any signs of amity or truce. If her mission was successful, a feast, given by the family of the man who had caused the dispute in the beginning, brought the matter to a satisfactory ending.

The weapons employed were the bow and arrow, the spear, war axes and clubs (some warriors being armed with one, some with the other), all of which are described in detail in the section dealing with handicraft. Cook's party saw the Eromangans armed with "darts" as well, and stones were hurled at his party (1st ed. pp. 46–7).

The bodies of district chiefs killed in action were removed by warriors of their own faction with the complete connivance and consent of the enemy, but any village chiefs who might be killed were carried away by the enemy and eaten. Cannibalism, here as in Tanna, was indulged in to give strength to the victors through a kind of contagious magic, while, in Eromanga, a distinct idea of gloating over one's enemy in this manner is confessed to by all the old chiefs today, in spite of years of Christian influence. The insistence of these same men that there were always men who refused to eat human flesh is difficult to account for. If these chiefs, all respectable elders of the Church today, are willing to confess to cannibalism in the past, why should they agree that certain men did not eat human flesh, if such were not the case? Robertson's contention (p. 393) that infant cannibalism prevailed in the old days is not in agreement with native opinion.

ECONOMICS

HORTICULTURE. While the land belongs to the district group, gardens may be made by any man, in the bush, on land that has been deserted by a former garden-maker, and these are the sole property of the maker as long as he continues to care for them, but directly they are allowed to lie fallow they return to the district group and may be used by anyone at will. In practice, of course, no native will use a garden site that is lying fallow unless a sufficient time has elapsed to ensure a good harvest, the native idea of the proper season being instinctive and varying in length according to the wetness or dryness of the seasons and other contributing factors. The fruit belongs to the man who cleared the garden, but all members of his district group may help themselves to the fruit to be eaten in passing, though they may not carry away fruit to their own villages, with the one exception that all fruit taken to the village of the owner is cooked, if cooking be necessary, in the general oven, and may be eaten by any member of that village. Public opinion is strongly against any breach of this rule and no infraction is known to take place.

Fruit trees in deserted gardens belong to the original owner of the garden site, the man who originally cleared and cared for the plot, and are inherited by his heirs and enjoyed by them in perpetuity, although the rule permitting any member of the district to eat of the fruit in passing is constant, and, in the case of bread-fruit and any fruit that may be cooked in the village oven, the rule of common enjoyment by any member of the village prevails. The gardens produce yams, the principal food staple, of which there are said to be twenty-six varieties, taro, with seventeen varieties, arrowroot, a kind of cabbage which is really a species of hibiscus, and beans, the fruit trees yielding banana, of which there are thirteen varieties, rose-apple and pawpaw, all of which seem to be indigenous. Robertson (pp. 376–7) says that the horse chestnut was grown in his time but there is no present evidence of it.

The making of new gardens takes place in July and August; any big trees that may be standing, if they are healthy, are left *in situ*, the soil being made fairly smooth and left to dry for one month, it being the dry season. At the end of this period all the men of the village repair to the new garden site, climb the trees and lop off the lower branches with which they cover the newly-exposed earth, which is now left for another month, when the entire site is burned over, the dried leaves and branches serving for excellent kindling. The ground is then broken by the use of digging sticks, the motion employed being peculiar, for the worker stabs the ground with the stick and then sits down abruptly, thereby tearing a large hole in the soil. The time of this performance seems to depend on the coming of the first rains and may be prolonged into December, this being in general accord with the practice in the other islands under consideration (Gunn, p. 197). At the same time the yam mounds are prepared, smoothed over neatly by the women, although the rest of the garden preparation is done exclusively by men. A yam kept for the purpose from the previous year is now set in the hole and the earth is replaced. The digging stick used for this purpose is of hard wood, about four feet in length and sharpened at one end. When the yam is about an inch above the ground, a long reed is placed with one end in the ground, at an angle of 45 degrees, and the young tendril is allowed to twine itself about this until it reaches the free end, which is then stuck in the ground, forming an arch of vine. Another reed is then inserted near at hand, and the tendril is led on to the new reed, which in turn is treated in the same manner, until the garden assumes the aspect of vines trained on trellises, with an average height of four feet. Cabbage, taro, sugar cane and banana are planted in the usual way without any use of mounds.

The first harvest depends on the date of planting, but has been known in seasons when rain has fallen during the cool weather to take place as early as November, the final harvest being usually at the end of April. The garden often is allowed to lie fallow after one season of use but no rule for this appears other than the whim of the maker, based on former experience.

INHERITANCE. The custom of burying with him all the weapons and other personal effects of a chief of the district, or even of a village chief, existed until a comparatively short time ago, and no son dared carry about openly anything which once belonged to his father. Trees are not cut down on the death of a man of the *Fanlo* class, contrary to the usual rule of inheritance in Melanesia (Codrington, 1891, pp. 255, 263, 285), although there seems to be doubt if the same rule is applied in the case of a man of the *Taui natimono*. For some years before his death, a man of the *Fanlo* speaks of his trees as belonging to this son or that, so that when he dies, everyone says that the trees are the son's, not the father's. This pleasant manner of cheating tradition is not unknown among people who have advanced further along the road to a complex civilization, in trying to avoid the payment of death duties, but it is impossible to state whether the native mind sees the wisdom of preserving the trees of the deceased, without too openly flouting tradition, or whether there was never any sign on this island of a custom that is otherwise uniform throughout Melanesia.

However this may be, it is certain that all the trees are inherited by the sons of the deceased while the daughters have nothing at all, any unmarried daughter falling to the care of one of her older brothers and living in his house with his wife and children, until a marriage is arranged for her. In the latter case, it is the brother who has harboured the woman who receives the bride price, and it is the wife of this brother who sleeps with the girl on the night when the bridegroom is expected to come to carry her to his village.

FISHING. The Eromangans are excellent fishermen and show a zeal in this activity that surpasses that of the Tannese (Gray, 1899, p. 128). Fishing is done with a line made of native fibre finely twisted, the spear, bow and arrow or with a native net. The line has a length of from ten to thirty fathoms and is usually baited with star fish, *nokuos*. A round stone is used for a sinker and is held in place, one foot from the hook, by several clever twists of the line; and a catch knot on the line near the sinker permits the fisherman to release the stone after the fish is hooked. The hook itself is described in the portion of the present chapter devoted to handicraft.

Fishing in the old days was done with native nets, and these are still in use. They are made of coconut fibre, strongly and nicely woven. Unfortunately, the use of dynamite is fast superseding the use of these nets and is preventing the building of new canoes as well, since the fish may be taken from the shore by this means. In June or July a fish something like a mackerel, *namat*, appears in the waters of the island. All canoes are put out at once, the school of fish is surrounded, and a large catch results.

Another method of taking fish is interesting. The *nehele*, a poisonous fruit, grows near the sea and, after it is cooked and thrown into the sea, has a curious effect on the fish, stupefying them so that the natives may go into the lagoon and take them. Here again, dynamiting is supplanting the older method.

Sometimes a whale is washed ashore on the reef, for in the month of November these mammalia appear off the island in great numbers accompanied by their young, and it rarely happens that one or more of the baby whales is not caught on some part of the reef or coralline coast of the island where the reef is missing. The baby is taken by the natives with the spear, carried ashore, cut up, cooked and eaten without further ceremony, but the natives have a wholesome fear of the mother whale and will not venture after the infant until it is left on the reef by the tide, out of reach of its frantic parent.

When turtle appear all the people of the district on whose beaches one of these creatures has first been seen repair to the sea, and the natives of another district to whom a feast is owed are sent for hurriedly. The turtle is ambushed, surrounded and thrown on its back, when it is quite helpless. Sometimes they are taken in the sea from canoes, but the writer was out with natives on several occasions and never saw one actually caught, although many attempts were made. When a turtle is taken in this way a man dives under the canoe, seizes it by the leg, rendering it helpless, and swims ashore with his catch. In either case, after the turtle is ashore, it is killed and hung up between two upright poles. One man only must use the knife for the despatch of the creature and afterwards make an incision in the shoulder of the turtle, through which he thrusts one arm up to the shoulder, removing the entrails with his hand. No man may take a turtle alone; he must send word to all the members of his district before he undertakes it. If several are taken at once, as is sometimes the case, the district invited to share in the feast will thereafter owe a feast of a corresponding number to their hosts. This debt may not be paid for years but it is never forgotten. The season when turtle are expected in large numbers is from late November to the end of January, for in the cool season the creatures seek the deeper waters off the islands.

Sharks are taken by tying a water snake to a creeper and fastening the free end of the creeper to the reef, the shark being speared when it scents the bait and comes into the more shallow water to take it.

According to Brenchley (p. 322) there are ninety-five kinds of salt-water fish and sixteen of fresh-water fish. He also says there are two kinds of snakes in the island, which is in accord with the writer's experience. One of these is a water snake which is seen rarely, of which the natives are much in dread, while the other, a large green land variety, seen occasionally coiled in the lower branches of trees, is sluggish in its movements and is apparently harmless.

HUNTING. Pig hunting, which today is carried on with fire-arms, was in the old days done entirely with spears. A group of men, often from several villages, go together on this expedition and great excitement sometimes prevails. As has been already shown, the wild pig of Eromanga is larger and seems more ferocious than that of Tanna. It is called *colibve talorun sai* and is eaten, although for special feasts the domestic variety is in great favour, and is bred by the natives primarily for such occasions, as pig is rarely eaten at the ordinary evening meal. As the gardens are protected by fences, the domestic pig wanders at will anywhere else, while the wild variety, as we have seen, is warded off by the big fences that protect and enclose the village and gardens together.

HANDICRAFT. The hand work of the Eromangan shows a considerable advance on that of the Tannese, though the houses strike one as being exceedingly crude. Ground is first raised about a foot above the surrounding level in rectangular form and somewhat larger than the projected floor space of the house, and when nicely smoothed over and solidly packed down, it is ready for the superstructure. Several branches of a certain native tree, *more*, are then sunk in the earth platform to the depth of about a foot, along two sides, at intervals of perhaps three feet. These are bent towards each other and are securely lashed together when they meet, fastened by a certain kind of creeper. A ridge pole, also of *more*, is laid above the lashings and is itself securely tied to them, in this case split sugar cane, *teru*, being sometimes used as well, additional beams being fastened at intervals, lengthwise, on either side. The ridge pole is not heavy but strong, and there are no upright poles in the construction. Woven reed, nicely plaited, is then laid over the poles, each piece corresponding to the space between the curved branches and the lengthwise beams. The whole is then covered with a thatch of sugar cane or reed, lashed by the same creeper that is used to lash the upright *more* branches where they meet. One end is then covered in by a woven reed or sugar cane screen, but there seems to be a difference of opinion whether the other end used to be open or not. Robertson (p. 374) says that he saw houses with a banana leaf door "hinged" with creeper, but no one now recalls any such construction. These houses average about 12 by 8 feet as a rule, and present a picturesque object to the observer, giving, as they do, the idea of a curved roof rising from the ground. A drawing of a house is shown on the opposite page. It is interesting that the fibre used for tying parts of the house, for which the usual creeper is too coarse, is made of pandanus and not of the usual coconut.

There are a few houses built with uprights, with regularly thatched roofs and plaited sides, but they are due entirely to Christian influence and need not be noted here. The *siman lo* is a different story. Although there is not a single one now standing, several old men recall them in the early days and some seem to have attained an enormous size. Robertson (p. 375) saw one still standing in the south part of the island, and reports it to have been 100 feet long, 20 feet wide and 25 feet high in the middle. Several of the old chiefs today, in tracing out a floor plan of one of the *siman lo*, pace off a length of between 40 and 50 feet and a width of between 15 and 20 feet. The *siman lo* of today, in which the single men still live, is only an imitation of the usual house, but in the old days it must have been, in its impressive size, the most important house in the community. It is available only to men of the *Fanlo* class, no *Taui natimono* man being allowed to enter it and it is of

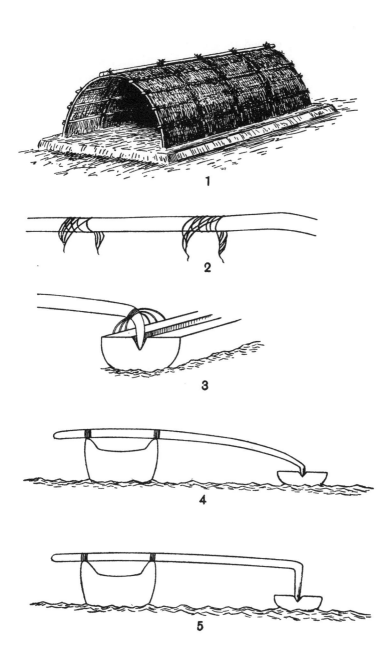

1

2

3

4

5

course entirely denied to women. The single men sleep there from the day of the incision feast until they marry and those who meet to drink kava sleep there as well, whether married or not.

The ease with which a house of the ordinary size is put up by the men of the community when there is need for a new one recalls the same condition in Tanna and has been noted by more than one observer[1], but the building of a *siman lo* in the old days, such as the one observed by Robertson, must have been a very different matter, and it is hard to see how a people so lethargic as the Eromangans today could have managed it. The only explanation is that they have degenerated physically and mentally, since the old fighting days.

Canoe making is not the prerogative of certain men and all men may work at this form of craft, although some have more proficiency than others as a matter of course[2]. When a canoe is desired a tree is cut down, generally the *leple* or the *nemaar* (bread-fruit), though others are used as well. On the east coast, however, the material is confined to the two noted above and no other is ever used, but in all other respects the canoes of the two parts of the island are identical. After the bark is removed from the tree an incision is made along the trunk and a hollow trench is made about 18 inches deep and for the full length of the trunk, the tree having been selected because of its proper length for the purpose, as well as for the condition of the wood. Fire is not used in Eromanga to any appreciable extent, although it is not possible to say that it is never employed as an aid to the hollowing-out process. As many holes are then made in the gunwale, on either side, as there are to be booms, or *mobok*, as they are called, and the booms are placed across the canoe at intervals resting on the gunwales, as shown in the drawing opposite page 156 (Figure 2). These are securely lashed with a native fibre called *walenevao*, which is passed and repassed through the holes and around the boom alternately. It is common nowadays to use imported twine for this purpose, although a fair number of canoes secured with the

---

[1] See Gray, 1899, p. 128.
[2] See O'Ferrall, p. 225.

walenevao are still seen. The float, *neleman*, is dug out much in the same manner as the canoe itself, on a smaller scale, the end of the boom having a sharp turn which is fitted into the groove or trench of the float and securely bound at the angle with the *walenevao*, fastened on either side of the boom, through holes prepared for that purpose, at two or three different places in the inner gunwale of the float (Figure 3). Sometimes the boom is carried out almost horizontally to the point where it turns at a right angle to meet the float (see drawing opposite page 156, Figure 5) and again it drops gradually to the point where it turns, as in Figure 4, although Figure 5 is the much more common type. Canoes are usually not more than 12 feet in length, the usual complement of men being not more than five or six.

The paddles, *walasowa*, are short, with a fairly wide blade and are made of several kinds of hard wood. In the old days, they were always made with stone axes, but these are now superseded by imported knives. There is no evidence of any ornamentation or carving nor is there even any recollection of it.

In houses and canoes the standard of workmanship in Eromanga seems to be about equal to that of Tanna, but when we turn to the making of the tapa cloth, of the skirts worn by the women and of the different weapons formerly used in warfare, we see a decided superiority. The tapa cloth is made invariably by the women. It is called *nemasitse*, and is made from the bark of the banyan or some other large tree, narrow strips of good length being stripped off with the aid of a bamboo knife. These are bound into bundles—rolled—to be kept till needed. One of these strips or bundles is laid across a log from which the bark has been removed and is beaten with a wooden implement and plentifully sprinkled with water so as to keep it entirely moist during the process. In the old days, according to Robertson (p. 368), the beaters were made of very hard wood and were beautifully carved, but there is no present evidence of any beauty of shape or design in them. New strips are added constantly and the beating and moistening go on until a pulpy, soggy substance is formed. The bark is constantly shifted about on the log, so that all parts shall receive the pounding of the beater. Then the piece is hung up in the open air and the design is made with a bit of charcoal before the material is dry. It is then dried and the dyeing process follows.

The root of the *nohorat* is scraped and, when mixed with ashes and water, forms a reddish-yellow substance which, when strained through coconut, forms a substance not unlike reddish mud. Into this the *nemasitse* is dipped and when it is removed the etched design has taken the colour and the rest remains in its former state. Sometimes a yellowish-brown effect is obtained by immersing the material in mud of the proper colour and leaving it for a time. The *nemasitse*, when finished, is worn across the shoulders by the women and is the only other article of dress beside the *namplat*, or skirt. In the hot weather it is usually dispensed with altogether, and seems to have a ceremonial use, for it appears in large numbers only on festive occasions, though babies are sometimes carried in it, fast asleep, while the mother does her work in the garden. There are two alternative names for the *nemasitse*, the *norok* and the *norolat*, but they seem to refer to the size of the article and not to any difference in the manufacture, which is uniform throughout the island.

While skirts of the nature of the one worn in Eromanga by all married women are common enough in the Pacific, the special long and trailing form in favour in this island makes it unique as far as is known. Green leaves of the pandanus are gathered by the women and bound together like sheaves of wheat. The women then sit in groups preparing what they have gathered, by stripping off the edges with a bamboo knife and removing the rough mid-rib by holding one end in the teeth, this work going on until a pile of material has been prepared. The next step is the decoration, which is done in one of two patterns, shown in the drawing opposite page 163 (Figures 1 and 2). The leaf is folded double and an oblique line is made with the point of the tree fern or with the teeth, which, when the leaf is unfolded, appears in duplicate, the multiplicity of lines being formed by the additional folds made in the leaf. The leaves are kept for several days immersed in water, which may be salt or fresh as convenient, but must be absolutely still, and they are then bleached on the beach in the sun. The result is that all colour has been removed and the material is quite white and very pliable. Next the leaf is fringed by making long slits throughout the entire length with a bamboo knife and all is ready for the plaiting. The plaiting is made with coconut fibre and is beautifully done, the end of the narrow leaf being bent back and the fibre twisted twice round it, the result being perfectly even as suggested by the rough drawing opposite page 163 (Figure 3). The colouring is done exactly as in the case of the tapa cloth. Some good examples of Eromangan *namplat* may be seen in the Melanesian collection of the Ethnological Museum at Cambridge. The description given by Robertson (pp. 364-7), practically the only other observer of the process, coincides with the above in all particulars.

Fish hooks are made of very hard wood, all of one piece, and are notched about 1 inch from the point, the entire hook being from 3 to 5 inches in length. A suggestion of the design will be found opposite page 163, Figure 4.

The bow is usually about 5 feet long and is made of the *more* and, occasionally, of other very hard woods. It is worked into shape with boars' tusks. A knife is never used, as the knife destroys the graining of the wood and weakens it as well, according to the native idea. Although nowadays the bow is often strung at both ends it seems probable that, in the old days, it was strung at one end only. The bow string is made of a particularly strong fibre prepared from the inner bark of the hibiscus.

The arrow, *negasau*, is made from the stem of a small but very straight reed, and the head is made from the tip of the tree fern, sometimes pointed and barred with four incised lines (see drawing opposite page 163, Figure 5), or simply pointed at the end and the grater-like stalk of the tree fern left otherwise in its natural state (see drawing, Figure 6). The head is bound to the shaft by an unbroken strand of coconut fibre of uncommon fineness and strength (see drawing, Figure 7) and the work is so well done that it looks as if it were done with fine copper wire, as noted by Robertson (p. 371). The winged end of the shaft is also wound with coconut fibre of a coarser quality, but in this case it is twisted in a geometrical pattern, as shown in the drawing opposite page 163 (Figure 8). There is no feathering of this end, and poisoning the point of the head

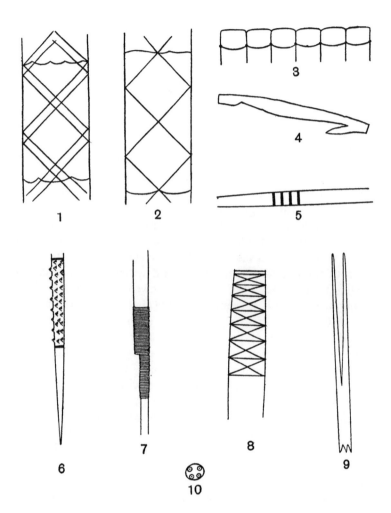

with any tangible material is unknown. Poisoning the arrow head by magical means was very common, however, as we shall see later in the consideration of magical practices. Cook, in his hurried visit to the island, noted (1st ed. p. 48) that the arrows had no heads of extraneous substance.

The spears are made of very hard wood; they are from 10 to 12 feet long and sometimes longer, with a diameter of about 1 inch. They are remarkable because the one piece of wood employed serves for the entire artifact, head, shaft and all. Four prongs, each carried to a sharp point, are cut in the wood, springing from a point about a foot and a half or two feet from the head. One would think that these prongs would be brittle and would break easily but such is most certainly not the case, for they are extremely stout and powerful in resisting strains put upon them. Nowadays a thick wire is sometimes wound around the flat end of the spear but it is not in any way necessary for strengthening purposes and is of recent introduction according to all the old chiefs. Drawings of two views of the spear are shown on the opposite page, Figures 9 and 10.

The war axes in the old days always had stone blades, but now an imported steel blade is used even if the handle is of native make. The stone blades were sharpened by rubbing two stones together and flints were sometimes flaked off for blades for smaller knives, the native name for a blade being *nonpunuis*, whether it be large or small.

The handle of polished *more* has a groove in one end, into which the blade is fitted and securely bound with coconut fibre, and these handles are common today, although the workmanship has deteriorated and the stone blades have entirely disappeared. There is no carving on the handle and it depends on the grace of its shape for its beauty. No knee-shaped handles were found.

Three kinds of clubs were made in the island in the old days, the *netnivri*, which seems to have been the most common form, the *novwan*, an oval-shaped club, now non-existent as far as is known, and the *telughomti*, or star club which is now a lost art and of which no example survives. All we know of these examples of Eromangan handicraft is that the *netnivri* had the head and handle exactly alike, the shaping being done with boars' tusks; the finished article was hung in the rafters of the houses until it had taken on a fine colour from the smoke of the fires, the polish being given by frequent rubbings with coconut oil between whiles. Of the *novwan* no description is now to be obtained. The *telughomti*, or star club, which seems to have been the *chef d'œuvre* of Eromangan workmanship, had an eight-pointed star at one end and a plain round knob at the other. While it is admitted that the star club had a place as a weapon in time of war, the ceremonial value of it seems to have been of greater importance. We have already seen it in use in connection with the arrival of the bridegroom at the house of his bride in the marriage customs.

TRANSPORT. Traffic by canoe between Eromanga and Tanna is fairly common and the canoes of the former island, on the return voyage, usually call at Aniwa in order to take advantage of the trade wind. No women ever accompany the men on these voyages and any intermarriage between the islands that may occur is the result of visits made by the men in every case. Canoes, even in the old days, were small and not suited to long voyages and very rough water, and it is certain that voyages to islands not in view are unknown today and are very unlikely to have taken place in the past. The stars are not used in steering by night and no Eromangan will be willingly caught in his canoe at sea after dark. If it happens that he is, he steers by the land outlines and not by the stars, a condition common to Tanna as well, where, as we have seen, the knowledge of the different constellations is extremely limited[1]. There is no record of any canoes being blown far away out of their course, as in Tanna.

CURRENCY. While pig is the general medium of exchange in Eromanga, as in so many of the islands of Melanesia, the *navela* has a use as a present for certain occasions, which inclines one to think at first that there is a monetary value to this as well. Further investigation reveals the fact that the *navela* is never given except with the expectation of a return gift in kind, and it is in the same category with the boars' tusks and *numpuri* shells,

---

[1] See Turner, p. 319.

which are sometimes given as presents in the purchase of a wife and can hardly be classed as ordinary currency, in spite of Brenchley's contention (p. 299).

There is no evidence of the use of the loom or of any pottery in the island.

Before leaving this part of our subject, a word must be added in regard to the cultural units credited to Eromanga by Speiser in his monumental work just issued. There (1923, pp. 449–50), in addition to the articles of handicraft already mentioned above or to be referred to later, the pandean pipe or flute, a light drum, and the spear thrower were not found by the writer. With the rest of Speiser's claim for Eromanga the writer is in entire accord, if dual organization be excepted. As has been already shown, it is too doubtful if it ever existed to any extent in the island to view its inclusion in the list of cultural units with composure. References are here given to the few artifacts illustrated by Speiser in his plates concerning Eromanga[1].

MAGICO-RELIGIOUS IDEAS AND PRACTICES

SPIRITS, GHOSTS, SUPERIOR BEINGS. Codrington's definition (1891, pp. 120–1) of the difference between spirits and ghosts holds good in Eromanga. Spirits are beings who were never human, or, if they had ever a human shape, it was so long ago that there is no remembrance of such an idea in the mind of the native; while ghosts, in the memory of man, or at least of tradition, had human attributes and were normal people, the supernatural parts of which wander about still. Sometimes they take the form of creatures, as for instance the glow-worm or fire-fly which is said to be a ghost; and all those people who wander at night are thought by those who remain in their villages to be of ghostly mould.

At Turaive, a part of Traitor's Head, there is a spot where the ghosts of the dead may be finally expelled from their old

[1] Fish spears ... Table 52, Nos. 14, 15, 16, 17
Spears ... ... Table 54, Nos. 23, 24, 25, 26, 27
Clubs ... ... Table 59, Nos. 2, 8
Throwing stones ... Table 59, Nos. 10, 11, 12, 13
Tapa ... ... Table 78, No. 7

haunts and, although it is admitted that the ceremony of throwing the ghost into the sea at this point is no longer practised, no native in a canoe today will speak in paddling over the spot, lest, as he says, the ghosts be disturbed. In the old days, this same condition of silence was practised in the vicinity of the *siman lo*, or sometimes in the vicinity of the house of the district *Fanlo* in which his wives lived.

In other ways fear of ghosts is very common today. When an old chief feels death to be approaching, he sends for all the members of his village and a feast is prepared, and the guests must be fed as long as there is life in the old man. In the old days, if a man was a long time dying, he has been known to ask that he might be buried before the breath had left his body. In this case he might be left in the bush in a partially made grave—this could only happen in cases of interment in the ground—but the earth would be left only partially covering him so that he might breathe. His friends frequented the place where the grave was dug, to see how matters progressed, but directly the breath had left the body everyone fled and the grave was deserted in its half filled-in condition for a long time. No native will go near a burial place today, be it cave or grave, if he can help it, and every man tells you that all ghosts are inimical to men and will harm them if they can, a state the more to be regretted since there is little that one can do in propitiation of the departed, except to keep away from burial places and to avoid walking alone through the bush in the dark. Very little other information is forthcoming about ghosts, and beyond the fact that they are always the souls, or supernatural parts of the deceased which wander for a longer or shorter period after death, no native will add any further information on the subject. This belief in a part of the human being that does not die with the body is common in other parts of the New Hebrides[1].

There is evidence of a superior being, *Nobu* or *Nabu*, recognized as the maker of all things, of whom nothing is known except that, after he had created the island and the men and women on it, he ceased to be an active director in the affairs of men, although he continued to exist and never was destroyed.

[1] See Rivers, *Folk-Lore*, 1920, p. 62.

One account says that he went away to another island to live after his work in Eromanga was finished[1].

MAGIC IN GENERAL. A class of men having power, or *mana*, is found in Eromanga as in all the islands of Melanesia which have been examined with any degree of thoroughness. The native name for these individuals is *Tavuwa*, and they have power both in beneficent and malignant magic, the process being very like that in Tanna, a *Tavuwa* usually transmitting his power to a successor before his death. It must be confessed that malignant magic is the commoner and the native mind is still terrorized by any evidence of it in Eromanga, as in so many other primitive parts of the Pacific[2]. It varies through the gamut from causing hurt to the gardens of an enemy to causing his illness and even death. Sometimes it is performed in a man's own district and against his own people, as in the case of a *Fanlo* who observed that the gardens of a certain village in his district were bringing forth fruit too plentifully, so that the waste would be terrific. In this case he went to the *Tavuwa* and asked him to take steps to injure the gardens of this particular village. This the *Tavuwa* agreed to do, the procedure in this case being as follows. The *Tavuwa* bound the roots of a certain tree with native fibre, the tree from which the roots were taken being like those in the offending gardens. They were then placed in a native basket and taken to the sea, where in quiet waters of the lagoon they were laid on the bottom, a few stones atop to keep them in place, the *Tuvuwa* at the same time uttering certain words over them. It was then made known to the people of the village that magical rites had been worked against them and that a big wind must be expected in consequence, but the name of the man who instigated all this was carefully withheld. Strangely enough, in this special instance, a hurricane arrived soon after, and the gardens of the unfortunate villagers received much damage and the crops were much depleted. It is hardly necessary to add that the *Tavuwa* worked this magic in the hurricane season and that on no account could he be induced to do so in the cool weather when hurricanes are practically unknown. All this is of course an excellent example of contagious magic and all natives take the

[1] This agrees with Brenchley, p. 320.   [2] See Deane, p. 162.

greatest care not to throw anything away that may fall into the hands of a *Tavuwa* and be used against them later on.

In the case of more serious manifestations of this magical power, in which illness or even death may be the result, the procedure is curious. Suppose a man wishes to cause illness or death to an enemy in another district, he first provides himself with something belonging to the victim, a banana peeling he has thrown away, if he is fortunate enough to find a thing so simple, or even a few blades of grass on which the victim has expectorated in an unguarded moment. This he takes to the *Tavuwa* who, when he has consented to act, wraps this object along with some stones, *natamas evai*, in a leaf. Sometimes the personal object is not wrapped with the stones but is kept near them; all are placed in a basket and the basket is hung to a tree in some remote place, where the victim and his friends are unlikely to find it. The victim is then informed by roundabout means of all this (the place where the basket is suspended being carefully concealed, as well as the name of his enemy), and that he is going to be ill or to die, as the case may be. The enemy and his friends make frequent visits to the place where the basket is hung, but at odd times and by night, so that the victim will not know where it is, although it is doubtful if the victim and his friends have the courage to seek out the place, even if its whereabouts happen to be revealed to them by chance.

The stones often represent a part of a man's anatomy or may suggest the entire man in miniature, as observed by the writer as well as by Gray in Tanna (1892, p. 653), but, in any case, the result is the same, and many cases where death or a serious illness resulted are reported. The name given to the stones is significant, *natamas* being the word for devil or evil spirit. In Eromanga, in the old days, no deaths from natural causes ever occurred, and all persons dying "in their beds" were done to death by black magic worked by some enemy in another district; so strong was this belief that the poor man was beaten with leafy branches to drive out the ghost before he had drawn his last breath.

The *Tavuwa* performed other rites as well. A woman five months along in child-bearing might have the sex of the infant determined by magical means, although no information as to the procedure in this case is given. If the sex determination was wrong it was of course the fault of the woman who had not carried out the proscribed rites in the correct manner, for the *Tavuwa* was never at fault, a usual condition in magical practices among primitive peoples[1].

It is pleasant to find magical means employed for the benefit of crops as well as for their hurt, the procedure being the same as in the case of the pieces of root producing a hurricane, very small pieces being used when the magic was to be beneficent, that is, if a small wind was desired so that it might bring rain. The application of the magic seems to be a question of degree. If the death of a man is intended in the beginning and the magical preparations are begun in the proper manner to compass that end, there is no chance to save the victim at the last moment, but if a severe illness is wanted, with recovery at the end, the mere fact that the personal article is not wrapped in the leaf with the stones seems to be sufficient to mitigate the result. Then the length of the illness and the propitious moment for recovery are controlled by the *Tavuwa* simply by regulating the distance between the stones in their wrapper and the personal object. At the end the stones are removed from the leaf and washed, but afterwards replaced in the basket, where they remain indefinitely, while the personal object is burned, thereby destroying all magical power. These *natamas evai* came originally from Tanna, but in transmitting the knowledge of their power the Tannese neglected to inform the Eromangans about any rites to counteract the magical properties of the stones. We have seen no evidence of any sort of control of, or antidote for, magical practices in Tanna, but the Eromangan is firmly convinced that the Tannese have the power to remove the bad effects of black magic while he, poor fellow, is unable to do so. In the old days, when fighting was still common, a Tannese came to Eromanga and lived there. Although the Eromangans practised all sorts of magic against him with all the power at the disposal of the *Tavuwa*, he lived entirely unharmed and died finally on the island, one of the few cases known of an absolutely natural death without magical influence. This

[1] See Woodford, p. 26.

contagious magic or, as Malinowski (p. 405) so well calls it, magic by impregnation, is world-wide in its distribution, the parts of the world where it is not found in one of its variants being few indeed.

Although the consensus of opinion now is that no woman may be a *Tavuwa*, it is admitted that certain old women have power to stop conception in a woman. In this case the magical rites must be begun at an early age, before the young woman who is to be made sterile has reached puberty. The procedure is, or was, for the natives stoutly affirm that this is never practised today, to place a stick in the house where the young woman lived. If the stick was used by chance for stirring the household fire, all the magical power in it vanished instantly, but, if it remained where the old woman placed it for a certain period, that is, until the young woman reached puberty, it was then cast into the sea and the woman never bore children. This custom is difficult to account for, and it would be omitted altogether here were it not that so many of the old chiefs insisted that it used to be successfully performed.

The bark of a certain tree is also chewed by women who wish to bear no more children, but this custom is not properly a magical one, and the medicinal effect of the tree is counted on to perform the act rather than the magical properties which it contains. Sterility in its natural state exists, but is rare, as in other parts of the New Hebrides, but a woman who bears no children is believed to have chewed the bark of this tree.

Magical practices, except those introduced from other islands, were not given to the Eromangans but have always existed, according to the older chiefs. This is in accord with the findings of ethnologists in other parts of Melanesia[1] and, indeed, in many parts of the world. Here the *Tavuwa* does not observe his own taboos as he must do in some parts of New Guinea (Malinowski, p. 425).

A mode of detecting a thief is simple. If anything is lost the district *Fanlo* calls all the men together and, producing a banana or yam, tastes a morsel himself and passes it to one of the village *Fanlo* near him, so that it makes the whole circuit of the com-

[1] See Malinowski, p. 398.

pany. The guilty man chokes over his piece and is thereby detected and caught. An example of this was given by a planter who has lived many years in the island. Many years ago he lost a new pair of scissors which, considering the speed with which such things become covered with rust, is a loss of considerable magnitude. He told the village *Fanlo* near his house, who promptly called all the men of the village together including, of course, the planter's house boys. They assembled on the verandah of the house where the planter lived and the ordeal commenced, the *Fanlo* swallowing a piece of banana and offering it to every man in turn. When it came to the native who was acting as cook for the planter, before he received the banana from his neighbour, he made a sudden dive under the table and, producing the scissors, pretended to have found them there. Nothing would induce him to swallow the piece of banana as he was firmly convinced that he would choke in doing so.

Some men have power to touch and handle snakes while others have not, but it is quite possible that this has no magical origin and is simply a matter of inclination or repulsion as with us[1].

The question of the *navela* stones, of which one is in the Museum at Cambridge, must hold us at this point for a few moments. They were given in the beginning by the *Nobu* for the use of man, and are kept as heirlooms in the families of the chiefs, to whom they exclusively belong, it being firmly believed by each chief that his *navela* was received by his first ancestor from the *Nobu* himself. They used to be kept in the ground in a place unknown to any but the *Fanlo* to whom the stone belonged, and his chief act in naming his successor was to tell the man where the *navela* was buried, so that he should find it, and, having seen it, bury it elsewhere. Sometimes the chief died too suddenly to impart the knowledge to anyone and the *navela* disappeared entirely. Fortunately, in this case, a series of *navela* of less potency always existed in each village, so that the loss was usually made good and the new stone was considered to have absorbed the virtues of the original one. *Navela* are still buried with the *Fanlo* when he dies and, in

[1] See Robertson, p. 339.

this case, it is always one of the inferior stones and not the one received directly from the *Nobu*, of which one must always be in existence. In the beginning, the special stones had markings which made them capable of identification by the men of the *Fanlo* class, and it is said that stones lost or missing for years, because a dying chief did not reveal their whereabouts, were found by chance long after and restored to the successor of the original owner. The use of *navela* as part payment for a wife and for presents was very common in the old days, and it is interesting that Brenchley (p. 304) found the price of a wife in his time to consist of one *navale*, as he calls it, a spear and a bow and arrow.

The *navela* are of all sizes, crown-shaped, round, like a crescent moon, long and thin or long and thick, the one in the Museum at Cambridge being of the first variety.

A word in regard to magical poisoning of arrows must be said at this point. The process was like that in connection with garden magic, some object discarded by one of the enemy's people being used, and the *natamas evai* in this case usually represented some part of the anatomy of an enemy, which it would be particularly unpleasant to have injured, such as the liver or the genitals. The stones and the personal object were wrapped together in a banana leaf and suspended in a basket where all the men of the district might go to look at it, and where the *Tavuwa* might perform his magical rites at his leisure. After a certain time the wrapping was removed and the heads of the arrows touched with the stones which had by this time become impregnated with the black magic, and it was implicitly believed to be fatal if a man received a wound from an arrow that had been treated in this manner. No other preparation of arrow heads by poison occurs in the island; all the evidence points to magical treatment here as in so many other places, which raises a doubt whether poisoned arrow heads, that is, treated by an actually poisonous substance, exist as frequently as has been supposed.

The commonest form of magic here, as elsewhere in Melanesia (Malinowski, p. 394), may be said to be the use of the elements, rain, sun, wind, for or against the gardens of the people, and the more serious form of black magic practised against the health and occasionally the life of an enemy.

There are a considerable number of taboos in the island that still have force and had great power in the old days. In connection with food there are the following. Before the yams are eaten at the beginning of the yam harvest, a man of the *Fanlo* class must twirl a yam around his head and throw it into the garden, or at least in the direction of it, the reason being given that any snake that may be in the garden must on no account be killed, and the yam is thrown as food for the creature. One of the old planters once started to kill one of the large green snakes already referred to in his garden and was restrained by one of his house boys, who told him that the garden would not thrive if the snake were killed. As snakes are very rare in the gardens of the natives, it is difficult to see how this custom began, unless snakes were formerly much more frequently found in the island than they are today, although, once the custom became established, it is quite easy to understand how it continued, even if there were no snakes to eat the yam. If a man from another village is present at the snake feeding ceremony and the same custom has not been observed in his own village that year, he must excuse himself when he is offered yam to eat, on the ground that he cannot partake of the new fruit until the ceremony has been performed in his own village.

Only certain men in each district may kill turtle and no man or woman with very young children may eat it, although there is no other prohibition against eating, and those who may kill are not prohibited from enjoying the result of their efforts.

In the old days, no man coming from the sea with fish which he had caught, or from the bush with game, might pass a man on the track without offering him a share of his catch. This custom has had a natural result, that almost all men now fish at night so that they may return through the bush in the dark and need not offer anything to anyone, it being quite impossible to see anyone on the track in the dark, especially if one does not want to do so. The only taboo against the eating of fish other than turtle is that no woman with child may eat of certain fish while other kinds are permitted[1]. It is to be regretted that the names of the taboo fish were not obtained.

Eromangans who have eaten pork at a feast or elsewhere, or who have been in the sea, may not go to their gardens for 24 hours; in this case a definite reason is given—that the yams suffer in consequence. The same prohibition applies to a man who has cohabited with a woman, and the same period of 24 hours' absence from the gardens is required of him in this case, although the prohibition does not apply to women. Again, during the menstrual period, no woman may prepare food, and no one may eat any food prepared by her at this time. Also, no one may give a name to a child until the father has cooked some food and given it to the infant.

While no native will willingly take food from the bare hands of another at any time, he may on no account touch his own food with his bare hands after he has had connection with a woman until 24 hours have elapsed and he has washed himself. All food, in this case, must be taken by holding a leaf in his hand and eating from the leaf.

Any relative who is called *etemarsi*, that is, corresponding to the in-law relationship in our civilization, must observe a certain taboo. He may not step over the feet or legs of his wife's mother under any circumstances, and in the old days the death penalty was given to the unfortunate man who thus insulted his mother-in-law.

There is a certain stone near the sea on the west coast which, if expectorated on, causes the death of the man who did the act within a month, and the present-day Eromangan is very careful not to go near this dangerous object. The native disclaims all knowledge why this particular stone is honoured with such special reverence, and there is no tradition extant about it, as far as one can learn, as in the case of many other stones in different parts of the island. In the case of the minor taboos, those connected with food and sexual intercourse particularly, the punishment for any infringement of the proscription is to deny the man the right to go in his canoe for a month, a heavy

---

[1] This occurs in San Cristoval, Fox, p. 337.

penalty in the case of an Eromangan, although he is not so frequently on the water as many of his island neighbours to the eastward and northward. If a man is drowned, the spot where he was last seen is regarded with awe for a full period between yam harvests—a full year—by all the people of his district, and no one can be induced to go near the exact spot in a canoe. This, of course, is not properly taboo, but fear of ghosts of the deceased and the malevolent influence incurred by the man who ventures near the spot.

Among the many coralline caves with which the island abounds, one on the west coast, not far north of Dillon's Bay, deserves special mention in this place. The cave is at the top of a coralline formation but is itself formed entirely of lime, with many stalactites depending from the roof, while the stalagmites below are practically non-existent to the eye, covered as they are with the deposit of powdered coral. There is a dome-like roof, 70–80 feet above the floor, and the depth is perhaps 60–70 feet into the cliffs, the entrance being rounded, about 14 feet high in the middle of the arch and 30 feet wide at the bottom. There is a raised apse-like formation of limestone around the circle of the cave, the floor enclosed by this being flat, with two lateral chambers in which piles of bones are still found, although they are not in any case lying in regular formation but have evidently been disturbed since the place was used for burial. There are no bones in the main chamber and no evidence that any were ever placed there, though the width of the opening and the lack of protection from molestation may account for this. At a certain time in the morning the sun pierces the limestone vault overhead and sends a ray of light down on to the floor but, though the cave has a large entrance, the thickness of the trees outside makes the light within much too dim for the use of the camera.

On some of the walls, which are fairly smooth and often stained dark green or even black by the natural percolation of moisture through the limestone, numerous impressions of human hands and a few of feet are made in solid colour, of about the shade of the coral powder of the floor, although they are not really made of that. They show up very plainly on the dark green surfaces. The hands vary from 9–12 inches in length to quite small examples not more than 7 inches over all and, wherever they occur on the dark green or black background, are quite distinct. There can be no doubt that they have been made by laying the hand on the dark background after it has been dipped in some preparation of the colour referred to above. Wherever they may be reached the substance does not rub off and is apparently indelibly stamped on the limestone. Most of the impressions are from 20–30 feet above the spectator who, standing on tiptoe on the raised formation of limestone referred to, can touch only a bare half dozen of the hands, the number increasing as one's eye travels higher up the walls of the cave. There is no incision of the rock in connection with the impressions as far as they can be felt, nor does there look to be in those out of reach. The flat surfaces of the walls have been taken advantage of, and the impressions are much more numerous where there is a flat stretch of wall space and they increase in number considerably around the entrances to the lateral chambers.

It is certain that these impressions of the human hand and, it may be added, in the case of the larger ones, of the hand of the male of the older or Papuan type of Melanesian, must have been made at a time either when the floor of the cave was at a considerable height above the present floor level (which is unlikely, since the cave is gradually filling up from the bottom today with a slowly accumulating deposit of powdered coral), or by men mounted on some sort of scaffolding, or on the shoulders or backs of other men. Some of the hands are small enough to be those of women, but may be of course of youths. The impression is invariably made by spreading the palm of the hand, flat, on the surface of the cave wall and the fingers are always complete, unlike the impressions found in prehistoric caves in some parts of the world. In one or two instances the forearm is indicated half way to the elbow; the feet are few and are not so well impressed as the hands. Many of the impressions are superimposed on others and there is no attempt at any order or regularity in the arrangement. At the very top of the cave there are a few round solid impressions of the same colour as the hands, not unlike one of the forms of the *navela* stones already referred to, these being about 9 inches in diameter, as far as one can judge, from the floor below.

While it is futile to suggest that the cave in question is of an age comparable with that of caves in other countries where hands occur, the present-day native knows nothing of the origin of the hands and will on no account accompany the visitor to the cave to have a look at them. As this avoidance of all burial caves is common to the Eromangan no special significance can be placed in the dislike to go near this cave in particular. It is curious, however, that the Tannese on Eromanga had no fears and went with the writer to the cave on several occasions, carefully exploring every nook and cranny of it with him, even to the lateral chambers with their piles of bones. Yet, on the west coast of Tanna, on one occasion, the natives hesitated to enter a cave where, it is true, one had to crawl in on all fours, trusting that nothing more unpleasant than bats would impede one's progress.

CEREMONIAL LIFE

The young are initiated into man's estate in Eromanga by incision and there is no evidence of circumcision in the island, in which it agrees with many other islands in Melanesia, notably San Cristoval, as noted by Fox (p. 364). The process is similar to that common formerly in Tanna and many other parts of the Pacific. It is done at puberty, or earlier, several boys being operated on at once merely as a matter of convenience, and to provide for a more general festivity than would be possible if one or two only were incised. The actual cutting is done in the bush not far from the *siman lo*, but no special house is built for the performance of the operation as in Tanna, and the entire period of seclusion is passed in the *siman lo*. Certain men have the reputation for skill in performing the operation, as noted by Gray (1892, p. 659) and the writer in Tanna. A small, flat stick is inserted under the foreskin and bound with native fibre. This is moved several times so that the foreskin is loosened on all sides. An incision is then made with a bamboo knife, or with an imported razor, which is much in vogue nowadays, the

H 12

foreskin being slit for its entire length from the top to the base of the glans in front, the parts thus loosened being bound on the under side of the penis and allowed to remain in this condition until a lump is formed. No part of the foreskin is ever cut off or removed in any manner. The boys remain in seclusion until the most stubborn case has healed completely and are fed by an older man assigned, in each case, to the care of a lad. No special relative has the prerogative to act thus, however, and it generally devolves on the father of the boy.

The *siman lo* is never in the village, although it may be close to it and, during the period of seclusion, no woman or female child may venture near the men's house under threat of severe penalties, although it is not possible to discover what the penalty is, for no case of a woman daring to approach the house has ever been known. So much a matter of custom has this avoidance become that no woman ever looks in the direction of the house as she goes about her daily duties, and on no account passes it closely.

When all are healed, preparations for a big feast are made, the boys are rubbed with coconut oil so that they shine, and the usual male adornments are put on them. Each boy wraps the penis in some leaves, binding the case thus made with native fibre, after which it is allowed to hang down in front, the assumption of this article of dress marking the time after which on no account shall the penis be exposed to the view of any man, as we have seen already. The boys have been well fed during the period of seclusion and are plump and well filled out, for the feeding of the boys is in the hands of one man— in addition to the man in charge of each boy—who cooks the food for them at a special oven, the actual feeding of the boy being done by the man in special charge of him. At the feast the women see the boys for the first time, the latter showing their transition to man's estate by a dignified disdain of woman and child, keeping entirely with the men in their groups. The boys live in the *siman lo* after the ceremony until such time as they take a wife and have a house of their own. A sham fight follows each incision feast and it has happened that a boy has been killed in the scrimmage, although no intention to do so is known to exist. No revenge for an accident of this sort is permitted and, in the old days when fighting was common, no appeal to arms ever followed.

It is difficult to account for the transition to circumcision in Tanna and for the absolute lack of it here. The fact that Eromanga came earlier under Christian influence than Tanna does not bear out the hypothesis that the transition is due to Christian influence, for there are still heathen people on Tanna, while all Eromangans were Christianized years ago. The difference, to whatever cause it may be due, must be a fundamental one in the people themselves, and we have seen already that incision and circumcision may exist side by side in other places besides Tanna[1].

Kava is prepared and taken in the following manner. The root of the *Piper methysticum* is grated into a wooden bowl by rubbing it with the stalks of the tree fern and it is then chewed by men of the *Fanlo* class; any man who has been incised may partake of the beverage and help in the preparation. In no case are virgin youths allowed to be present at the ceremony, even for the purpose of chewing the root, as is the custom in some places. This is in direct opposition to the testimony of Robertson, who says (p. 393) that the root was chewed during the process by virgin boys, and that even virgin females sometimes took part in the ceremony. The liquid is then passed around, before it is strained, and each man holds his coconut shell cup covered by a strainer of coconut for the reception of his share of the drink, which he quaffs at once without further ceremony. There is no evidence of any grinding process in the preparation, as found by Fox (pp. 216–17) in San Cristoval, although the rest of the process there is similar to that in Eromanga.

Each village has its kava house somewhere in the bush not far away, and there is nothing to distinguish it from the usual house today, although in the old days it seems that the kava house must have existed as well as the *siman lo* which it resembled in plan and outline. The village *Fanlo* acts as host at the drinking ceremony, any guests from other villages or even from other

---

[1] See Brewster, p. 313.

districts of the *Fanlo* class being invited to be present and to partake. The ceremony is confined to the kava house and takes place usually towards evening, after which most of the men sleep in the house all night, many men sleeping away from their families in this way most of the time. The *Fanlo* at whose village the drinking takes place sends to his village for food after all have drunk kava and the men eat, then smoke, then sleep. It is a noticeable fact that the drink affects the appetite and that the men eat very moderately after they have drunk.

The kava prepared from the *Piper methysticum* is light in colour. It is made occasionally from another root producing a dark liquid, but the use of this variant is dying out today. Tales are told of the sudden effect of this dark variety, but they must not be taken too seriously. At any rate, the effect is different from that of the usual kind which, as we have seen above, affects the limbs of a man but not the clearness of his head. The sleep following indulgence in the ordinary variety is deep and untroubled by dreams, and it is said that a rude awakening causes nausea and great discomfort. The awakening after natural sleep is delightful and can only be appreciated by those who have tried it, the men being able to rise at once and go about their affairs with no bad head or other signs of a debauch. It is different if the drink has been taken to excess; intemperance robs a man of all desire for sexual enjoyment as well as of the power to perform the sexual act. It is believed that a woman who drinks will not bear children, and this is said to be the reason for prohibiting them from the indulgence. An alternative to the use of a wooden bowl for the mixture is to dig a hole in the ground and line it deftly with taro leaves. Sometimes the individual cups are of banana leaves, instead of coconut shell. It is insisted that the drinking never takes place in the *siman lo* of the unmarried men and that the men of the *Fanlo* class are eligible only, although this latter prohibition is not a usual one. There is no evidence of tossing a few drops of the liquid to the ghosts of the dead in Eromanga as in so many places in Melanesia (Codrington, 1891, p. 128).

Return feasts, *nisekar*, were common in the old days, but they are practically unknown now, and the Christmas and Easter Church festivals supply the native with the *joie de vivre* that he used to get from one of his *nisekar*. The preparations of the old form of *nisekar* sometimes took several months, and on the day appointed for the beginning, yams and taro in great numbers were piled high in the spot chosen, which was not the dancing ground by its banyan tree, for this did not exist in Eromanga as it did, and does still, in Tanna. Pigs had been cooked in anticipation and fowls as well, and all the food was brought together in one place, where it must have made a great show. The first event in the order of exercises seems to have been a sham fight which was undertaken in play directly the guests from the district to whom the *nisekar* was being given arrived. This developed into a real fight occasionally, although only clubs were used, spears, bows and arrows and knives being forbidden, and there were no warlike disturbances as a consequence afterwards. Sometimes the feasts lasted for several days or even weeks, and lending of women to the visiting men was a common custom in the old days.

During the progress of the *nisekar*, as we have seen already, all fighting between districts must cease, and no feast was ever used as a trap to entice the enemy and take him by surprise. Such treachery seems to be unknown and the idea is quite beyond the comprehension of the native mind. At times the return *nisekar* was given at the close of the one given by the district owing the original feast, as soon as the preparations were made. At times for months nothing but preparations for *nisekar* and the enjoyment of them was heard in the land; then, for months, no feasts would be held and wars took their place in the mind of the native. Fighting or *nisekar* seems to have been the chief matter of interest at all times, outside the usual local concerns of each village or district. Only one rule concerning the return *nisekar* is outstanding, and that stipulates that a number of pigs must be provided by the people giving the return feast, equal to that given them in the beginning.

Naming the child of a man of the *Fanlo* class is the occasion for a feast in the island, the father bidding all the men of his district in the case of a village *Fanlo*, or even the *Fanlo* of other districts if he be a district chief. The great preparations for the proper *nisekar* do not take place in this case, but kava is drunk by all the men of the *Fanlo* class in the kava house, one of the visitors asking the name of the child just as he is in the act of drinking. A man of the *Fanlo* class of the village of the father then pronounces the name of the child in a loud voice, it being the first time, presumably, that anyone has heard it spoken or known what it is to be, although the use of names in the line from father to son has a distinct uniformity which makes it easy to guess what the name will be. Two chiefs told me that, in the old days, a boy sometimes received the name of his mother's mother's son which, if true, is the only suggestion of the existence of anything like matrilineal descent in the island.

No ceremonial connected with the disposal of the afterbirth or of the umbilical cord exists, nor is the birth of the first child celebrated beyond that of subsequent children. Twins are not received in any manner that is unusual, although a female twin used to be neglected and sometimes left to die in the bush in the old days. Twins are very rare in Eromanga. Nail parings have no special significance, beyond the care that is taken to conceal any part of the human anatomy that is thrown away, so that it may not fall into the hands of the *Tavuwa*.

When we turn to disposal of the dead, we find three forms existing in the island today: the first and most widespread is grave burial in the ground, on the back with the legs extended, earth being at least partially filled in over the body; cave burial, the second variety in importance, in this case always on the back in an extended position, in many of the coralline caves in which the island abounds; and an interesting form of recess burial, which seems to be common only on the east coast of the island, the other two forms having a more general distribution. Other forms of burial are either sporadic cases or of too doubtful authenticity to be considered. Interment in a sitting posture is unknown, and does not exist, even for men of the lower class, as in Northern Melanesia[1].

The first form is confined necessarily to the parts of the island where the presence of broken coral in the soil is not sufficient

[1] See Fox, p. 224.

to prevent the digging of graves; the place, called *nahur*, is chosen by the *Fanlo* of the district, and all bodies of members of the district are laid there until the place is full and a new site must be chosen. The only rule for the interment of the people using this form is that the head must be toward the sun. After the body is laid in the grave, on its back with the legs straight, as we have seen, one of the *navela* of the late man, if he be of the *Fanlo* class, is laid by him in the grave. The people of Sufu, on the east coast, place the *navela* on his breast. Nowadays the grave is entirely filled in but, in the old days (although the old men are not agreed on this point), only a partial sprinkling of earth over the body, probably just enough to cover it, was made. Although the name *nahur* suggests the prerogative of a chief, all men are interred in this place whether they are of the *Fanlo* class or not.

Cave disposal is invariably carried out in the same manner; the body is borne on the shoulders of men of the village of the deceased to the cave which is used by the people of that vicinity as a burial place, and is laid in the extended position, on its back, in the most level place that can be found in the cave. In this connection it must be admitted that very often the body is left in a place that is far from level, but the intention to leave it on the back is plain, and there is no evidence of any inclination to set the body up or to flex the legs, either temporarily or permanently, as is found in many parts of Melanesia and other places. The testimony of one chief that the legs were sometimes flexed and bound in order to carry the body to the cave is too unreliable, in this special case, to be trusted, for no evidence of burial in the extended position after having once flexed and bound the legs of the corpse is extant. The Mafulu of New Guinea inter in a grave on the back, having flexed and bound the body before carrying it to the grave, but the bindings are not removed and the earth is thrown into the grave, leaving the body on its back with the legs still tightly flexed (Williamson, p. 246). Once a body has been deposited in a cave there is no danger that it will be desecrated even if left entirely exposed, for nothing will induce a man, friend or foe, to go near these burial caves. There is no distinction in this form of disposal between the men of the *Fanlo* or the *Taui natimono*, but *navela* are laid on the breasts of the former before the cave is quitted by the burial party. This form of disposal was noted by Brenchley (p. 320) during his visit to the island.

The third form, that of recess burial, consists of a pit 5 or 6 feet deep, circular in shape, perhaps 10 or 12 feet in diameter. The graves were dug—for this form of disposal is no longer carried on, although the places may still be seen on the east coast of the island—in the circular wall of the pit, and the body, in a wrapper of woven coconut leaves, was interred, feet first, in the hole, the head remaining near the opening, which was closed in by a filling of earth, the pit itself never being filled in. When all the possible graves were full, a few coconut leaves were tossed into the open space and it was left entirely alone, the same inhibitions, or rather dislike to go near any such place, prevailing as in the case of the burial caves.

A child dying soon after birth is buried in the house, a hole being dug in the smooth ground under the mats, if there are any, and the body disposed of in that way without further ceremony or ado. One sporadic case of burial is worth mentioning. In this case an old *Fanlo* was buried in the recess of one of the pits on the east coast in his canoe, the outrigger having been removed. This is admitted to be a most unusual performance.

The mourning customs of the Eromangans are interesting. When a man of the *Fanlo* class feels that death is approaching— and there is rarely any doubt of the outcome once a native becomes convinced that he is going to die—he sends some of those about him to his gardens to gather fruit and tuberous roots as quickly as possible, for, if the gatherers fail to do their work before the man draws his last breath, the food is wasted, since it cannot be eaten. After the burial, all those who were about the man at the time of his death, as well as those who helped to dig his grave (in those cases of disposal where a grave is necessary), partake of a feast of the food that was gathered on the eve of the death, a custom found as far afield as the Wagawaga people of New Guinea (Seligmann, p. 620).

The work of the women all this time mainly consists in

weeping and wailing at the time of the death and until the obsequies are performed, a special woman usually being in demand for this function in the district, living in anticipation of being called upon at any moment. It seems to be only in the case of a district *Fanlo* that she exerts herself to any great extent, the death of a village *Fanlo* being attended usually by mourning women of the village only. But in any case these women receive a substantial part of the food served at the feast in reward for their services. It is quite common for the weeping women to stand around the body of the dying man, if he be a *Fanlo*, both before and after his death, uttering their lamentations and singing his praises as well. A few years ago, in the case of a much beloved *Fanlo* of one district, the body was passed about among his people, standing in double line, up one side and down the other, to the accompaniment of the weeping of the women.

In the old days the wives of the *Fanlo* of the district or of the village mourned for a year on the death of their husband, and during this period were not allowed to leave the house where they had lived during the lifetime of their lord and master. Some women were deputed to look after the widows in their seclusion but the retirement seems to be purely voluntary to-day. At the end of the prescribed period of mourning a feast was held and the widows came forth from their seclusion. At this feast the bow and arrows, spear, club, penis wrapper and any other effects of the deceased that had been kept for this purpose, were burned in a hole in the ground, in the presence of the widows and all the people of the district. The *namplat* of the widows were now cut short, reducing them to the status of an unmarried and marriageable woman again. Among the Tubetube people of New Guinea this same custom prevails (Seligmann, p. 620). These women belong to the brother of the deceased as wives and, in the old days, he usually exercised his prerogative or sold them to the man who offered the most for them, if he was already well supplied with women. They became his property on the death of the late *Fanlo* but did not pass to him until the period of mourning was finished.

In the case of the *Taui natimono*, there is no set period of mourning for the widow (for there was usually only one, a poor

man not being able to afford more than one wife), although very
often the woman used to go into voluntary seclusion for a period
of two or three months. But in this case, when she came forth,
no feast was held, and as she had no value as a wife for a man
of the *Fanlo* class, she usually became the property of one of
the unmarried or widowed men of her own rank.

MYTHS AND TRADITIONS

There are three accounts of the creation of the island and its
people. In the first, the *Nobu* made a man in each district,
where there was later a district *Fanlo*, and each man took a
woman, although there is no definite account of her creation.
These district *Fanlo* all had children and, when they were
grown, one was named as the successor of the original *Fanlo*,
the others being also of the *Fanlo* class but ineligible to hold
office unless the nominated man died before the death of his
father, the original *Fanlo*. This is the origin of the *Fanlo* class,
but where the people of the *Taui natimono* came from is not told.

Another account says that the *Nobu* made a man and then,
seeing that he was lonely, made a woman from a part of the
man's body. As the children which the woman bore to the man
grew to puberty they were sent to different parts of the island
and there founded families, although nothing is said of the
presence of any women in the island, beyond the woman
created for the first man. This is so suggestive of Christian
influence that the writer was on the point of abandoning it altogether, but the insistence of three or four of the old men that
it had nothing to do with Old Testament narrative, which they
knew very well, finally influenced him to retain it.

The third tale says that the *Nobu* created men of earth in the
ground and that they remained there warmly bedded until they
reached puberty, when they painfully pushed themselves up
through the surface of the ground and, scattering to different
parts of the island, were the foundations of the different district
Fanlo there. It is curious that no women appear in any tale,
except the second, and then only in the case of the wife of the
first man.

There have been three peoples in the island. The *Nompo* or

Nombo were a very light-skinned folk, who still live in the centre of the island, although no one ever sees them nowadays. They were the first-comers and were followed by the *Losorvu*, a very dark-skinned, woolly-haired folk, much like the present-day Eromangans. These second people saw the *Nombo* working in their gardens with the digging stick. Not knowing horticulture, they asked what those women, pointing to the digging sticks, were doing, and seeing that they were good called out, "Give us that woman." As a result they learned the use and care of gardens and became agriculturalists. The third people are the present Eromangans.

There is a tale that the Tannese gave the Eromangans kava in exchange for some of the red earth found in both islands nowadays, which is used by the Tannese, or used to be, as a pigment for decorating the face.

A story of the beginning of warfare is told. Fighting was unknown in the beginning but, one day, a man happening to clear and plant a garden at some distance from his own village and quite close to the village of another district, came to words with his neighbours about the rights of the matter and in the dispute that followed was killed. The men of the *Fanlo* class of the district of the deceased held a long consultation over the matter, and it was decided that, since a life had been taken in their group one must be taken in the other group to make all even and well again, and this led to the policy that prevailed ever after of "a life for a life."

Several tales are told about a blind fellow, or sometimes two, TAUIA and NUNPUNAIS, who are constantly being plagued by a mischievous fellow named NAMPUNOAI. The tales are usually of the lightest and most frothy nature, often quite obscene and with an indelicate climax at the end of each. There seems to be nothing in common between the RAMSUMAS of Tanna and NAMPUNOAI. The former is wicked and ill-natured, while the other is mischievous but not really vicious. NEVOYOI, another little fellow who plays pranks in the same manner, seems to be of different origin and not the same as NAMPUNOAI. Robertson (pp. 385–8) tells of a dwarf who plays pranks on stupid people.

Only one pure folk tale was obtained. An old woman had a niece, but whether she was brother's or sister's daughter is not stated. This old woman was the only person in the island who could give a pleasant taste to food and was in great demand at preparations for feasts. When the little girl was ten years old she followed her aunt into the bush one day and, hidden in a clump of bamboo, watched the old woman lift a huge stone from which pure, white water gushed forth so that the bamboo water carrier which she had with her was soon full. Carefully replacing the stone the old woman returned to the house, but the niece remained in concealment until the woman was well out of the way and then tried to lift the stone herself. Although it took a great deal of effort she succeeded finally and, when she tasted the water, she found it had the exact flavour of the food which everyone liked so much when prepared by the woman's hand. But the water, which had poured forth in a steady but moderate stream at first, now came with more and more volume and power and, although the girl tried to replace the stone she found herself utterly unable to do so. This frightened the child and, when the water rose in such force that it carried away the stone, she ran to the house of her aunt and told her what had happened. The woman shrieked in her distress, "You have flooded our whole land!" She sent her husband in one direction and she went in another, while the child ran in still a third. The waters, rising all the time, swirled around the place where the persons were running and then became gradually quiet again, leaving a human being on the bit of land surrounded by water, while water stretched as far as the eye could see, with the exception of the three islands that had been formed, where all had been land before. In this way Eromanga and two of its neighbours were created and a human being supplied to each. The tale ends here and no account of creation of a mate for the lone islander or of the descent from each is given.

KNOWLEDGE AND ART

There are several forms of medical practice in the island that show a certain amount of attention to different kinds of malady and their alleviation. The marks that might easily be taken for evidence of scarification on the bodies of the natives are, in every case, scars resulting from bleeding, which is done today as formerly for all sorts of ailments. A pointed bamboo knife is still used—or a pointed splinter of hard wood—and never an imported one, the incision being made by the sharp point of the wood and the blood allowed to flow freely, the idea being that, as the incision is made near the afflicted spot, the withdrawal of blood cannot help having a beneficial effect. The blood is received in a coconut shell and the native recounts with pride that, in his case, a certain amount was taken from him, indicating on the coconut the point to which the blood rose. When a man is nearing his end, bleeding in the same manner is resorted to in order to see if the blood is still flowing, for, without the least knowledge of anatomy, the native knows that, when the blood ceases to flow, all is over. There is no doubt that bleeding has a salutary effect and in cases of blood poisoning has, on more than one occasion, saved the life of the sufferer.

Blistering is used to reduce inflammation by the application of a certain plant to the tender spot, a plant with a leaf so powerful that it removes all the skin, leaving a sore that is long in healing and may cause the native the greatest discomfort, although he never doubts that the effect is beneficial, no matter how much or how long he has to suffer. In cases of an inflammation of the chest, this treatment often cures the trouble entirely, although the poor native carries a very sore and raw spot on his breast for some time afterwards.

A baking process for the cure of certain ailments is resorted to and resembles in general procedure a form of treatment popular in our civilization. A big hole, or oven, is dug, or the usual oven of the village is used, the hot stones being removed after it is heated to its full capacity. Some fresh leaves are scattered over the hot stones, and on these the patient reclines; hot earth, that has been preparing in the vicinity of other hot stones is heaped on top of him, leaving only the head visible. The perspiration induced is profuse and after an hour or so the patient comes out much benefited by his course of treatment, if only by the copious perspiration. In rheumatic complaints this treatment is wonderfully successful, and there is no doubt that it is an ancient custom and does not owe its introduction to imitation of the white man.

Five colours are named by the native and all others are variants of these: *nesuva* is white, *narumsu*, black, *telemte*, green, *nemeliau*, yellow, and *nabla*, red. For blue there is no name and it is called *narumsu*, black, by the native. No case of colour blindness was detected in any of the fifty-nine males measured.

There is a name for the sun, *namunka* on the east coast, *nipminem* on the west coast; for the moon, *itais* throughout the island, this being the same name as that used for "grandfather" in the second person singular direct address. The morning star is *iaros*, and the stars in general are *mosi*, while the evening star has no special designation and the constellations are not named or, apparently, noted at all.

Counting is in multiples of five, and there are names for the numbers from one to five inclusive. There is also a special number for ten, but six is 5 plus 1, seven, 5 plus 2, etc., eleven being 10 plus 1, twelve 10 plus 2, etc. to fifteen, which is 10 plus 5, sixteen being 10 plus 5 plus 1, seventeen, 10 plus 5 plus 2, and so on to twenty, which is "two tens." Above twenty counting is rare and in the old days it is admitted that after one had indicated the total number of fingers and toes, there was no use in going further and all beyond this was called "a lot." Thirty, now, is called "three tens," and thirty-one is "three tens plus 1." When the fingers are held up to indicate a number the left hand is used first, beginning with the thumb, then the index finger and so on in order to the little finger, but the fingers are touched by the index finger of the right hand throughout and are not turned down or raised by themselves. From five to ten the right hand is used and the index finger of the left indicates the number. Never were the toes touched, but this used to be done according to all the old chiefs. Probably the native rarely had occasion to count above ten in the old days, but, when he did, had recourse to the toes in order to do so. Today the natives are taught to count in English but it is rare for any one of them to be able to go from one to ten quickly and accurately. Knowledge of English figures is extremely limited, and it is common to hear a native speak of a number of men as "Many people he stop, p'raps ten, p'raps more, p'raps sixty, seventy, ninety, p'raps twenty, he stop."

The numbers from one to ten are as follows:

1	*Sai.*	6	*Sokrum mesaki.*
2	*Duru.*	7	*Sokrum-duru.*
3	*Desel.*	8	*Sokrum-desel.*
4	*Devat.*	9	*Sokrum-devat.*
5	*Sokrum.*	10	*Naholem.*

Mesaki—6—is sometimes used alone without *sokrum* and is the only exception to the logical sequence. It seems to be fairly recent, however, and in the old days was not used without the *sokrum* before it. *Sokrum-sai* for 6 is never heard and means nothing to the native mind whatever.

LANGUAGE

There are six or possibly seven dialectal groups in the island, but there is no evidence of more than one fundamental linguistic stock in Eromanga, and no reason to believe that the survival of an early non-Austronesian tongue may be found today. The native names for six of the dialects are *Eniau, Etio, Adiau, Sorung, Seimo* and *Tanempenum*. There is a seventh, according to WARIS, BILLIE and one other old chief, but no one recalls the name of it. At first the division of the people into three groups, quite distinct from the six or seven mentioned above and not concerning them in the past, was given by two chiefs as a linguistic division of the people, but concentrated inquiry on this subject settled the matter to the satisfaction of the writer that these are geographical divisions and not linguistic. The *Owilia* of the east coast, the *Nuru elongas* of the west coast, and the *Elevate* of the north part of the island, that in sight of the distant island of Efate on a clear day, may then be considered as non-linguistic. There are also some *Nuru elongas* people on the south-east coast. It would be interesting to know if there is any affinity between the dialect spoken by the *Elevate* people on the north coast and that of the island of Efate to the northward, but no knowledge of this was gathered by the writer during his stay in the island. A journey across the island on horse or foot is practically impossible nowadays and my only opportunities for exploring were by boat, up and down the west coast, and once around to the east coast by schooner when, unfortunately, no opportunity was afforded to touch at the north part of the island at all.

CHAPTER VI

CONCLUSIONS

GENERALIZATIONS concerning migrations of people to the five islands which are being considered in this work may carry us only a short distance on our way to a complete and accurate knowledge of the order in which these migrations occurred. The precise region whence each came and the cultural units of which each was composed cannot, certainly, be stated at present with scientific accuracy; there are, however, certain outstanding facts from which an hypothesis may be formed and the following is submitted as a suggestion.

The woolly-haired people, the taller branch of the Oceanic Ulotrichi, made little impression on the five islands in question, with the possible exception of the island of Tanna. By the time the Austronesian-speaking people had fused with them in other parts of Melanesia, these islands became permanently populated by the dual people resulting from this fusion. Later the dual people became modified in their turn by the arrival of the kava folk who brought with them many new cultural elements. The influence of these people in Futuna and Aniwa was tremendous, and the culture of these islands became much changed by the new element. In Tanna and in a less degree in Eromanga, this new influence was not felt so strongly, although on the east coast of Tanna it made a lasting impression. In Anaiteum we must assign it to a place midway between the two bi-insular groups. This influx of kava folk came almost entirely from the north-east, from Tonga and Samoa, as a reflex migration, and the modification of the culture of the dual people by an original easterly drift of the kava folk appears to have been very slight. This, in brief, is the hypothesis which we suggest. Let us see how far the material gathered in the five islands bears it out and how far the evidence is contradictory.

In the first place, however, it will be well to state briefly the different migrations into Papuasia, Polynesia and Melanesia in the past, according to the present belief of ethnologists.

The first people to enter this region at all were the Oceanic Ulotrichi. Wherever they came from, the earlier smaller people of pygmy stature scarcely penetrated into Melanesia, and there appears to be no trace of them in the New Hebrides, though they left their impress among some of the so-called pygmy peoples of New Guinea, and appear in the regions further to the west, as the Andaman Islanders and the Semang of the Malay Peninsula. The taller branch spread very extensively in New Guinea and possibly reached Tasmania by way of the Australian continent and they arrived in Melanesia in large numbers and formed there the aboriginal population.

Although the second great migration into this region did not affect Melanesia at all, it may be mentioned in passing that a great wave of pre-Dravidian peoples, proceeding from the west, reached the Australian continent at some period later than the Ulotrichi migration into Tasmania. We can trace them pretty well along their track, in the Vedda of Ceylon, the Sakai of the Malay Peninsula and some groups in Celebes and other islands of Indonesia.

The third great migration into the region was made up of Austronesian-speaking peoples who, wherever they originated, spread into Indonesia and Melanesia in large numbers and reached Polynesia, where they formed the aboriginal population in many of the islands. As they interred their dead in the sitting position they have been called the Sitting-Interment people, and it was they who, by fusion with the Ulotrichi, formed the dual people leading to the dual organization of society and its important results in Oceanic culture. These Austronesian-speaking people are also credited with having introduced many new cultural units such as a belief in spirits, the practice of magical rites, circumcision and the outrigger canoe. Descent was through the mother, with the result that, when the dual organization of society became firmly established, matrilineal descent combined with exogamy remained an important element in this culture complex.

The fourth movement of peoples may be divided into two classes, those who used kava and those who used betel. The kava folk are assumed to have brought with them, among other things, patrilineal descent, secret societies, extended interment, preservation of the body, and megalithic monuments, as well as cremation. The betel folk never got beyond Santa Cruz and it is unnecessary to give them any consideration here. These migrations, it must be borne in mind, brought different complexes at different times and the whole movement covered a long period. For example, the kava folk who introduced cremation had associated with it extended interment, while those who introduced megalithic monuments were worshippers of the sun.

A glance at the map of this part of the Pacific shows that no intervening islands lie between the five we are considering and the Fiji group, and that a south-westerly movement of people from Tonga and Samoa, which might be absorbed by the islands of the Fijian Archipelago to a considerable extent, might also pass by these islands and reach the Southern New Hebrides and even the Loyalties. It is an established fact that the Samoan group was an important centre of distribution at some period for the proto-Polynesians, and it is quite easy to believe that kava and some of the combinations of its culture complex came into Aniwa and Futuna, and, to a lesser degree, Anaiteum, Tanna and Eromanga, entirely from the north-east. The almost complete saturation of Polynesian culture in the two small islands, which would be the first reached by people coming from Samoa, and the extent to which it influenced Tanna, particularly the east coast, and Anaiteum, tend to confirm all that we have claimed for our hypothesis. The fact that the influence in Eromanga is less strong adds strength to the argument, since the influence of the kava folk is less as one proceeds northward through the group of the New Hebrides, so that, by the time Efate is reached, we find it confined to two or three small islands (of which Meli is the most conspicuous example) close to, but separated from, the larger island.

Part of our hypothesis is that the fusion of the taller Ulotrichi with the Austronesian-speaking people to form the dual people took place largely in the other islands further to the northward, and that the dual people had been tolerably fused by the time they arrived at the five islands in question. The primary reason for this contention is the lack of evidence of a more primitive folk living in the interior of the larger islands, as would be likely, especially in an island the size of Eromanga, had the fusion taken place by conquest or peaceable absorption, after the arrival of the Austronesian-speaking people. Had this been the case, it is hard to believe that some of the earlier folk would not have escaped and lived in the higher parts of the island, and that some survivors of them would not be found today. Of course there is always the chance that the arrival of large groups of Austronesian-speaking people led to resistance on the part of the Ulotrichi, which resulted in the extermination of the men of the latter and the possession of the women but, granting this, it is hard to believe that no remnant would survive in some part of a mountainous island like Eromanga, and of this there is no evidence at all. Strangely enough, there is evidence of such a survival in Tanna, where the *Kauyamera* of the south-west part of the island speak an entirely distinct dialect of the Austronesian tongue, so different from that of the *Numrikwen* folk that one is not intelligible to the other. The most probable explanation of this is that, for some reason, Tanna was settled by the Ulotrichi before the arrival of the Austronesian-speaking people and that the final fusion of the two peoples into the dual people actually took place in Tanna itself, although it is very unlikely that it had not been begun elsewhere. In this case, the *Kauyamera* people represent the descendants of the Ulotrichi who were overcome by the Austronesian-speaking immigrants and who left their mark in the language of the people resulting from the blend, while the *Numrikwen* represent the descendants of the dual people, who, having fused elsewhere, developed a dialect of the Austronesian language, quite different from that of their fellow islanders. If this be true we have still to account for the reason why the Ulotrichi reached Tanna and settled there while neglecting the other islands in full sight of it. If the Ulotrichi came from the north as we suppose, the coral-line nature of much of the coast of Eromanga might act as a deterrent to people who were prospecting for a comfortable place in which to settle, while the rich, volcanic soil of Tanna would have a contrary effect, but the surmise must not be pressed too far. On the whole, there is nothing to upset our hypothesis, that the fusion of the two peoples took place mostly outside the islands in question, if we admit the possible exception in the case of the *Kauyamera*.

We have seen that the existence of totemism in these islands is of the most nebulous sort, but that there are certain objects in Tanna and Aniwa which are closely akin to, or derived from, a system of clan symbolism, with a more or less clearly defined belief in descent from the symbol itself and, in some quarters, a certain reluctance to eat it. Now clan symbolism is rare in Polynesia, although it exists in Tonga and Samoa and is very strong in Tikopia, with its Polynesian culture, but it becomes increasingly common as one proceeds north-westerly through the New Hebrides and the Solomons to the Shortlands and the Melanesian islands to the north. The only simple explanation of its practical disappearance in the islands we are considering is that the influence from the north-east which came in with the kava folk brought little of this element of culture, and it finally became what it is today—only a memory of its former power as a taboo and a genealogical explanation at the same time. Considering the strength of totemism in certain parts of the Solomons, notably in the coastal regions of San Cristoval, it is possible that the kava folk who introduced totemism in its pure form came south-easterly through the Solomons to the New Hebrides, while those who reached the Southern New Hebrides by way of Tonga and Samoa were less impregnated with totemistic ideas and practices. Fox (1924) distinguishes between a bird totem people in San Cristoval and a people who were probably earlier but whose totemism can hardly be called a pure form, and it is possible that we have here the explanation of the variation in totemistic beliefs throughout the Pacific.

When we turn to the question of chieftainship, we find that the usual Pacific form of a tribal chief with village chiefs under, or subservient to, him prevails throughout the Southern New Hebrides, with the single and significant exception of the east coast of Tanna, where there is a decided tendency to equality of all the chiefs of the tribe, although today the suzerainty of one chief is gaining in favour. Now the prevailing form of chieftainship in these islands is akin to that of Fiji and Tikopia, and is found, with modifications, throughout Polynesia, even as far away as Hawaii, while the form which has prevailed on the east coast of Tanna until now is quite like that in the Banks' Islands. In Northern Melanesia, this form of chieftainship occurs usually in conjunction with secret societies, which have entirely disappeared in Tanna. It must be confessed that one would expect the Banks' Island form to be stronger in Eromanga than in Tanna, since the influence of the kava folk from the north-east was less strong in the former island; and finding it on the east coast of Tanna and not on the west coast weakens still further the argument, for the influence of the kava folk ought to have been uncommonly strong on the east coast of that island, if their main movements came from a north-easterly direction. We have seen above that there is reason for supposing that the fusion of the taller Ulotrichi with those who spoke an Austronesian language took place, at least partially, in Tanna, so that the dual people were actually fused in that island while the other four islands received them after their fusion had been accomplished. In that case the struggle between the two elements of the dual people would be more bitterly contested in Tanna than in the other islands and might account, in one part of the island at least, for the survival of the kind of chieftainship which was introduced by one of the peoples before the amalgamation took place, even if it disappeared elsewhere under stress of pressure from the kava folk. If the *Kauyamera* people represent, as we suppose, a survival of the Ulotrichi who mixed with the Austronesian-speaking people in the island, we should have to presume that they offered such resistance that the form of chieftainship which the latter introduced never became common in the part of the island where the *Kauyamera* dialect prevails, but was securely intrenched on the east coast by the arrival of some of the dual people who already practised this form of chieftainship. This is pressing the point too far, and if dependence on chieftainship alone were necessary to support our hypothesis, it must be confessed that it could be maintained with little confidence. Happily there are other and stronger arguments and to some of them let us turn.

The physical characteristics bear out our hypothesis fairly well. On the east coast of Tanna there is a decided average of brachycephalism—79·1 for 54 adult males. On the west coast the average is only slightly less—78·6 for 133 adult males—the average for the 187 males measured being 78·7. In Eromanga the average for the 59 males measured is 74·9 and shows a decided tendency to dolichocephalism emphasized by the further fact that, of the 59, only 4 have an average of over 80, while 32, or a little more than half the total measurements taken, are under 75. In the case of Eromanga, the figures represent about half the adult males of the island, which is now reduced to a little over 400 souls. It is to be regretted that no measurements from Aniwa, Futuna or Anaiteum are available, but the measurements recorded are sufficient to indicate the high average of brachycephalism in Tanna. This is precisely what one would expect if large numbers of kava folk came in from Tonga and Samoa, where the brachycephalic element is very strong. The fact that the east coast has a higher average than the west coast is additional argument for the hypothesis, since the brachycephalic influence would naturally be less on the west coast if it came in from the north-east as we suppose. The dolichocephalic character of the head measurements in Eromanga is also exactly in line with what one would expect, considering the greater influence on it from the north-west than in the case of Tanna.

If Speiser is right in maintaining that the tapa belt, the penis case and the fibre or grass skirt worn by the women form an invariable culture complex (his *Nambus Kultur*), the fact that they occur in Tanna and Anaiteum as well as in Malekula is interesting and significant. The route taken by this complex is obscure but, since the three elements occur in the northern island with a combination of other elements, some of which are entirely missing in the south, it seems fair to presume that the influence containing these units came from the north-west and became a vital part of Tannese culture before the influence of the kava folk reached the islands. Speiser's suggestion that the head rest for dressing the hair of the males, which was so common in Tanna in the old days, came in from New Caledonia is of great significance, since it is not a part of the Malekulan complex, and the fact that the curious mode of dressing the hair adopted by the Tannese has no counterpart in Malekula points certainly to its introduction from some other source. Is it presuming too much to suggest that the hair-dressing and its attendant head rest came in an easterly drift from Papuasia, since something akin to this mode of dressing the hair is found in parts of New Guinea? If this be true, it must have been a part of the complex introduced by the Ulotrichi who reached Tanna, and very likely Anaiteum, before the fusion with the Austronesian-speaking people had begun. In this case we should assign the *Nambus Kultur* of Speiser to a later migration of the dual people coming from the north-west, the blending of the two cultures (*i.e.* the head rest and the *Nambus Kultur*) taking place before the kava folk made their first appearance.

In the islands in question the marriage regulations show strong influences of the dual people. The necessary consent of the chief, the prohibition of marriage with certain relatives—of a man with his mother's sister's daughter, for example—the former practice of polygyny, setting apart certain relatives for certain unions, the monopoly of the young women by the old men, all point to an origin which had its inception in a dual society which practised exogamy combined with matrilineal descent. Even if the evidence at the present time in Eromanga is contradictory, we have seen above that there is good reason to suppose that the dual organization of society prevailed there in the past, and the evidence is stronger in the other islands, culminating to a practical certainty in Tanna. Now all this marriage regulation came in with the dual people; and the later influence of the kava folk, which introduced the more communistic form of Polynesian marriage, made little headway, except possibly in Futuna and Aniwa. Indeed, it may safely be asserted that what slight changes there may have been in marriage regulations in the islands have been due more to Christian influence than to the kava folk. The marriage regulations and prohibitions of the dual people were so strong and so firmly rooted in their cultural life that they were never successfully displaced by the kava folk, and the Christian form of marriage by the missionaries has merely been superimposed upon it, as the missionaries generally seek the advice of the chief as to whether from the native point of view a certain man may marry a certain woman.

Handicraft is now of a much finer quality in the islands which received the greater influence from the kava folk, that is, in Aniwa and Futuna, but this was probably not true in the old days, for there is ample evidence of superior workmanship in certain important artifacts in the past, such as the *siman lo* and the star-shaped club of Eromanga and the finely-made tapa beaters of Tanna. When one recalls the fine canoes of Malekula and the Solomons in the old days, one is astonished that there is not more survival of fine workmanship in the southern islands today. Indeed, one would think that the Polynesian influences which have come in since the kava folk began their migrations into this part of the group would have accentuated the beauty of the handicraft in all the islands in question, rather than assisted in their degeneration, as seems to have been the case. The survival of a few fine examples of Eromangan handicraft makes one think that the south-westerly movement of the dual people must have brought with it much beauty and skill in craft of this kind but it is difficult to understand why the degeneration set in.

Let us look at two more elements of the culture of the kava folk—disposal of the dead and the use of kava. If Eromangan cave disposal of the dead, which, for geological reasons perhaps, seems to be a sporadic form in the five islands in question, be eliminated, the simple explanation of the common form in the other four islands—interment on the back in the earth, with or without the knees flexed—is that this custom is very common in Tikopia, Tonga, Samoa and many other parts of Polynesia. In this case we must claim that the form of disposal introduced by the kava folk, for some reason or other, superseded entirely the sitting interment of the dual people, which is commonly supposed to be an important element in the earlier culture complex. The most plausible explanation is that the kava folk introduced a practice so revolutionary in its influence that important elements of culture, such as disposal of the dead, became completely changed to the form practised by the new-comers; also that the dual organization of society itself, with its descent through the mother, began to change to the new order of patrilineal descent, except in some of the marriage prohibitions and the survival of the kinship terms in Tanna and Eromanga, although these gave way to new forms in Aniwa and Futuna; and that chieftainship, except on the east coast of Tanna, changed its form. It was only the old and fundamental elements of the complex of the dual people which survived the fusion. Warfare never changed from the single combat idea to the massed fighting practised by the people of Polynesia, as occurred in the Hawaiian Islands before the arrival of the white man. Perhaps there was a good reason for this if the conquest of the islands by the kava folk was peaceable as has been suggested by Rivers. In this case inter-tribal warfare would tend to be conducted on the old lines rather than on those common to the kava folk, if the dual people had never seen massed fighting in actual use. Preparation of food was carried on in the manner introduced by the dual people, although it is probably true that it was the mode of the kava folk as well. However this may be, it is true that the kava folk effected a complete overturn in the culture of the dual people in the islands in question. It is possible, also, that these migrations, being in the nature of reflex movements south-westward from Tonga and Samoa, lost many of their original elements in transit, so that our islands emerged with a new and rather erratic culture complex distinct from the nearest groups in any direction. It is certain that cremation, which we expect to find associated with extended interment, never accompanied it to Tanna; and the group which introduced sun-worship and megaliths, which are commonly thought to have gone together into the Pacific, never reached these islands at all.

Is it not possible that we have in Tanna, Anaiteum, Futuna and Aniwa at least, a sidewash in the main stream of the great movement of kava folk, influenced largely from Samoa and Tonga (partly by way of Fiji and partly avoiding that group) but introducing no complete complex of the various migrations that brought kava on its eastward way?

Whether or not the fusion into the dual people took place in the islands to the north-west of those which we are considering (according to our hypothesis), or partly in the islands themselves (which is also according to our hypothesis, as far as Tanna is concerned), there can be little doubt of the tremendous influence which the dual people exerted in Eromanga and Tanna and probably in Anaiteum, Futuna and Aniwa as well, an influence which, in the two last-named islands, was later almost completely wiped out by the kava folk, who seemed to have a special liking for small islands lying close to or in sight of a larger one.

If, as has been suggested, the penetration of the kava folk was largely peaceful and composed mostly of males, the survival of the older form of warfare would be accounted for, as we have suggested above, and the lack of secret societies in these islands easy to understand. Rivers has offered the suggestion that the secret societies flourished, after their introduction by the kava folk, only in those islands where the arrival of the men was more or less opposed, and that in the islands where there was little or no opposition, there was no need for them to practise their rites in secret. If this be true, the complete lack of these organizations today and the presence of the men's house close to each village, in Tanna at least, strengthen the argument. If we search diligently for any survival of the secret societies in these islands, we can find the only suggestion of it in the *siman lo* of Eromanga which bears some resemblance to the large men's houses of New Guinea.

It is certainly true that all the foregoing applies less well in the case of Eromanga, but that island is more akin to Efate in its culture and characteristics. The physical measurements tend to confirm this, and the language of the north point of the island, by its construction and native name, so much more like that of Efate than like Southern Eromanga and the islands to the south, suggests that perhaps we are wrong in including Eromanga, other than geographically, in the group of five southern islands of the New Hebrides. The relatively high percentage of brachycephalism in Tanna certainly suggests an influence from some other region where the same form of head index prevails, and Samoa and Tonga have this index in good measure. The average in Eromanga, on the other hand, being, as we have already seen, under the average for dolichocephaly, shows more affinity with the Northern New Hebrides and the rest of Melanesia.

While the writer is very far from claiming that the arguments presented above are in any sense final, or that further investigation may not upset the present opinion altogether, he hopes that the hypothesis which he has here supported may lead to a further discussion of this fascinating subject, and the solution of the whole problem of the Pacific and its movements of peoples about which we must admit, while taking note of the increasing amount of work that is being done in this region each year, that we still know very little indeed.

BIBLIOGRAPHY

BRENCHLEY, J. L. *The cruise of the Curaçoa*. London, 1873.
BREWSTER, A. B. "Circumcision in Noikoro, Noemalu and Mbou-mbudho." *J.R.A.I.* XLIX. 1919.
CLAVEL. *Les Marquisiens*. Paris, 1885.
CODRINGTON, REV. R. H. "Notes on the customs of Mota." *Trans. Proc. Roy. Soc. Victoria*, XVI. O.S. 1880.
— "Social Regulations in Melanesia." *Rep. Brit. Ass. Adv. Sci.* Bath, 1888.
— *The Melanesians*. Oxford, 1891.
COOK, CAPT. J. *A Voyage towards the South Pole*. London, 1777. 1st and 2nd editions.
COOMBE, F. *Islands of Enchantment*. London, 1911.
CRUMP, REV. J. A. "New Ireland." *J.R.A.I.* XXXI. 1901.
DEANE, REV. W. *Fijian Society*. London, 1921.
DIXON, R. B. *The racial history of man*. New York, 1923.
ELLA, REV. S. "Some physical phenomena of the S. Pacific Islands." *Rep. Aust. Ass. Adv. Sci.* 1890.
ELLIS, W. *Polynesian researches*. London, 1829.
ERSKINE, J. E. *A cruise in the Western Pacific*. London, 1853.
FINSCH, O. "Die Rassenfrage in Oceanien." *Verh. d. Berl. Ges. f. Anth., Eth. u. Urg., Z. f. Eth.* 1882.
FISON, L. "The classificatory system of kinship." *Trans. Proc. Roy. Soc. Vict.* X. O.S. 1874.
FORSTER, A. *A voyage round the World*. London, 1777.
FOX, REV. C. E. *The threshold of the Pacific*. London, 1924.
FRAZER, SIR J. A. *The Golden Bough*. Abridged ed. New York, 1923.
GRAY, REV. W. "Notes on the Tannese." *Rep. Aust. Ass. Adv. Sci.* 1892.
— "Notes on the Natives of Tanna." *J.A.I.* XXVIII. (N.S. I), 1899.
GUNN, REV. W. *The Gospel in Futuna*. London, 1914.
GUPPY, H. B. *The Solomon Islands and their natives*. London, 1887.
— *A naturalist in the Pacific between 1896 and 1899*. London, 1903.
HADDON, A. C. *Report of the Cambridge Expedition to Torres Straits*. 1912.
HOBHOUSE, L. T. *et al. The material culture and social institutions of the simpler peoples*. London, 1915.
HOWITT, A. W. *The native tribes of S.E. Australia*. London, 1904.
HUBERT, H. and MAUSS, M. "Théorie générale de la magie." *L'Année Soc.* § 7, 1902-3.
HUTCHINSON, H. N., GREGORY, J. W., LYDEKKER *et al. The Living races of man*. London, no date.
INGLIS, REV. J. *In the New Hebrides*. London, 1887.

JACKSON, J. R. "Des arts et inventions de la vie sauvage." *Mém. de la Soc. Eth.* I. O.S. 1841.

KEANE, A. H. *Man, Past and Present*. Cambridge, 1920.

KRUSENSTERN, A. J. VON. *A voyage round the world*. London, 1913.

LANG, A. "The origin of totem names and beliefs." *Folk-Lore*, XIII. 1902.

LANGSDORFF, A. H. VON. *Voyages and Travels*, 1803–7. London, 1813.

LAWRIE, REV. J. "Aneityum and its Customs." *Rep. Aust. Ass. Adv. Sci.* IV. 1892.

LAWRY, REV. W. *Friendly and Feejee Islands*, First visit. London, 1850.

McDONALD, REV. D. "Early Arabic and Oceania." *Rep. Aust. Ass.- Adv. Sci.* XII. 1909.

MACMILLAN-BROWN, J. *Maori and Polynesian*. London, 1907.

MALINOWSKI, B. *Argonauts of the Western Pacific*. London, 1922.

MARINER, J. M. *An account of the natives of the Tonga Islands*. London, 1817.

MARZAN, B. J. DE. "Le totemisme aux Iles Fiji." *Anthropos*, II. 1907.

MIKLUCHO MACLAY, in O. Finsch's "Töpferei in Neu Guinea." *Verh. d. Berl. Ges. f. Anth., Eth. u. Urg., Z. f. Eth.* 1882.

O'FERRALL. "Native stories from Santa Cruz and Reef Islands." *J.R.A.I.* XXXIV. 1904.

PAIN, H. E. "Aboriginal art and its decay in Australasia." *Trans. Proc. Roy. Soc. Victoria*, X. O.S.

PATON, REV. J. G. *An Autobiography*. London, 1891.

RADIGUET, M. *Les derniers sauvages*. Paris, 1852.

RAY, S. H. "Some notes on the Tannese." *Inter. Archiv f. Eth.* VII. 1894.

— "Stories from the S. New Hebrides." *J.R.A.I.* XXXI. 1901.

— "The people and language of Lifu, Loyalty Islands." *J.R.A.I.* XLVII. N.S. 20, 1917.

RIVERS, W. H. R. "Totemism in Polynesia and Melanesia." *J.R.A.I.* XXXIX. 1909.

— "The father's sister in Oceania." *Folk-Lore*, XXI. 1910.

— "Genealogical method of anthropological inquiry." *Soc. Rev.* III. 1910.

— "Sun cult and megaliths in Oceania." *Rep. Brit. Ass. Adv. Sci.* Birmingham, 1913.

— "The Contact of Peoples." *Essays and Studies presented to William Ridgeway*. Cambridge, 1913.

— *The History of Melanesian Society*. Cambridge, 1914.

— "Melanesian Gerontocracy." *Man*, XV. 1915.

— "The Boomerang in the New Hebrides." *Man*, XV. 1915.

— "The Concept of Soul-Substance in New Guinea and Melanesia." *Folk-Lore*, XXXI. 1920.

ROBERTSON, REV. H. A. *Erromanga, the Martyr Isle*. London, 1903.

SARASIN, F. *Neucaledonien und Loyalty Inseln*. Basle, 1917.

SELIGMANN, C. G. *The Melanesians of British New Guinea*. Cambridge, 1910.

SITTIG, O. "Compulsory migrations in the Pacific Ocean." *Smithsonian Reports*, 1895.

SPEISER, F. "Reisebericht über Tanna, Neue Hebriden." *Z. f. Eth.* XLIV. 1912; XLVI. 1914.

— *Ethnographische Materialien aus den Neuen Hebriden und den Banks-Inseln.* Berlin, 1923.

SPENCER, B. and GILLEN, F. J. "Notes of certain of the initiation ceremonies of the Arunta tribes of Cent. Australia." *Trans. Proc. Roy. Soc. Victoria*, x. N.S.

SUAS, P. J. "Mythes et légendes des indigènes des Nouvelles Hébrides." *Anthropos*, VI. 1911.

THOMAS, N. W. *Kinship organisations and group marriage in Australia.* Cambridge, 1906.

THOMSON, B. *The Fijians.* London, 1908.

TURNER, A. *Samoa a hundred years ago and long before.* London, 1884.

WEBSTER, H. *Primitive secret societies.* New York, 1908.

WHARTON, W. J. L. *Captain James Cook's Journal: a literal translation.* London, 1893.

WHITEHOUSE, L. "Women in primitive society." *Soc. Rev.* VII. 1914.

WILLIAMS, T. *Fiji and the Fijians.* London, 1858.

WILLIAMSON, R. W. *The Mafulu: mountain people of British New Guinea.* London, 1912.

WOODFORD, C. M. *A naturalist among the head hunters.* London, 1890.

INDEX

Abortion, 50
Adoption, 34, 37, 107, 115, 132, 133
Adultery, 44, 45, 108, 115, 144–5
Afterbirth, disposal of, 88, 182
Amulets, 67
Ancestor worship, 112
Andaman Islanders, 194
Anklets (Leg bands), 136
Anointing, 76
Arm bands, 39, 66, 87, 136
Arrows, blunt, 57, 65, 67, 101, 104,
 145, 161–3, 181, 185
 poisoned, 57–8, 65, 161–3, 172
 sharp, 57, 64–5, 95–6, 101, 104,
 116, 148–9, 150, 153, 161–3, 181,
 185
Art, 100–1, 159, 188–91
Austronesian-speaking people, 193–4,
 196, 200
Avoidance, 43–4, 46, 47, 49–50, 80,
 108, 115, 140, 143, 145
Axes, stone, 66, 150, 159, 163

Bailing implement, 116
Baking process (cure), 189–90
Banana, 14, 63, 72, 81, 86, 109, 111,
 139, 151, 152, 180
Banyan tree, 56, 57, 84, 91, 138, 159
Basketry, 68, 116, 121, 136, 168
Bathing, 38, 76–7, 80–1, 135
Betel, 146, 194–5
Birds
 garafi (long-tailed tit), 14
 melikom (hawk), 14
 mianuhu (black hawk), 14
 takaskisi (wagtail-flycatcher), 14
Birth ceremonial, 115
Bleeding, 189
Blistering, 189
Boars, *see* Pigs
Boomerang, 66, 74, 146
Bow (weapon), 57, 64–5, 67, 95–6,
 101, 104, 115–16, 145, 150, 153,
 161, 181, 185
Bread-fruit, 63, 68, 91, 94, 109
Breast ornaments, 66, 115, 183
Brenchley, J. L., 40, 101, 106, 107,
 109, 146, 149, 155, 165, 167, 172
Brewster, A. B., 76, 179
Bride price, 48, 61, 115, 141, 143,
 153, 172
British Museum Handbook, 52, 90
Brother-sister relation, 47, 145

Brown, Macmillan, *see* Macmillan-
 Brown
Bull-roarer, 74, 146
Burial customs, *see* Death and burial

Cannibalism, 59, 60, 83–4, 109, 150
Canoes, outrigger, 64, 67–9, 110,
 112, 153, 158–9, 164, 184, 194,
 201
Castes (Eromanga)
 Fanlo, 132–4, 142, 144, 148, 149,
 152, 156, 166, 167, 170, 171,
 172, 173, 179–87
 Nasimnalan, 132–3
 Nefore, 132
 Nevsen, 132
 Taui Natimono, 132, 142, 145,
 152, 156, 184–6
Cat's cradle, 52, 146
Cave disposal, 89, 175, 182–4, 201
Caves, 96, 175–7
Cephalic index, 3–4, 124. *See also*
 Measurement tables
Ceremonial life, 74–92, 177–86
Chieftainship, 34–7, 55–6, 60, 61,
 106, 107, 114, 120, 132–4, 150,
 197–9, 202
Childhood, 50–2, 53, 115, 146–8
 Musukmusuk (game), 51
 Noaniberiba (game), 51
Circumcision, 45, 46, 47, 57, 74–81,
 88, 110, 111, 117, 177, 179, 194
Clan, 14–15, 44, 45, 107, 114, 120,
 129
Clan symbolism, 14–15, 37, 107, 129,
 197. *See also* Totemism
Classificatory system, 17, 114
Clavel, 83
Club, star, 144, 163–4, 201
Clubs (weapon), 57, 67, 104, 115,
 150, 163–4, 165, 181, 185
Coconut, 41, 58, 59, 61, 86, 91, 94,
 109, 121–2, 139, 180
Codrington, Rev. R. H., 2, 34, 36,
 39, 41, 42, 43, 44, 46, 47, 50, 52,
 55, 58, 59, 61, 68, 71, 74, 78,
 79, 82, 84, 86, 90, 92, 110, 145,
 146, 149, 152, 165, 180
Colour blindness, 2, 190
Colouring, *see* Dyeing
Colours, 105, 190
Combs, bamboo, 66, 135, 136
Concealment of penis, 38, 134, 178

H   14

For EU product safety concerns, contact us at Calle de José Abascal, 56–1°, 28003 Madrid, Spain or eugpsr@cambridge.org.

www.ingramcontent.com/pod-product-compliance
Ingram Content Group UK Ltd.
Pitfield, Milton Keynes, MK11 3LW, UK
UKHW010043140625
459647UK00012BA/1583